STRATEGY

Transforming War | *Paul J. Springer,* editor

To ensure success, the conduct of war requires rapid and effective adaptation to changing circumstances. While every conflict involves a degree of flexibility and innovation, there are certain changes that have occurred throughout history that stand out because they fundamentally altered the conduct of warfare. The most prominent of these changes have been labeled "Revolutions in Military Affairs" (RMAs). These so-called revolutions include technological innovations as well as entirely new approaches to strategy. Revolutionary ideas in military theory, doctrine, and operations have also permanently changed the methods, means, and objectives of warfare.

This series examines fundamental transformations that have occurred in warfare. It places particular emphasis upon RMAs to examine how the development of a new idea or device can alter not only the conduct of wars, but their effect upon participants, supporters, and uninvolved parties. The unifying concept of the series is not geographical or temporal; rather, it is the notion of change in conflict and its subsequent impact. This has allowed the incorporation of a wide variety of scholars, approaches, disciplines, and conclusions to be brought under the umbrella of the series. The works include biographies, examinations of transformative events, and analyses of key technological innovations that provide a greater understanding of how and why modern conflict is carried out, and how it may change the battlefields of the future.

STRATEGY

CONTEXT AND ADAPTATION

FROM

ARCHIDAMUS TO AIRPOWER

EDITED BY

RICHARD J. BAILEY JR., JAMES W. FORSYTH JR.,
AND MARK O. YEISLEY

NAVAL INSTITUTE PRESS
Annapolis, Maryland

Naval Institute Press
291 Wood Road
Annapolis, MD 21402

Library of Congress Cataloging-in-Publication Data

Names: Bailey, Richard J., Jr., editor, author. | Forsyth, James Wood, Jr., editor, author. | Yeisley, Mark Owen, 1960– editor, author.
Title: Strategy : context and adaptation from Archidamus to airpower / Richard J. Bailey Jr., James Wood Forsyth Jr., Mark O. Yeisley.
Description: Annapolis, MD : Naval Institute Press, 2016. | Series: Transforming war | Includes bibliographical references and index.
Identifiers: LCCN 2016000958 (print) | LCCN 2016001466 (ebook) | ISBN 9781682470039 (alk. paper) | ISBN 9781682470176 (epub) | ISBN 9781682470176 (mobi) | ISBN 9781682470176 (ePDF)
Subjects: LCSH: Strategy—History. | Strategy.
Classification: LCC U162 .S84 2016 (print) | LCC U162 (ebook) | DDC 355.02—dc23
LC record available at http://lccn.loc.gov/2016000958

♾ Print editions meet the requirements of ANSI/NISO z39.48-1992 (Permanence of Paper).
Printed in the United States of America.

24 23 22 21 20 19 18 17 16   9 8 7 6 5 4 3 2 1
First printing

Chapter 2 was originally published in a slightly different form as "An Imperfect Jewel: Military Theory and the Military Profession," *Journal of Strategic Studies* 34, no. 6 (2011): 853–877, and is reprinted by permission of the author, Harold Winton, and the publisher, Taylor & Francis Ltd, www.tandfonline.com. Chapter 7 was originally published in a slightly different form as "Beyond the Horizon: Developing Future Airpower Strategy," *Strategic Studies Quarterly* 8, no. 2 (Summer 2014): 74–95, and is reprinted by permission of the author, Jeffrey J. Smith, and the publisher, Air Force Research Institute.

To the students of the School of
Advanced Air and Space Studies
for their intellectual curiosity,
dedication, and selfless service.

We are not schooled in the useless over-intelligence which can make a brilliant verbal attack on the enemies' plans but fail to match it in consequent action. Rather we are taught to believe that other people's minds are similar to ours, and that no theory can determine the accidents of chance. It is always our principle to make practical plans on the assumption of an intelligent enemy, and not to let our hopes reside in the likelihood of his mistakes, but in the security of our own precautions. We do not need to suppose that men differ greatly one from another, but we can think that the strongest are those brought up in the hardest school.

ARCHIDAMUS, KING OF SPARTA
THUCYDIDES, 1.84

CONTENTS

FOREWORD

The School of Advanced Air and Space Studies (SAASS) may not be the "hardest school" Thucydides refers to in the epigraph, but it would likely rank high on the list. For twenty-five years the school's hard-nosed teaching faculty, composed entirely of PhD-level officers and civilian academics, has delivered a curriculum of stunning breadth and depth. The curriculum is focused on educating carefully selected field-grade officers to be tomorrow's strategists and senior leaders. Subjects taught are designed to "kit out" would-be strategists with an intellectual panoply suitable for the modern-day Pericles. They range from military theory to international politics, from organizational behavior to technology and innovation, and from history to the heuristics of argument. While this volume does not attempt to summarize the SAASS curriculum, a careful reading could lead to an understanding of its structure and to a representative sample of its content. As with any first-class graduate school, the key to the reputation and ultimate success of SAASS has always been the faculty. As noted above, all its members are "card-carrying" PhDs, and all are teaching within their specialties. As demonstrated in this interesting collection of essays, their research and writing interests are quite eclectic. Note, for example, that included in this collection of articles are such diverse offerings as: a Socratic dialogue; a historian's notions on educating airpower strategists; and musings about cyberspace and cyberpower. Eight other outstanding articles round out the bill of fare.

I am sure you will find all of the articles interesting, informative, challenging, and skillfully presented. They are worthy contributions to the published body of literature. They are the work of serious scholars doing a serious job. Enjoy! Learn!

DENNIS M. DREW,
COLONEL, USAF, RETIRED
EMERITUS PROFESSOR,
SCHOOL OF ADVANCED AIR AND SPACE STUDIES

INTRODUCTION

Widening the Aperture

The Quest for Strategic Understanding

RICHARD J. BAILEY JR.

> Our knowledge of circumstances has increased, but our uncertainty, instead of having diminished, has only increased. The reason of this is that we do not gain all our experience at once, but by degrees; so our determinations continue to be assailed incessantly by fresh experience; and the mind, if we may use the expression, must always be under arms.
>
> —Carl von Clausewitz, *On War* (1832)

❋

As Dennis Drew mentioned in the foreword, every author contributing to *Strategy* is a current or former faculty member at the School of Advanced Air and Space Studies at Maxwell Air Force Base, Alabama. SAASS is often touted as the premier strategy school in the U.S. Department of Defense (if not the country at large). And yet, as will be evident throughout the pages that follow, each of us defines strategy slightly (and sometimes not-so-slightly) differently. Herein lies the central challenge of teaching and learning strategy: the journey is never complete—the best we can hope for is to continue the quest. For over two millennia, serious thinkers have tried to define timeless strategic principles. But as Clausewitz notes above, our human experience sheds light on knowledge only in piecemeal. And while that knowledge grows, our own understanding of what is *unknown* grows as well. This is not meant to sound pessimistic or defeatist. On the contrary, awareness of our own shortcomings is one of the cornerstones

1

of strategic thinking. Thus, strategy is not just about amassing knowledge; it is also about recognizing our imperfect understanding of the environment and respecting the complex nature of adaptation to the unforeseen or unexpected. In essence, the quest continues ad infinitum.

With that thought in mind, we, as the editors of this new book on strategy, decided to take a unique approach. Rather than providing a rigid framework for each contributing author, we purposely took off the shackles and encouraged complete freedom of thought and expression. As stated above, each contributing author to this work has his own definition of strategy. But all of us agree that strategy is dependent, in one way or another, on *context* and *adaptation*. Therefore, to explore the strategic application of national power, we need both a foundation of understanding and an intellectual flexibility. By that, I mean that we should understand the salient frameworks inherent in air- and spacepower, for example, but that we should also understand temporal and historical frameworks, theoretical underpinnings, and social dynamics. To put it another way, we should attempt to understand the tools of national power but also gain an appreciation that the use of these tools must be adaptive and sensitive to a dynamic environment.

Therefore, we hope that what results in the following pages is twofold. First, the book offers a way of thinking strategically about each particular subject matter, from classical history to cyberpower. As practitioners in the profession of arms, we must think strategically about the application of power on land, at sea, and in the air, space and cyberspace. In the following chapters, the authors present their own perspectives on fields related to the strategic application of power. In doing so, each presents his view of the relevant and important topics within a particular subdiscipline. Every exploration of strategy must begin with an understanding of context and environment, so the following chapters provide key concepts in each area worth contemplation. Secondly, and more importantly, this work illuminates different *approaches* to *thinking* about strategy, choices that have implications beyond the profession of arms. For example, in chapter 3, James Forsyth relies on *theoretical* underpinnings to explore the world through a realist lens of strategy in international relations. In chapter 6, Richard Muller uses a *historical* narrative (and pedagogical approach) to highlight the development of strategic airpower thinking and teaching; in chapter 9, Richard Bailey focuses on the *social* aspects of cyberspace and cyberpower. Thus, we hope that this book not only contributes to a greater understanding of the strategic aspects of the employment of power but also widens the aperture in recognizing different ways to explore new concepts.

It is our contention that only through a willingness to explore different intellectual approaches do budding strategists make the most of their journeys.

John Warden, widely considered the architect of the airpower strategy that contributed to U.S.-coalition success in the first Gulf War, once stated that while tactics are necessarily tailored to specific ventures, strategic principles have much broader applications. He now serves as a strategic adviser to corporations and civilian agencies, where he uses many of the same skill sets he honed while on active duty in the military.[1] If Warden's contention is true, the concepts revealed in this book have applications well beyond the military arena. Without question, the various approaches to strategic thinking presented here can serve as a guide to approaching complex problems from different angles, thereby offering a greater understanding of their contextual parameters.

While our intention as editors was to encourage creativity among our contributors, we nevertheless painstakingly deliberated over the optimal arc for the book as a whole. We hope that the result is an intentional full circle academic journey. In the opening chapter, Everett Carl Dolman presents a thoughtful exploration of strategy itself, focusing on the complexities inherent in defining it as a concept and the perils of equating strategy with tactics. In chapter 2, "An Imperfect Jewel," Harold Winton provides both an appreciation for the utility of military theory and a cautionary tale as to its misapplication. In chapter 3, James Forsyth explores the geopolitical big picture and looks at how one of the major schools of international relations—realism—interprets strategic thought. In addition, he explores the role that morality plays (or should play) for the grand strategist. Following that, in a dramatic twist, James Tucci presents a Socratic dialogue in chapter 4. In it, he presents a hypothetical discussion about classical strategy and the development of strategic thought. (Perhaps more importantly, he uses that dialogue to reveal options for how one might go about learning and teaching strategy.)

Stephen Chiabotti then provides a chapter on the symbiosis of technology and strategy. He demonstrates how successful strategists adapt to technological advances through a keen knowledge of environments and systems. In doing so, Chiabotti provides a foundation for the four chapters that follow it. In chapter 6, as mentioned above, Richard Muller gives a historical pedagogical review of the development of airpower thinking and elucidates its importance to the study of strategy. Next, Jeffrey Smith in chapter 7 builds on Muller's work with an explanation of the relationship between airpower theory and airpower strategy, followed by contemporary thoughts on airpower and prescriptions for its future use. In chapter 8, M. V. Smith tackles the conundrum of spacepower and the challenges of articulating strategy in an environment devoid of clearly defined military objectives. And in chapter 9, Richard Bailey completes the technology discussion by exploring the social dynamics largely missing from the current literature on cyberspace and cyberpower.

In chapter 10, Mark Yeisley brings us back full circle to the present dilemmas facing the military strategist, namely the ubiquity of irregular warfare and the increasing complexities of preparing for the unexpected. Finally, in our concluding chapter, Stephen Wright tackles the seemingly impossible task of operationalizing strategy. His personal experience fuels a conversational narrative to explore the difficulties in translating strategy into definable (and measurable) actions. As Andrew Jackson once said, "Always take all the time to reflect as circumstances permit, but when the time for action has come, stop thinking."[2]

Economist Peter Drucker once stated, "Strategic management is not a box of tricks or a bundle of techniques. It is analytical thinking and commitment of resources to action. But quantification alone is not planning. Some of the most important issues in strategic management cannot be quantified at all."[3] The essence of strategy, ultimately, comes from the facilitation (and encouragement) of strategic thought. Today's strategists must approach complex problems with an intellectual curiosity, an appreciation for the unknown, a willingness to battle their own biases, and (perhaps most importantly) respect for a multitude of perspectives, all in order to widen the aperture and better understand the context of their environment. In the pages that follow, we offer you a sample of these differing perspectives. As the book's title suggests, the journey of the strategist is not an easy one. But that does not relieve the strategist of his or her duty to continue on the quest for contextual understanding. Ultimately, success or failure of the strategic endeavor hangs in the balance.

NOTES
1. Col. John Warden, USAF (Ret.), interview by the author, 13 March 2013.
2. Jon Meacham, *American Lion: Andrew Jackson in the White House* (New York: Random House, 2009), 262.
3. Fred R. David, *Strategic Management Concepts: A Competitive Advantage Approach* (Upper Saddle, N.J.: Prentice Hall, 2013), 173.

CHAPTER ONE

Seeking Strategy

EVERETT CARL DOLMAN

The idea is timeless; the act is historical.

✳

The manner in which states link political intent with the use or threat of violence is the subject of this essay. Although strategy as a concept can be applied to any human endeavor that requires critical decision making, the focus here is on its application in a military context.

The word strategy, drawn from classical Greek, has changed meaning considerably over time. Originally limited to describing the art and skills of generals (*strategós*), strategy (*strategía*) was differentiated from and placed hierarchically above the science (*epistéme*) of tactics (*taktiké*), or battlefield techniques and maxims—distinctions that are still widely held.[1] Accordingly, until the mid-nineteenth century, when writing about strategy authors tended to title their works along the lines of *The Art of War*, or a suitable variation, focusing on the characteristics and instincts of notable commanders and, more recently, on the difficulty of connecting the policies of civilian leadership with the *use* of military force. In discussions of tactics the tendency is to shift to more systematic analyses under the rubric of military science. And yet, despite all the ink spilled and effort spent on the subject, there is no clear or prevailing authority on what strategy is or how to do it.

With the demise of classical learning in the Middle Ages, the ancient texts were for the most part lost, then forgotten, in the Western world, and the art of strategy was subordinated to acts of piety. From Constantine's conversion following a dream in which he led Rome to victory by placing the symbol of a cross at the head of his overmatched armies, until at least the disastrous battle of Tannenberg (1410), when Grand Master Ulrich von Jungian led a force of Teutonic Knights and assorted volunteer noblemen to ruinous defeat at the hands of a much larger Polish and Lithuanian army, planning for victory was decidedly less valued than praying for it.

By way of Islamic libraries and scholarship (and a scattering of Irish monasteries), many of the surviving Greek and Roman texts returned to the West in the fifteenth century, and the intellectual appetites of Europe ignited a renaissance in all matters of systematic inquiry.[2] No one had more of an influence on secular politics than an ambitious civil servant from Florence. Ever since Machiavelli cleanly severed the connection between politics and religion, in what has been aptly dubbed the "Machiavellian Moment," and took the further step of separating completely the notions of strategy and religious or godly favor, successful military thinkers have looked to the latest paradigms of science to inform their ideas about the art and conduct of war.[3] Accordingly, this chapter includes a description of several adaptations into military affairs of concepts from emerging sciences, including the mind-bending facets of quantum physics and complexity theory but also insights that linger from the more intuitive constructs of the physical and social sciences, to include evolutionary change, problems of cause and effect, and the curious realm of paradox.

DEFINING STRATEGY

It is curious that an authoritative or universally accepted definition of strategy has been so elusive, given its extended lineage and lengthy etymology.[4] The pithiest description of the process, that of simply matching means to ends, is a reasonable start, but its universality makes it broadly unsatisfying.[5] For state-centered military strategy, it neglects the widely accepted view that although war has an essential *nature* amenable to broad and enduring principles, such as unity of command, the *character* of war is in continual flux. Theorists today thus predominantly assert that strategy is a concept that must be continually prodded, poked, investigated, adapted, and then elevated to fit the circumstances of the times—because the times always change. From such a perspective it is reasonable to assert that seeking strategy is vastly more important than finding it.

Seekers of strategy, like seekers of philosophic or scientific truth, are notoriously critical. For them, finding the truth is anathema, as it ends their quest and with it their purpose. Once truth is declared there is no more need for investigation, no lack of surety in its rightness, no room for doubters. For the seeker, a solution is merely an excuse to cease thinking, for thought is no longer needed; it has no more value to the problem now solved. The solution becomes dogma or doctrine, to be followed precisely and without dissent. Continued questioning interferes with dogma's efficiency. And yet seekers continue to prod and poke, investigate and adapt, ultimately settling on a practical solution that works for the time being but retains too many shortcomings to be declared unassailable. These seekers tend to be considered, for the efforts, cantankerous pains and can easily become ostracized—or worse, denounced as heretical. Regardless of the popularity or profit of the accepted truth, the seeker retains doubt, continuing to ask questions, forever assessing and evaluating the edifice that undergirds the accepted canon, never quite accepting its certitude and thereby constantly suspicious of its authority.

Strategy may be especially prone to predisposing outcomes through definition. Defining a thing bounds it, and strategy may "no more be bound by a definition than the wind can be shut in a box without ceasing to be wind. Thus any attempt to write on [strategy] may seem an absurdity from the beginning, but that is only so if either reader or writer imagines that [strategy] can be contained in a set of ideas. A book about London is in no sense London itself, and no sane person would dream of thinking it is."[6] A book—or in this case a chapter—about strategy should not be taken as a substitute for strategy.[7]

Definitions are not required in order to think deeply about a subject, though they are extremely useful for productive debate. When two sides are arguing past each other, it is generally because they have not agreed on basic terms. To break such an impasse, working definitions can be agreed on, allowing the finer points of an argument to go forward. In attempts to discover new information or gain fresh knowledge, however, definitions can prove harmful. By defining a thing or idea, the description channels investigation into predetermined directions or outcomes. And so definitions can either help or harm; the point here is simply that they may not be necessary. For instance, in response to the statement "You haven't even bothered to define the word 'consciousness' before embarking on this [study]," Dr. Francis Crick said, "I'd remind you that there was never a time in the history of biology when a bunch of us sat around the table and said, 'Let's first define what we mean by life.' We just went out there and discovered what it was—a double helix. We leave matters of semantic hygiene to you philosophers."[8] The latter point is rather dismissive of the high regard most of us have for the importance of semantics—we insist words have meaning and thus value—but it does help clarify my insistence that *it is not necessary to define strategy before we study it or even before we discover profound implications of it.* Indeed, it may be part of the human condition that we cannot help but meddle with things we don't fully understand; otherwise, how would anything get done? I once heard of a fellow who refused to go into the water until he learned how to swim. Such an attitude is hardly dynamic and unlikely to allow the fellow to swim well when he finally does attempt it. In favor of the old sink-or-swim rubric, Pablo Picasso used to insist that he was constantly trying to do that which he could not do, in order that he might learn to do it.

While there is no consensus definition of strategy—the opening line of this essay is about as useful as any—each of us undoubtedly has a personal working definition of strategy, one that appeals to us and gives meaning to our efforts, but ideally not so pedantic as to declare this or that definition the final solution, the end of inquiry. The bulk of definitions that have gained traction in academic and military practice, nevertheless, do share several essential assumptions about war and strategy. For example, most hold that certain aspects of war have persisted through time, can be identified, and subsequently can be stated as enduring principles (if not laws) of war and strategy. These generally cleave to the Clausewitzian notion that the character or conduct of war evolves but the essence or nature of war is unchanging. In this way the immutable principles of war, the adaptive agents of strategy, find success in context.

Beyond this limited consensus, however, there is little agreement among theorists and plenty of doubt—a very desirable condition for any study of strategy. This brief interlude of shared notions also allows a mea culpa for the rest of this essay, which comprises an attempt to present some of my own thoughts on the essential principles of strategy and some more recent beguiling aspects of its study that all of my colleagues have assisted in developing over the last decade at SAASS (but for which none of whom can be blamed).

I begin with the highest level of strategy, commonly referred to as grand strategy. At this level, the state is bound by its purpose, by the reason for which it exists—to enhance the welfare and security of its people.[9] This applies to all states, regardless of leadership's effectiveness or intent in pursuing this aim, and it helps the strategist differentiate *good* from *bad* strategy. Tyrannies or dictatorships can act as they please only so long as they maintain the power to keep the population politically inert; power is the metric of their legitimacy, just as popular support is the metric of legitimacy in representative and democratic government. Note there is no so-called end state, no static objective to be reached in politics. There is no point when the state can announce that the security and welfare of the population has been achieved and it is time to move on to something else. Strategy, like politics, never ends.[10]

Military strategy—the focus here—is subordinate to grand strategy. It conforms to the dictates of higher-level strategy but must be differentiated from other forms of state power, including diplomatic, economic, and information power the grand strategist employs to pursue continuing advantage. As with grand strategy, military (like other forms of) strategy is best defined by its *purpose*. Accordingly, I have declared elsewhere that the purpose of military power is to be prepared, and when called upon by the legitimate governing authority, to maximize violence within the constraints and limitations placed upon it.[11] The military strategist must ensure that the force available to the legitimate governing authority is the best that can be procured in the circumstances, with the resources and within the direction provided, and is maintained at the highest level of proficiency. The functions of military power and strategy thus serve the compatible interests of the grand strategic level above it, but are limited to martial means and methods.

Without question, military violence is but one means of power the state may have at its disposal, and it is quite often inappropriate for the task at hand. A worthy grand strategist will consider all pertinent means individually and in concert to achieve the continuing health and advantage of the state. The military strategist should be aware of and coordinate with the strategists dealing with other forms of state power, but unless the military is limited by law or policy to martial functions requiring external violence (a legitimate monopoly on internal, or domestic, violence is properly the police power of the state, and such force or violence by military organizations should be applied sparingly—if at all—by liberal democratic states) it quickly can be tapped to take over the duties and responsibilities of the other forms of power.[12]

Note too that the purpose of military force is not to go to war—that would be absurd, for whenever it was not at war the military would not be fulfilling its purpose and would be worse than useless. Rather, its purpose is *preparing* for war, which requires organizing, training, and equipping in peacetime. It requires maximizing the capacity for violence in the (perhaps paradoxical) belief that this is the best manner in which to ensure that violence does not have to be unleashed. In the classic Roman adage, *si vis pacem, para bellum.*

As one moves down the scale of organization, a strategy becomes necessary for any subordinate functions or capabilities that are different enough to require unique expertise or functional capabilities. Thus within military power there is room for land, sea, air, and now space (and possibly cyber) power. The purpose of each should be nested (again) within the overarching purpose of military power, which, as asserted above, should be focused on external violence. Unfortunately, this hierarchical nesting is rarely the case.

Typically, the military is organized into branches or services to deal separately with each warfighting domain: an army for land and a navy for the sea, and today an air and/or space force for the others. As new domains are discovered, or perhaps created, they may require additional service entities.

Paralleling this organizational separation is a tendency to define the services by platform/function (ships for navies, aircraft for air forces) or by the physical characteristics of the medium in which they operate (fluid dynamics for the water, orbital mechanics for outer space), even though doing so stresses the relationships between these organizations in predictable ways. Which branch should command joint operations, for example, is routinely contested; in the U.S. military today the services for the most part simply take turns or, worst of all, insist that all are represented equally in every operation, campaign, or war. Who is in charge ought to be based on which service is providing or tasked with the predominance of effort, but since budget allotments are argued on the basis of participation in whatever current activity is deemed most vital, American military operations appear to follow the rules of Little League baseball—everybody suits up, everybody plays.

When medium as a characteristic is the determinant of service priority, intra-service budget battles and rivalries are multiplied. It may seem obvious that platforms operating in the air should be assigned to an air force, for example, but does this mean that the navy and army should have no aircraft? The organizational mess that would ensue if aircraft on aircraft carriers were owned, maintained, and operated by some organization other than the one that owns, maintains, and operates the carrier is equally obvious. So too should be the conundrum of a platform that routinely operates in or on more than one medium. Should control of an intercontinental ballistic missile launched from a submarine—passing through the water, then the air, and then outer space before arching over and falling back through the air to a target on the land—be passed from the navy to the air force then to the army in the course of its flight?

If the logic of purpose for determining the role of military power helps us to understand the proper roles and functions of the military in the context of state power, the same logic should apply to the roles and functions of subordinate military services in the context of military power. The medium of operations becomes dominant not because of its physical characteristics (as described above) but because of the capacity to *use* or *contest* the medium.

Thus the purpose of military land power is to take and hold territory. Any operational command issues or functional differentiations disappear when this mission is assigned to the army. Likewise, the purpose of military sea power is to command the seas; that of military airpower is to command the air; and that of military spacepower is to command space. It is of the utmost importance that if command of the land, sea, air, or space cannot be achieved (or is undesirable), then it is vital that an enemy does not command it. This is called contestation of the domain.

Accordingly, the service assigned to control or command a domain in times of conflict or to deny that control to an opponent if one's own command cannot or should not be achieved must have the capacity to contest the littoral (or adjacent) domains to prevent (or at a minimum add a cost to) an opponent from operating freely there. This allows, for example, an army to maintain air-defense weapons so that the skies above it are not open for opposing air forces to strike. The navy must maintain ports on the land, and the air forces need air bases there, and so both properly have ground troops to help secure them. When purpose determines organization, the functions of subordinate military services are clarified.[13]

Such purposeful deliberation helps further to assign proper use and roles for military operations at the level of state power. Specifically, is actual or latent (implied) violent command and contestation an intended effect of the use of military forces in any particular state-contemplated action? If so, military power should be considered and, where determined necessary or useful, employed. If not but military power is the most expedient or available form of power that can be effectively put to use, then it is to be used sparingly and temporarily. For example, military forces can and should be used to provide humanitarian aid in areas where civilian resources are limited or unavailable, but this should be thought of as an expedient only, not a new or desirable function of military power.

Sea transport is a vital function of navies, for example, as is air transport for air forces, but not all sea and air transport is military power. Although commercial transport can be and sometimes is appropriated and placed directly in the martial service of the state when dedicated military transport is insufficient for the task at hand, and a robust maritime or air commerce is extremely helpful in crises (just as military aircraft can assist in humanitarian missions, as described previously), their primary purposes are economic, and their organizations and functions should be maximized for and controlled by civilian entities. Likewise, a bomber can be used to transport passengers or deliver informational pamphlets, but this does not make it a commercial or propaganda platform; to believe that its role is not necessarily violent confuses the purpose for which it was designed and built. Along these lines, to insist that when the military bombs a factory it is conducting economic warfare is as ludicrous as arguing that if it bombs a school or church the state is conducting educational or religious warfare. It is this ironic and euphemistic cause-and-effect reversal that makes missions palpable; the U.S. Air Force services targets when it destroys them, a nice way of putting it but divorced from the meaning by which, say, a Maytag repair technician would service an appliance.

Attempts to place function or platform or even effects and targets as the characteristics of strategy denies the importance of the *value* of thinking as a strategist and supplants it with the *utility* of thinking as a tactician. When purpose is at the forefront, the effects of military power, the uses to which it can be employed, are limited only by the creative genius of the strategist. This does not mean, however, that strategy is superior to tactics or to the way of thinking that maximizes the use of means within prescribed boundaries to achieve assigned goals. Strategy and tactics work synergistically to maximize both utility and value.

SEPARATING STRATEGY FROM TACTICS

Perhaps the most difficult thing for a strategist to accept is that there are no meaningful ends, goals, or targets in strategy—at least, there ought not to be, for including these forces the strategist to set aside purpose and focus on objectives. It is simply not effective (and may not be possible) to think as a tactician and a strategist at the same time. The strategist determines the means, establishes the boundaries, and provides the goals for the tactician. Within these, the tactician maximizes—most efficiently and/or effectively—results. The most that can be hoped for is the capacity to switch nimbly back and forth, but in practice such movement is difficult at best.

This exposition of strategy began at the top and worked down, but this is not necessary. At the bottom of any organizational human endeavor is the individual, and here there is ample room for strategy, because the realm of activity is unique—every person is different. And despite the enormity of individual differences, a good strategy for any individual is the same, just as it is identical for every state—to grow, to get better, to improve. It is an overarching purpose in life. It is also not necessary to start a discussion on tactical thinking from the bottom and work up, but it is at the bottom that tactical thinking can be shown as different from strategic thinking but equally valuable and necessary. Tactical thinking is focused on utility, on ends or goals. It is eminently measurable, and determining a proper metric is vital in assessing success. Thus the typical misunderstanding of strategy, as a matching of means to ends, is properly tactical—regardless of the size of the organization, the breadth of control, the length of time desired or required, or the variety of twists and turns in the plan to reach some end state.

At an individual level, my desire is to become *more*. I may want to be healthier, stronger, kinder, wealthier, and the like. This is the purpose for my strategy. But I cannot realize a continuing advantage if I do not achieve results along the way. Thus I set goals and I measure my performance. For example, I wish to be educated, and so I determine that I will go to university. I set as a tangible goal a degree, and I dedicate a portion of my resources to achieving a diploma. I measure my success by grades, the time in which it takes, and the employment I get upon graduation. There are, of course, numerous effective ways to become educated; I have selected this as a means by which I attempt to accomplish my goals. If, however, I accept the goal as the end of my strategy, then upon graduation I will have completed my education and learning will no longer be needed. This is absurd, of course. Education—learning—is a lifelong process that is never finished. As soon as I believe that some achievement, a piece of paper, completes my education and that now I can move on to the next goal or task, I am no longer a strategist. I am a fool.

On the other hand, if I think I can become educated without setting interim goals and objectives, or if I demand a college degree simply as evidence of my education—or worse, to validate myself as educated—then I am no better than the scarecrow who receives a diploma from the wizard and believes he now has a brain.

Two more examples should suffice. The first concerns the American fascination with weight and dieting. On the one hand, any reasonable weight-loss program will get a dieter to a predetermined weight if he or she sticks with it. On the other, if lifestyle changes are not part of the diet, once the weight is achieved and the diet cast off, it is very unlikely that the target weight will be maintained. Typically, crash-dieters who achieve their goals eventually balloon up to weights greater than those from which they started. Much of this failure can be ascribed to the poor strategy that determined the tactical diet. If my goal is to fit into a swimsuit for the summer, the best diet is the one that gets me there quickest and cheapest. I shall declare victory and proudly march out onto the beach. If my goal is to become healthier and weight loss is a valid part of my strategy, *how* I diet—the tactical element—is critical. It must be sustainable and must be done in such a way that health problems associated with rapid weight loss and bounce-back gain are avoided.

This is better illustrated in the social problem of drug and alcohol addiction. Too often an addict is sent to a rehabilitation facility to dry out, to force a period of abstinence that allows the physical addiction to drugs or alcohol to dissipate, and after a suitable four- or six-week program is released as "cured." This tactical success is overcome by the strategic failure of recidivism, a return to drug or alcohol use and the requirement to be cured again. What is needed is a strategy that combines the tactical necessity of first getting addicts clean and then keeping them that way. Logistician Derrick Niederman describes the confluence of sound tactics and strategy in his description of Alcoholics Anonymous, which "has long recommended that its followers view alcoholism as a never-ending struggle, [that] this prescription, far from an admission of defeat, was recognition that alcoholics do better by *developing strategies against a constant adversary than through the premature declaration of victory.*"[14]

STRATEGY AND TACTICS AS PARADOX

Human beings live in perpetual paradox; every fundamental principle of life can be expressed in two opposing ways.[15] Life is thus dialectical, and so are people. So is their output. A consistent and remarkable observation is that every strategy and every stratagem has a counter that is directly in opposition and is just as valid and persuasive in the same context. For example, a common rule of thumb (a stratagem) offered by Sun Tzu is that the pinnacle of strategic success is to put oneself in such a superior position that war or combat is unnecessary: the outcome is foregone, and the opponent acquiesces. Thus, to "win a thousand battles without dulling the sword" is the mark of a great strategist.[16] But what kind of military force will be left after a thousand potential battles in which fighting is superseded by excellent command? (In any case, why is the state potentially engaged in a thousand battles? Is it doing something wrong?) An army that has not fought, regardless of the keen edge of its weapons, has not been battle tested and is unlikely to counter successfully a less-well-equipped or smaller force of hardened veterans. Sometimes the strategist must find a battle to keep the state's military forces sharp.[17]

A true paradox exists where individual components, each of which is rational and logical on its own, cannot coexist. To the strategist, this is generally evident where opposing solutions are equally logical and no compromise is possible. For better or worse, most of the great questions and important aspects of human existence are paradoxes. Does the good of the one outweigh the good of the many? Is it better to allow a possible criminal to go free than potentially to imprison an innocent person? Can a war now stop a greater war later? These questions are simply insoluble—the only thing worse than doing either is doing neither. This is not some curious aside; it seems that at some level rational life *must* be so, for paradox expresses the necessary polarity inherent in every self-regulating system.[18] Therefore paradox, which cannot be solved, has one of two outcomes: either the conflict continues in perpetuity, which is pathological, or it must be *outgrown.* To get past paradox, paradox must be accepted and moved beyond.

This growth beyond the pathological is the essence of understanding strategy as a dialectical or paradoxical counter to tactics, an opposing way of thinking. It is not that they compete (necessarily); they interact to form a conceptual whole. Strategy and tactics are the yin and yang of military operations. The whole is incomprehensible without both and irreducible to one or the other. Xeno's classic paradox is a fine example. He argued that the essence of reality is continuous but that the essence of thought is discrete. Xeno asked whether an arrow fired from a bow can ever hit a tree if it first must travel half the distance to its destination before reaching it. If it must, as reality dictates, it must also travel half the remaining distance before hitting the tree, and then half that, ad infinitum (or possibly *nauseam*). Since it must always travel half the distance before hitting the tree, it can never hit the tree. The logic is impeccable, and the only thing an observer can do is point out that the arrow does, in fact, hit the tree. But this is not a solution to Xeno's paradox; it is simply an observation. What is needed is not an answer but a better question.

In this case, Xeno highlighted a recurring paradox of nature, between a digital (discrete) and an analog (continuous) framework of reference. Until Newton (and Leibnitz) solved the equation using fractions—by inventing a new form of mathematics called calculus—Xeno's paradox could only be dismissed.

STRATEGY AND CHOICE

Strategists have practical needs that must be met. Choices are made that affect the future health of the state, and the first area of study or practice is decision making. For this reason, as already stated, strategy is commonly defined as effectively or efficiently matching means to ends. Such thinking is child's play at worst, tactical genius at best. It stems from the notion that as political and military leaders rise through the ranks they make decisions for increasing spans of control. In this view, strategy is simply tactics at a grander scale; experience in making choices is completely transferable from one level to the next.

It is also widely accepted that the more information or options a decision maker has, the better the choice ultimately made. But this is rarely the case. It is simply *easier* to choose profitably between a limited set of choices than an infinite number, but this does not mean having fewer choices has merit in itself. There are many situations in which I make myself better off by limiting my own choices—for example, when I cut off my own retreat so my army will fight with greater desperation (not something you want to induce in the opponent) or by strictly adhering to treaties and conventions regarding humane treatment of prisoners so that the opponent is less likely to continue fighting for fear of torture. While strategy is about making more choices for myself and quite often for my opponent (though it is a bad idea to interrupt an enemy who is making poor choices), tactics is about *constraining* the opponent's choices to one—surrender or die.

Proper strategy is more than simplified choice selection; strategy is different and requires an alternative, effectively opposite, way of thinking. To illustrate, great generals are primarily known for winning battles—that is, in situations in which forces (or means) are fixed and the end is unchanging, victory in the battle space.[19] In this view, the general is a master tactician, using the forces available to achieve the ends provided most effectively and efficiently. This in no way diminishes the role of the tactical commander. Quite the opposite, it is the hallmark of great generalship, as without competent tacticians few strategies will be successful. But it highlights the opposing thought processes that dominate strategic and tactical thinking. An appropriate analogy is with chess. In this game, forces—the strength of pieces and their movements—are perfectly understood by all sides, the battlefield is rigid and contained, and the objective of both is clear: take the opponent's king. Within this tightly regulated contest, genius can emerge, as epitomized by the grand master. Within the game, the grammar of chess is perfect, its logic supreme. But it is outside the game that strategy as I perceive it truly takes place. Why chess as a form of competition? Should I win every game? When should I play knowing I will lose? These are all questions of strategy. They are *external* to the game.

The tactician seeks to bring events to culmination, whether in victory or in exit strategies or end games. This is appropriate. But only that which is capable of change is capable of continuing indefinitely. Thus the strategist's realm, which has no end or culminating point, is the realm of change. It is the strategist's purpose to manipulate the boundaries and rules of competition, to make them fluid, to change them as readily as needs dictate. In such a realm of the possible, the strategist enters into a relationship with the goal of continuing it, on favorable terms, and accepts that every choice made and acted on redefines the rules and boundaries of the interaction. This is anathema to the tactician, for if the rules and boundaries of the conflict change in midconflict, carefully made plans are disrupted. Imagine a game of chess in which halfway through pawns were allowed to move as queens. The master chess player would be frustrated to no end—and more important, if the conditions of conflict are not fixed, it will be impossible to agree on a victor! The conditions for victory could change at the moment of triumph, in which case the winner is determined not by skillful play but fortuitous interruption.

Hence it is vital to the tactician that the rules not change during the course of battle, and many of the tactician's actions are directed toward that end—establishing a consistent combat environment that is congruent with the strengths and knowledge of the tactician. Expecting and adapting to change is the essence of the strategic thinker's planning, however. A strategist without at least the possibility of change has no function within the conflict. In the chess analogy above, once the terms and decisions that get the players in position to begin the game are agreed upon, strategy is subordinated to tactics (but never over). Prowess within the rules will determine a winner of that match. Play may conform to an overall strategy—to win decisively, for example, or to perform credibly even in losing—but neither outcome is predicated on a future change in the structure of the game. If the future will be like the past, boundaries are set and immutable. The master tactician can hone his or her craft through experience and in a study of history alone. Everything important is already known.

In fact, savvy chess players do not seek to take the king. They force situations in which the king *must* move, and that move *must* be to a vulnerable square. Great players gain control or dominate a space next to the king, not the king's space, and then force the king to move into it. The chess master is thus a tactical thinker. When the opposing player understands that within the rules and boundaries of chess the outcome is certain, resignation occurs before the final moves are made. When there is no action allowed in the rules that would reverse the coming defeat, surrender will be offered. Tactics are triumphant when choices are eliminated.

To the extent that the game of chess has master strategists, they would not be concerned about the outcome of a particular game or tournament. For them, the outcome of each game establishes new conditions and boundaries for subsequent play. The desire is not to win but to continue playing chess on favorable terms. Permit me to continue the chess analogy from the perspective of a strategist. Perhaps I have decided to teach my daughter to play chess. I do this because I enjoy chess and would like a partner, but also because I believe learning and mastering chess is good for my daughter, that it will assist in developing analytic skills and stronger capacity for logical reasoning. Thus I have no end state; my goal is to enhance my own and my daughter's futures, regardless of the circumstances that may present themselves in the future.

If I were to go over the rules of chess carefully and then win every game quickly and decisively, she would soon grow bored and refuse to play. I would have demolished my opponent, satisfying the conditions of victory, but I would have lost my strategic purposes of enhancing her mental development and eventually playing a substantial game with my daughter—in other words, sharing some quality time. If I were thoughtful, however, I would carefully develop my daughter's skills so that she would become an able opponent—so that she developed a taste for the game and someday became a master herself—in order that someday she could teach me new options, ultimately enhancing my play. No matter how much better we mutually get at chess, there is no conceivable point at which we would be good enough and the games would end. In fact, as I get older and my skills erode, my daughter may continue playing for enjoyment and as an excuse to spend time with me in my dotage. At that point, she may even let me win now and again. Even upon my death, the game will not end. My daughter will teach her children, and they will play on.

This metaphor for conflict and war is not a clean fit. It seems a bit strained to try to equate the desire of the chess player to play in the future and the state strategist's desire to continue positive future interactions with other states, but the mental leap is not overwrought. The tactician plays chess to win, the strategist to play in the future. The tactician wages war to win; the strategist anticipates waging war in the future.

Hence the ideal tactical decision-making situation is one in which all courses of actions are known (surprise is impossible) and the rules and boundaries are clearly established. Battle is a foregone conclusion, and so entering into it (or not) is the initial strategic decision. The game of tic-tac-toe provides an analogy here. Between skilled opponents, the side that goes first will win. While there is no best strategy *for* playing the game, there are infallible tactics *within* it. It would even be possible to create a short guide that would list all possible moves and the optimum counters to each. All the tactician must do is recognize the situation on the board and counter appropriately. In a few iterations, it becomes apparent that the superior player will attempt to put the opponent in a position that requires a choice: block one of two winning moves. Since either block allows the other to win, it is not even a meaningful choice. It is merely interesting. Therefore neither how the game was played nor its outcome is relevant to the strategist. What is important is how the decision was made as to who goes first. This critical competition outside the boundaries of the field of play is what connects the tactician to the strategist.

Hence the tactician strives to eliminate choice, to ensure that no surprise can occur. All possibilities are included in the ideal battle plan. The best of these anticipate outcomes that are foregone, that are sureties. The perfect plan is therefore perfected prediction. Accordingly, if the outcome is not in doubt, choice has been eliminated. If no action the other takes will forestall victory, those actions are meaningless. The strategist strives instead to expand options, even for the opponent (by leaving an honorable exit, perhaps, or making available an alternative game), to maximize the available choice set. The tactician seeks closure, the culmination of the plan. The strategist rejects closure, seeking instead to continue. It is the interaction of war, its dual nature, that forces this view: no matter how careful my planning, no matter how comprehensive my plan, the opponent could do something unanticipated. The boundaries could change. The rules could evolve.

Choice again becomes the operational descriptive of power and meaning. As human beings, we reference our lives not by the *boundaries* that begin and end them, notions of birth then death, but by the major events that shape them: graduations, marriage, births of children, new jobs, and the like. These are events and accomplishments that define us, and they are always subject to change and reinterpretation. They are representative of the free choices made and rejected that continuously shape our existence. So long as life goes on, there is choice, and where there is choice, hope. A single act can redeem a life of evil or condemn the good person to ignominy. More than this, a life ends in death only in the physical sense. The choices and accomplishments of a profound life can shape the future long after the body is dust. Birth too is not seen as a sudden creation of life. Each person is the result and extension of generations before, the manifestation of a physical, cultural, and political evolution that gives shape and meaning to the newest life.

The state is a manifestation of this logic. Its decisions are based on a past history and accomplishments. It is understood not as a simple descriptive of its existing characteristics (size, population, resources, etc.) but as a culmination of these and its culture, ideology, mythology, and more. Since the state is what makes war, its power has meaning only in the context of its accomplishments and the events that shaped it. But history is not deterministic for the state any more than it is for the individual. It shapes and guides behavior, but the likelihood that a certain action will or will not be taken is a probability only. It is in fact this mutability of time that makes strategic thinking incompatible with the notions of victory or defeat. For the tactically defeated, this means that the possibility of rising to challenge again exists. For the tactical victor, it means there will be new challenges and new challengers. Nothing is ever truly finished.

Strategy is thus always about the game or competition. Within are tactics only. The absurdity of a strategy *within* a game is highlighted by the example of a game of solitaire. The only unknown, the order in which the cards are revealed, is tactically all-important and strategically meaningless. The conclusion of the game is immaterial to the play or outcome of subsequent ones, with the exception that patterns might emerge that could reveal or prompt a preference (or habits) for certain moves. Since no other people are required to engage in solitaire and the decision to play is entirely internally motivated, strategy is absent. The game is a time-filler.

On the other hand, in interactive games with players of differing skills, strategy is always present, even if only implicitly so. Poker is the exemplar here. When and where to play, what limit to place on bets, which variation of the game to use, what opponents to engage, these are all serious strategic questions. Once *in* the game, knowledge of odds, skills of card counting, and awareness of other player's tells (and one's own) are critical to increasing the chances of winning. Even a decision to throw some games (that is, once it is recognized that the other players are outmatched, so as to increase the take at the end of the night) is a tactical move toward ultimate victory. To throw some games because the other players are friends or family and the most important thing is to keep them playing week after week is a strategic choice, however. Examples abound. A poor player who engages in poker to win, playing to the best of his or her ability, may lose repeatedly yet still desire to play on. In this case, the external strategy may be to gain experience. Future advantage is the goal, to become a better player, and so near-term reversals are expected as part of the process toward that end.

At this juncture it may be useful to change the analogy from games to occupations. It is useful to think of the strategist's role as akin to that of a gardener: "To garden is to design a culture capable of adjusting to the widest possible range of surprise in nature. Gardeners are acutely attentive to the deep patterns of natural order, but are also aware that there will always be much lying beyond their vision."[20] The garden itself is a perpetual thing, and a "successful harvest is not the end of a garden's existence, but only a phase of it[;] . . . gardens do not 'die' in the winter but quietly prepare for another season."[21] Like a gardener, who creatively monitors and cares for a parcel of ground, the strategist perceives a continuity of interactions that must be tended to from one generation to the next. Just as master gardeners creatively and experimentally draw all the sources of nourishment and variety to enhance the continual output of the garden, master strategists must take an active part in the maintenance and health of the many political systems that encompass military actions. It is necessary to prune the tree to keep it healthy, but too vigorous cutting will kill it. "Inasmuch as gardens do not conclude with a harvest and are not [planted] for a certain outcome, one never arrives anywhere in a garden. . . . [One] does not bring change to a garden, but comes to a garden prepared for change, and therefore prepared to change."[22]

STRATEGY AND STRATEGISTS

For the most part, the study of strategy is the study of plans and actions of noted military and political leaders. Strategy is, in this view, an intrinsic thing that can be assessed and critiqued. But it is unrealistic to separate strategy from those who practice and promulgate various forms of it. Strategists as agents are products of their times, their cultures, societies, and governments—in short, interactive products of their structures. The study of strategy is therefore incomplete without a study of strategists in their time, a relationship that is a coequal if not dominant influence on the evolution of strategy through history. This helps to explain why the dominant view of successful strategy changes so much over time—not because strategy is mutable (in theory it need not be) but because strategists live and think in a contextually constrained space and time.

Strategists and tacticians are by necessity observers of the world around them. They cull from reality and the database of history justification for their choices. But strategists are human, and humans are flawed. People see what they expect to see and tend to ignore what does not fit into their worldviews. This is neither good nor bad; it simply is. One cannot observe with perfect objectivity, not in the social sciences or in history. A bias exists in all observations—a bias generated by the desire or reason for the observation. Whenever strategists seek data, prejudice and bias limits their ways of observing. I observe the outcome of battles, for example, to study the efficacy of strategy. But why start (or end) there? I presume the outcome of battles is necessary to understanding the strategy under examination, but what of the influence of cockroach populations in Alabama? I don't even take a look on the off chance it might be important. As an investigator, I choose avenues of inquiry that I believe will lead to insight. I have to.

Not only personal or psychological biases eliminate observational objectivity. Nature seems bent on eliminating it as well. One of the most confounding aspects of theory or strategy is the paradoxical logic of duality when assessing cause and effect. The conventional view is that every effect has a prior cause. The explanation is naturalistic and grounded in empiricism; it asserts that no cause can be preceded by its effect. This seems sensible enough, at first, but the world seems to be filled with causes that do not precede effects. Whenever purpose or emotion is factored in, cause and effect are routinely misinterpreted.

As Werner Heisenberg observed: "Causality law has it that if we know the present, then we can predict the future. Be aware: In this formulation, it is not the consequence but the premise that is false. As a matter of principle, we cannot know all determining elements of the present."[23] This brilliant observation comes from Heisenberg's mathematical proof that the more accurately one determines one aspect of nature, another aspect becomes necessarily obscured. In the case of quantum physics, the location of a subatomic particle cannot be determined accurately if one also knows precisely the velocity of that particle. Observation of one aspect makes simultaneous knowledge or observation of another aspect impossible. Indeed, quantum physics shows a world that is not deterministic, not empirically established until the observer intrudes on reality. Erwin Schrödinger's cat-in-a-box metaphor describes the fundamental problem—quantum events occur all at once and are not resolved until the observer fixes an event by the act of observation.

Quantum theory describes the physicist's attempt to understand and explain the basic nature of reality at the submicroscopic level, at the level of quantum mechanics. As such, it is appealing to strategists, who have always adapted freely from the sciences, even when they have been convinced that a perfected science of war could never truly be achieved. Clausewitz, more a product of the German Romanticist tradition than of the Enlightenment, may have done so intuitively. He could have accepted the tenets of probability and uncertainty that quantum physics would identify more readily than his Newtonian counterparts in the West.[24] This is not surprising. Some of the outcomes of quantum analysis are so foreign to the Western intuitive sense of reality that they have only been reluctantly applied. Those strategists educated into Enlightenment values and holding a faith in scientific positivism (holding that a thing exists only if it can be observed and measured) could not so easily accept that nature, at its core, could be unknowable.

If the world were truly governed by natural laws that could not be violated, then the essence of science should be entirely based upon observation and prediction. The more carefully we define our experiments and the more keenly we measure and chart changes over time, the closer we get to a perfect comprehension of reality. The most perilous strategic connotation may be the always-present implication that reality is rational, explainable, and perfectible. Implicitly or stated plainly, this view must lead to the belief that the universe can be comprehensively understood. One has only to know the fundamental laws acting upon the fundamental material particles (atomic structures) and one could, in theory, predict future events with certitude.[25] This belief imbues tactical notions in which combatants attempt to make the outcome of battle, and ultimately war, assured. If the individual soldier is trained to clockwork precision and will perform all tasks flawlessly, a perfect calculation of battle is conceivable. The dilemma for the Newtonian physicists and Maurician grand tacticians is plain. If the outcome is certain, the future is predestined. There is no choice, and so there is no power.

The Copenhagen interpretation of quantum physics claimed, among many other dazzling notions, that perfect prediction is impossible not only in practice but even in theory. Because the future cannot be known, the new physics predicted probabilities only. This is partly because we can never know precisely the reality in which we exist. We comprehend the universe by interpreting (with our brains) the senses of our bodies and the measurements of our instruments. Thus, it is possible to know only the shadow of reality, much as Plato insisted in his famous allegory of the cave. Some philosophers go so far as to state that *all* notions of reality are equally valid, as each is merely the individual interpretation of sensory and data input, and so all realities are created. Any reality is possible. The response of the realist, like that of the Zen master, is to smack the philosopher on the head with a stick. ("Interpret *that* reality!")

Nonetheless, the quantum model is a powerful one that spawns an incredible array of insights. It stems, innocuously enough, from Einstein's resolution of the centuries-old dispute as to whether light is composed of particles, and thus mass, or of energy, like a frequency wave. The result of so-called double-slit experiments, repeated and verified innumerable times, showed that light acts as both a particle *and* a wave until it is acted upon by observation—at which point it displays the characteristics of *either* a particle or a wave—not both. Einstein's solution was radically simple. He envisioned a new physical construct called a photon that at times exhibits the characteristics of a particle and at other times those of a wave. The problem was that the characteristics they exhibit depended on the *means* one uses to measure them.

The activity of the photon is indeterminate until one decides to measure the activity. This must lead to the notion that a fundamental basis of nature is its inherent unpredictability (and its reliance on the perspective of the observer!). Not that we have too little understanding to be able to predict the future with certainty but that even if all the relevant information were available, it would not be possible to do so. This is the essence of Werner Heisenberg's extraordinary Uncertainty Principle. This indispensable principle of quantum physics states that it is impossible to know simultaneously both the precise location and the velocity of any object. Quantities of position and momentum, when measured in relationships, generate uncertainties. We can know one or the other exactly, but the more precisely we determine one, the vaguer our knowledge of the other.

Much of the uncertainty of nature comes from our own intrusive attempts to measure it, and conjectures drawn from Heisenberg's principle for information gathering are startling. If the subatomic (micro) realm proves to be a better model for information flow than the macro one, the limit of what is even possible to know is severely constrained. First, the easy part: since one cannot know all things precisely, only approximately, strategists must become comfortable with knowledge of the world stated in probabilities, not absolutes. We cannot say with certainty that a war will occur, much less precisely when, where, or with whom such an event will transpire. But, with increasing reliability, we *should* be able to predict the exact likelihood that a certain type of war, perhaps in a certain region and with specified foes, will occur within a given time and prepare accordingly. We simply cannot know the specifics. The phenomenon is highlighted in the process of radioactive decay.[26] In this case, precisely predictable overall behavior (rate of decay) is based on the patterns observed in completely unpredictable individual events. Wars of attrition are fought this way. Predictions of success are based on the numbers of one's own troops that will be killed in a given situation (versus the opponent's). Without knowing who will be killed, the total casualty rate can be quite accurately projected. It is a grisly calculus but at times a useful one.

Now the more difficult notion: our very attempts to determine the likelihood of an event happening alters the probability of that event happening. Not only do we alter the probabilities of reality by observing it, in the act of observing we choose the future in which we will act. This is clearly counter to the Newtonian view based on universal laws that govern mass and movement. Prequantum physics adheres to the belief that nature is fixed, that our measurements of it have no effect on what is or what will be. This real world is external to us, at least to our inquiring minds. It is what it is. Moreover, it is indifferent to us. In this image, the course of human history is akin to a rudderless boat floating down a river. Its course is buffeted and complex, it goes from right to left and back again, but its progress is inevitable, and the desires or observations of the people on the boat have no effect on the outcome of its journey.

Quantum mechanics tells us it is impossible to know precisely the future of any phenomenon, only the probabilities that lie ahead. The quantum vision sees humanity as a part of nature, an element in its journey that continuously interacts with and influences it, with or without intent. Any choice the strategist makes changes nature. Staying with the river analogy, imagine the boat has oars and a rudder, as well as a crew to operate them. The people on board look downstream for the best passage through rapids and shoals. The boat is moved in anticipation of the perceived danger, and the course is different than it would have been without the observation. And the river has changed too. Eddies and currents are altered minutely. There will always be the image of what might have happened if we did not steer from right to left, and even though we will never float through that section of the river in precisely the same way again, that image will affect future decisions as much as does the physical lay of the stream. Strategists are no different from the quantum physicist in this regard. They cannot be objective, for they are elements within the world of war. What they choose to examine will change the future, because every choice is real and reality cannot be observed without changing it.

This notion of choosing one's reality is undoubtedly more tenable to the strategist than to the tactician. It is difficult to persuade a naval battle planner that the enemy is both over the horizon and *not* over it, for example, and that both realities will remain in being until we choose (or are forced) to look for one or the other. This is because the enemy ships are things, or objects, and our experience tells us the thing is there or it is not, regardless of my attention. Whether or not I choose to look does not change the reality of its coming. I cannot avoid being struck by a bullet by closing my eyes.

But strategists do not deal in their planning with things or objects (aspects should be left to the tactician); they seek instead a condition or situation of advantage. This world of ideas and possibilities is more compatible with the microphysical world of the quantum physicists than the macrophysical one of Newton, because quantum particles should not be thought of as things. They are more correctly understood as "tendencies to exist" or "tendencies to happen."[27] They are events, phases, and fields. The smallest of reality's building blocks may not even have mass; they may simply be rules of interaction.[28] The strengths of these tendencies are expressed as probabilities. The result is that careful study and examination of aggregate characteristics over time, the province of statistical analysis, cannot provide with assurance a prediction of the actions of any one individual; it can, however, give an uncannily accurate projection of the future behavior of a group. Political pollsters have long known this phenomenon and have established methods that work extremely well. They collect data to determine the characteristics of voters likely to be swayed by particular arguments, or they use the data to make projections of future elections. They recognize that not all the members of the target group will be equally swayed and that the decision of any one voter is not known with any greater accuracy than intuition. But a particular group decision of a large number of likely decision makers, and by what size plurality, can be known with astonishing accuracy.

The notion that a group acts in predictable ways but that an individual does not has far-reaching consequences for the military planner. It points to the *patterns* inherent in actions as the sources of true understanding, and not the actions themselves. Perhaps most disconcerting, the tactician's correct and proper search for perfect knowledge in the conduct of campaigns and battles could prove to be suboptimal as one moves toward the level of strategy. If we follow the logic to conclusion, however, it may prove that the more we attempt to know about one characteristic of the enemy, the less we can know about another. The more we try to get perfect knowledge about the enemy's intent, for example, the less we may be able to know about the enemy's actions. The more a planner looks to the micro level of battle to influence or simply observe a single engagement, the less that can be known about the macro level of the war.

It is desirable, for example, to know which of two individual combatants will win. But it is not yet possible to predict accurately every action or event in the course of the fight. These can be stated as probabilities only. The outcome of any single engagement is thus unknowable in advance. But the aggregate outcome of thousands of similar actions or events can be known with a high degree of reliability. In other words, planners cannot know which aircraft will make it to an assigned objective, which ordnance will hit its target, which of the enemy will be killed, but over time they can determine how many aircraft of a certain kind carrying what type of load are needed to achieve the desired effect with near certainty. One of the functions of doctrine is to assist the tactical and operational planner in calculations like this for specific engagements, and they are commonly performed. It is quite rare to see them done for entire battles—as components of campaigns or wars—and rarer still for wars as components of grand strategy.

The ability of the battle planner to predict the aggregate outcome of numerous indeterminable tactical engagements efficiently is extremely useful in the effort to maximize the probability of achieving broad tactical goals. For the operational planner, an ability to determine the aggregate outcome of numerous battles is equally valuable in campaign planning. For the operational planner, however, reaching down to the level of engagements to increase the probability that specific battles would be judged successful would skew the probability set for aggregate outcomes of *all* battles and so must be scrupulously avoided. The temptation to reach down multiple levels to increase control over variables should be even more shunned. Strategists should thus abandon any attempt to exercise control at the micro level (the individual soldier, sailor, or airman), entrusting that function to the commander on the scene. Operational strategy or grand tactics raises the aggregate level of success through better training and equipping, and the strategist must support these efforts, but the strategist should guide military matters so that the tactical outcome of any war, much less any individual battle, is not critical to success (or continuing advantage). To be sure, a strategist whose plan rests on a specific action working out in a precise way is not thinking strategically. Such a mind-set locks the strategist into predetermined choices, and the capacity to control events is lost.

It was classical logic that placed on us the rules of either/or, not the world of experience. Greek philosophers demonstrated the fallacy long ago, with two confounding paradoxes.[29] The first was Epimenides' famous Cretan paradox, in which a traveler from Crete states that all Cretans are liars. The paradox can be boiled down to the statement by a Cretan, "I am lying," or simply, "This statement is false." In a world of either/or logic, where A and B are clearly defined and existence of one cancels the other, the statement is logically insoluble. To a significant extent, Gödel's Incompleteness Theorem, which states that "all consistent axiomatic formulations of number theory include undecipherable propositions," is a mathematical investigation of the Cretan paradox.[30] Gödel demonstrated that for any logical system, statements could be formulated that cannot be proven true or false (they are "undecidable") from within the system, starting with the statement, "This statement is unprovable." This is actually the First Incompleteness Theorem. The Second Incompleteness Theorem proves that the statement "The axioms of arithmetic are consistent" cannot be proved by using those same axioms.[31]

Gödel's theorem concerned self-referencing systems and holds sway in the logic developed here to separate tactics and strategy. One of the significant steps in scientific analysis is to differentiate when one is making hypotheses and taking measurements from *within* the system being studied from when one is doing the same from an observational vantage *outside* the system. Such a distinction cannot always be made. At the strategic level, it is possible to step outside the arena of combat and make decisions about war. At the tactical level we are by definition within the system of war and must make rational decisions that impact individual lives directly. Tactics is in effect a self-referencing milieu and can usefully be portrayed in that manner. But it will cause paradoxes to develop—of necessity—because decisions are made within the system. A tactician might see the current battle as the most crucial event on the road to victory, for instance, and be perfectly convinced of the truth of that. Even if the statement were true, there is no way to prove it from within the system of reference—the tactical level of war. More to the point, it is a meaningless assessment at the level of strategy. This is because the strategist instead recognizes the war for what it is: an event or series of events that has become part of the context of what is now the structure of decision making—a structure that will change with the next event.

Likewise, victory is a self-referencing notion in tactics, as is evident in the statement, "This war is winnable if politicians do not interfere." Since the decision maker at the tactical level cannot step outside the circumstances of his or her condition, anything that appears to confound the established criteria for victory is absurd. If one could withdraw from the immediacy of one's experience for a moment, an order to withdraw from a well-fortified position (for example) might make perfect sense. From the tactical perspective, doing so will put the unit at risk of heavier casualties—in addition to giving up territory that may have come at a stiff price—than staying put would. In an overall battle plan, the movement could be part of a ruse to draw the enemy into a losing position elsewhere. But what of the decision by a government to withdraw or remove its forces from combat despite having won (by the standards of victory) every battle of the war?[32] This can make no sense at all to the tactician, for the standards of victory in war do not apply to the strategic-level requirement that war is to support policy.

The physical sciences are generally perceived as focusing on objects of inquiry, the social sciences on observers or inquirers. Both emphasize the relationship between observers and observed, but their foci are opposite. Hard-science physicists tend to study empirical phenomena, the things observed, and to reject motives or justifications. Historians, on the other hand, tend to study strategists, using biography to understand the roles of individuals in time. Social historians focus on the output of societies rather than individuals but still tend to elevate the individual (in the aggregate) to prominence. As the softer sciences explore human activity that is hidden from direct view, they tend to look more equally at both the practice and the practitioners of strategy. Medical doctors and psychiatrists study the patient as well as the disease. Social scientists study both politics and politicians, culture and celebrity, and wars and warriors, and yet even within these groups there are notable divisions. Behavioralists study actions, or outputs, while Traditionalists study motives, justifications, and reasons. The real difference, again, is one of emphasis. The more the field relates to human behavior, the more its scions tend to study the observer.

The bottom line is that is impossible to observe or investigate without some point of view. Objective research does not mean that the investigator has no idea what he or she shall find, for that would make research all but futile. When one does not know where one is going, any road will take you there. Without an idea of what will be found or of what is related to the phenomena under investigation, observers nevertheless have implicit theories or explicit working hypotheses to guide their observations. Karl Popper would famously emphasize this to his students by starting class with a simple command, "Observe!" "Well," students queried, "observe what? Why? To what end?" Popper would stand mute, and eventually students would make observations such as the room is cold, the table is hard, there are fifteen males in the room. So what? Popper knew that all useful observation is guided by some theoretical perspective or belief and that this is as it must be. He would point out to the students that they were not making observations outside of the room, as they probably thought there would be some sort of exercise to follow, and that limited their observations. Some students tried to make observations that were connected to the subject matter of the course, believing that was the intent of the assignment. In the end, Popper would relent and highlight to his students that the highest integrity of objective observation is not perceiving the world with a blank mind—even if such a thing were possible, it would be more important to chart the manner in which the mind was filled with data to isolate bias or presumptive theory than to accept the random and uncoordinated observations likely to emerge. The highest integrity comes when the observer thinks she or he knows what data and information are needed to understand the situation and seeks it out but does not hide or ignore observations to the contrary or reject alternative explanations. Only when there is a theory to guide the observation can observed data and facts provide meaningful support. Only in the light of a theory, a problem, the quest for solution, can they speak to us in revealing ways. Facts can never speak for themselves, some wag wrote—they are always spoken for.

STRATEGY AND CHANGE

Change is the constant of our time, and so theories of change play heavily in the formulation of strategy. Because change is constant, no end state can profitably be contemplated by the practicing strategist. Static conditions exist only in theory. There are, of course, goals and ends in tactics, but wherever they appear in strategy the grammar of war will subsume the logic of war, to paraphrase Clausewitz, and perversions will result.[33]

For example, what is so excellent about stability that it is so popular in current U.S. strategy? The current U.S. peacekeeping and nation-building operations are based on a notion called "stability operations," or "crisis stability," the latter an oxymoron of the first rank.[34] What is it about a crisis that would lead anyone to want to stabilize it? Crises should be defused, solved, or overcome, but for what purpose should they be preserved?

Stability in international relations is the desire of the dominant persons or states to maintain their positions at the top of the extant world order. This is quite understandable, but why would those at the bottom of the order prefer stability? Shouldn't they desire upward movement?

> The actions of nations were in this view not determined, or capable of being judged, by right or wrong: the haves preached peace and the sacredness of international law, since the law sanctioned their holdings, but this code was unacceptable to virile have-not nations. The latter would rise and overthrow the degenerate capitalistic democracies, which had become the dupes of their own pacific ideology, originally intended to bemuse the underdogs.[35]

Stabilizing any system that is defined by change is a poor strategy. The best one can hope for is to postpone the crisis to a later time, when it will undoubtedly come to a head. The longer the crisis is stabilized, the greater the passion—and likely violence—for change or reform. Change is in fact the only thing that matters. Stability is a chimera, and static goals are hopeless causes.

Huge efficiencies in perception and assessment are possible because of change. Indeed, humans have become so adept at perceiving and reacting to change that they may not even be able to comprehend an end state or static condition should it present itself. People react to movement, which is change over time. It is also easily demonstrable. What we really perceive is motion, or to be more precise, changes in velocity (or Δv). Not only is change the thing that catches our attention, but it may be impossible to perceive a thing that has no change in velocity. Indeed, once change is perceived humans have a tendency to impart intrinsic meaning to it. There must be some reason for the change, some prior cause that demands change.[36]

Movement is simply change over time. Where no time passes, no movement can occur. This is obvious enough, but we can also reverse the statement and declare with utmost certainty that where there is no movement, no time passes. And this is true. All movement is a function of space and time, and humans are constructs of the real world. But even constant movement imparts no meaning if there is no Δv. Movement, or velocity, is something that makes sense only by comparison. We say something is moving with respect (or relative to) some other thing, and it is the change in distance between them we really notice. But even such constant change as this becomes static over time and less and less noticeable. A thing in constant movement is predictable; it becomes part of the scenery and deserves no further notice. But an unexpected change in direction or velocity catches our attention; it is an effect, and we look for what caused the change. We want to give the change meaning.

THE EVOLUTION OF STRATEGY

The evolution of strategy shows the dynamic interaction between context and strategists over time. Evolution theory applies to biological entities and environments, of which humanity is a part, but the metaphor is so powerful that it works its way into social constructs and physical systems as well. The primary insight is that success is fleeting. Organisms that dominate their niche will be successful only so long as the environment remains stable, and the longer an environment is perceived as stable—that is, the longer a single species dominates a niche—the more catastrophic the collapse of the perfectly adapted when change inevitably occurs.

The process is relatively simple. Organisms adapt to their environments and develop strengths and capabilities that are rewarded in their special contexts in two ways, within generations and across generations. Characteristics that are rewarded in the extant environment (specific strengths, cunning, camouflage, etc.) are heightened within the organism, and its success attracts mates. These characteristics are passed on and enhanced. But there is another key. When copying the dominating individuals and species, nature introduces slight-to-significant variations in each successive generation and lets these mutations loose. When the environment is static, most of these variations do not repeat (they die off), for they represent departures from the ideal of the perfectly adapted niche. But nature also provides an ever-changing world (in which the rules of competition keep shifting). In such a context, the mass of modifications to each generation allows optimal solutions to new problems to arise. Thus diversity is the most valued attribute of a species in a changing environment—not ideal adaptation to a specific environment. Darwin never claimed that the species best adapted to its niche will survive (which would be an extension of Herbert Spencer's notion of survival of the fittest). Darwin said the species *most able to adapt to changes in the environment* will survive.

This is how evolutionary adaptation works. Organisms interact and collect information about the world. Adaptations increase the yield of resources from the environment specific to the organism's survival, which in turn modifies the environment. Through its ability to gather and process information about the environment, the organism embarks on creating an environment that is conducive to providing more of those resources. Different adaptive problems give rise to alternative environments, and so environments and organisms are mutually adaptive. Much in the same way, successful strategy changes the context for which it was devised, making context at least partially strategy dependent. So now we are all constructivists, of course.

Conclusion

How does one explain the relationship between strategy, a plan for continuing advantage, and tactics, maximizing means toward given ends? If the outcomes of battles are the means of the strategist, as Clausewitz tells us, how do the myriad of interactions that take place between individuals in combat relate to the strategy of the state? The new science of complexity may hold the key. Metabehavior, which cannot be predicted from the interactions of components, gives meaning to those interactions. No matter how carefully we observe and describe neurons and synapses that constitute interaction in the brain, we cannot project consciousness from them, much less emotions, such as hate or love. No matter how intensely we examine the cells of an organism, we cannot project what it means to be human— or just what it means to be alive, for that matter. No matter how carefully we describe individual letters—symbols for sounds—we cannot understand the meaning of speech or predict the Gettysburg Address.

An emergent property—and strategy fits that definition—does not exist in the components of the system from which it derives. It forms as a result of the arrangement of those parts and *the myriad of interactions* between them. Craig Reynolds has pointed out that the flocking behavior of birds, an emergent property, cannot be understood by observing the characteristics that make up a bird— wings, feathers, bone structure, etc.[37] But it can be perfectly understood by the simplicity of the rules that guide their interaction. First, leave a minimum separation between yourself and the next bird (don't crowd your neighbor); second, align yourself with the average heading of everyone else; and third, steer toward the average position of the birds adjacent to you. When automata are modeled on these three rules, they exhibit the extraordinarily complex movement of flocks of birds with perfect precision.

In this way strategists can promote positive emergent properties from the myriad of individual interactions at the tactical level by providing sound rules of engagement that both properly constrain and enable the broader conduct of war along lines amenable to the state. This is not an easy task. Whenever the strategist meddles with rule sets, unintended consequences also emerge. A city or county that decides, in order to save money, to pay members of a fire department according to the number of fires it puts out rather than fixed salaries is likely to find a number of arsonists in its employ. Unfortunately, as my old history professor James B. Oviatt used to opine, "Hind-sight is better than foresight by a damned sight."

The problem of unintended consequences is inherent to situations in which strategists attempt to influence real-world systems with a lot of moving parts. Any change to these environments will have unforeseen outcomes, because the calculations necessary to determine all of them accurately are beyond current computing capacity. Thus thinking about second- or third-order effects is useful but fraught in practice with dangerous assumptions and impossible calculations: the more interactions with a complex system, the more unforeseen and unforeseeable effects.

How do strategists make unpredictability beneficial? First, they recognize there are fundamental limits to what can be known. Second, they seek out conundrums—especially paradoxes—that challenge what is accepted as true. Third, they plug away. And there are good examples of this strategy. The discovery of quantum indeterminacy in physics and mathematics—at first a frustrating conundrum—in turn fostered an unprecedented increase in our knowledge and understanding of nature.

If complex systems science could help to determine fundamental limits to the predictability of war, commanders and decision makers could refocus efforts from trying to anticipate fundamentally unknowable events—the search for the so-called silver bullet that efficiently and permanently solve problems—to increasing the resilience and adaptive capacities of their forces. The ability to adapt will provide greater responsiveness to stimuli and limit the risk of systemic or catastrophic collapse. Understanding how predictability decays over time and space is needed if we are to shape operational tempo and information dissemination policies. By challenging the simplifying assumptions of traditional approaches to preparing for future conflicts, complex theory could stimulate a much richer and valuable understanding of the phenomena of war.

NOTES

1. See Beatrice Heuser, *The Evolution of Strategy: Thinking War from Antiquity to the Present* (New York: Cambridge University Press, 2010), 3–4.

2. An excellent popular account is Stephen Greenblatt, *The Swerve: How the World Became Modern* (New York: W. W. Norton, 2012).

3. John Pockock, *The Machiavellian Moment: Florentine Political Thought and the Atlantic Republican Tradition* (Princeton, N.J.: Princeton University Press, 1967), 1.

4. Lawrence Freedman states the case flatly in his magnificent *Strategy: A History* (New York: Oxford University Press, 2013), xi: "There is no agreed-upon definition of *strategy*" [original emphasis].

5. See Edward Luttwak's *Strategy: The Logic of War and Peace* (Cambridge, Mass.: Belknap, 1987), 239–41, which includes more than a dozen accepted military definitions. Colin Gray, *Modern Strategy* (Oxford: Oxford University Press, 1999), 17–23, adds considerably to the list.

6. From the argument of Francoise Jullien, *A Treatise on Efficacy: Between Western and Chinese Thinking,* trans. Janice Lloyd (Honolulu: University of Hawaii Press, 1996), 57.

7. Nor should anyone proclaim him- or herself a strategist simply for penning a book or chapter on the subject. I have most certainly not reached that status. Strategy is still too difficult for me, evident in retrospect but awkwardly laborious in prospect. Nonetheless, I continue to study, practice, discuss, write, and learn in the hope that one day it might be so.

8. V. S. Ramachandran, "Genes, Claustrum, and Consciousness," in *This Explains Everything: Deep, Beautiful, and Elegant Theories of How the World Works,* ed. John Brockman (New York: HarperCollins, 2013), 88–89.

9. This is clearly not the *raison d'état* of Cardinal Richelieu (who extended Machiavelli's insistence that the *only* end that justifies *any* means is the continued health and benefit of the state and) who insisted that *any* end the state pursues is by definition in the national interest and that therefore the means to achieve it are morally and ethically unassailable.

10. Politics, which never ends, has its analogy to tactics in the political process culminating in selection of a leader or representative. In a democracy, the political campaign ends with an election. Candidates must achieve victory in order to govern, as tacticians must achieve objectives in the battlespace during war. But *good* military strategy is about war *in support of* sustainable peace; *good* politics goes *beyond* winning elections and is about governing in support of sustainable security and economic well-being.

11. For a fuller exposition, see Everett Dolman, *Pure Strategy: Power and Principle in the Space and Information Age* (New York: Frank Cass, 2005).

12. A point made much better by Clausewitz, who asserted that those who shy away from the violence necessary to proper military activities may feel

better about themselves but do their states and their politics no favors: see Carl von Clausewitz, *On War,* ed. and trans. Michael Howard and Peter Paret (Princeton, N.J.: Princeton University Press, 1976), 1.

13. Though not eliminated. For example, the U.S. Air Force's A-10 aircraft is designed and intended for close air support (CAS)—that is, direct ground combat support in the U.S. Army's mandate to take and hold territory.

14. Gary Bateson, "The Cybernetics of Self," cited in Derrick Niederman, *The Puzzler's Dilemma: From the Lighthouse of Alexandria to Monty Hall, a Fresh Look at Classic Conundrums of Logic, Mathematics, and Life* (New York: Penguin, 2012), 47 [emphasis added].

15. Jullien, *Treatise on Efficacy,* 37.

16. Sun Tzu, *The Art of War,* trans. Ralph D. Sawyer (Boulder, Colo.: Westview, 1994), 177.

17. A point emphatically made by Niccolò Machiavelli in *The Art of War,* revised edition of the Ellis Farneworth translation with an introduction by Neal Wood (New York: Da Capo, 1965).

18. To self-regulate, a system—for example a home furnace—must have polarity of opposition. This is the essence of the control mechanism, in this case a thermostat, which keeps a room consistently pleasant—a constant compromise between too hot and too cold.

19. Victory in this case is bounded by the political aims that employ force or the threat of force as the means. Commanders are provided with forces and capabilities, as well as limitations (for the most part rules of engagement that can also, though less often, be established as enabling broader action under specified conditions). Victory may not be destruction of the opponent or even serious incapacitation. It may be simply delay of the opponent, attrition of forces, a feint, or seizure of a particularly valuable position. Regardless, the objective is set externally to the battle, and judgments of its effectiveness to the larger campaign or war goals are determined outside the requirements of any specific battle. When one wins the battle but loses the war, the logic of tactics has *replaced* the logic of strategy.

20. James Carse, *Finite and Infinite Games: A Vision of Life as Play and Possibility* (New York: Ballantine, 1986), 152–53.

21. Ibid., 153.

22. Ibid.

23. Cited in Henry de Claude, "Scientific Uncertainty and Fabricated Uncertainty," in *The Stockholm Lectures* (Stockholm: Royal Swedish Academy of Sciences, 15 December 2011), http://sciences.blogs.liberation.fr/files/texte-de-claude-henry.pdf.

24. A point made by Alan Beyerchen, "Clausewitz, Nonlinearity, and the Unpredictability of War," *International Security* (Winter 1992/93): 59–90,

and Barry Watts, *Clausewitzian Friction and Future War,* McNair Paper 52 (Washington, D.C.: Institute for National Strategic Studies, 1996).

25. Clearly articulated by astronomer Pierre Simon LaPlace, *Philosophical Essay on Probabilities,* translation of the 1812 fifth edition by Andrew Dale, in *Sources in the History of Mathematics and Physical Science* (New York: Springer Verlag, 1994), vol. 13.

26. Gary Zukav, *The Dancing Wu Li Masters: An Overview of the New Physics* (New York: Morrow, 1979), 34–35.

27. Ibid., 32.

28. If this is true, then everything in existence may be made of nothing. Brian Green, *Elegant Universe: Superstrings, Hidden Dimensions, and the Quest for the Ultimate Theory* (New York: Alfred A. Knopf, 2000).

29. See Douglas Hofsteder, *Gödel, Escher, Bach: An Eternal Golden Braid* (New York: Basic Books, 1979).

30. Ibid., 17.

31. Stephen Wolfram, *A New Kind of Science* (Champaign, Ill.: Wolfram Media, 2002), 1158.

32. This example, of course, refers to the American military experience in Vietnam.

33. Clausewitz, *On War,* 605.

34. For example, Robert Powell, "Crisis Stability in the Nuclear Age," *American Political Science Review* 83, no. 1 (March 1989): 61–76; Dean Wilkening, Ken Watman, Michael Kennedy, and Richard Darilek, *Strategic Defenses and Crisis Stability* (Santa Monica, Calif.: RAND, 1989); Barry Posen, "Crisis Stability and Conventional Arms Control," *Daedalus* 120, no. 1 (Winter, 1991): 217–32; and Forrest Morgan, *Crisis Stability and Long-Range Strike: A Comparative Analysis of Fighters, Bombers, and Missiles* (Santa Monica, Calif.: RAND, 2013).

35. Michael Polyani and Harry Prosch, *Meaning* (Chicago: University of Chicago Press, 1975), 13.

36. See Brian Green, *The Fabric of the Cosmos: Space, Time, and the Texture of Reality* (New York: Vintage, 2005), 24–25. "A magnetic force field provides a magnet what an army provides a dictator and what auditors provide the IRS: influence beyond their physical boundaries" (40).

37. Craig Reynolds, "Flocks, Herds, and Schools: A Distributional Behavioral Model," *Computer Graphics* 21, no. 4 (1987): 25–34.

CHAPTER TWO

An Imperfect Jewel

Military Theory and the Military Profession

HAROLD R. WINTON

Again, the kingdom of heaven is like a merchant man, seeking goodly pearls, who, when he had found one pearl of great price, went and sold all that he had, and bought it.

—Matthew 13:45–46

Whatever argument can be drawn from particular examples, superficially viewed, a thorough examination of the subject will evince, that the Art of War, is at once comprehensive and complicated; that it demands much previous study; and that the possession of it, in its most improved and perfect state, is always of great moment in the security of a Nation.

—George Washington[1]

✳

These disparate texts illuminate the subject of theory and the military profession. For many military theorists and practitioners have, like the merchant of New Testament times, sought a theory that could so perfectly guide practice that it was worth selling everything to obtain it. And America's first commander in chief thought that perfection of the art of war, which presupposed at least some theoretical knowledge, was so important that the fledgling nation required a military academy where its study could be advanced. But theory used inappropriately can also be a very blunt instrument—it should carry with it a warning label, "handle with care!" This chapter expounds upon the theme of why theory is potentially useful but should be handled with caution by military professionals. First, it explores the general and somewhat problematic relationship between theory and the military profession. Next, it examines what theorists and academics say about the utility of theory. Finally, it seeks to determine what utility military theory actually has for individuals and institutions.[2]

THEORY AND THE MILITARY PROFESSION

Webster's defines theory as "a coherent group of general propositions used as principles of explanation for a class of phenomena."[3] This construct highlights the essential task of explanation and the desirable criterion of coherence. But theory has additional functions. The first two occur before explanation. Theory's first task is to define the field of study under investigation—in the words of the definition cited above, the "class of phenomena." In the theory of war, for example, Clausewitz offers two definitions. The first states baldly, "War is thus an act of force to compel our enemy to do our will."[4] After introducing the limiting factor of rationality, Clausewitz expands this definition as follows: "war is not a mere act of policy but a true political instrument, a continuation of political activity with other means."[5] In short, war is the use of force to achieve the ends of policy. Although the utility of this definition has been argued at some length, it leaves no doubt as to what Clausewitz's theory is about.[6]

The next task of theory is to categorize. Again, reference to Clausewitz is instructive. War had two temporal phases: planning and conduct and two levels: tactics and strategy.[7] Wars could also be categorized as offensive or defensive and as limited or total.[8] Categorization is part of theory's continuous evolution. Theory evolves in response to two stimuli: new explanations of old phenomena and changes in the field of study itself. An example of the former is the Copernican Revolution in astronomy.[9] An example of the latter is the early twentieth century discovery of the "operation," which emerged from the Industrial Revolution's influence on the conduct of war, as the connecting link between a battle and a campaign and subsequently led to the study of "operational art" as a new category of military art and science.[10]

Explanation is the soul of theory. It may be the product of repetitive observation and imaginative analysis as Copernicus's was, or of "intuition, supported by being sympathetically in touch with experience," as Einstein's was.[11] In either case, theory without explanation is like salt without savor—it is worthy only of the dung heap.

Theory performs two additional functions. It connects the field of study to other related fields in the universe. This marks the brilliance of Clausewitz's second definition of war, noted above. Although war had been used as a violent tool of politics since before the Peloponnesian War, Clausewitz's elegant formulation, which definitively *connected* violence with political intercourse, was perhaps his most important and enduring contribution to the theory of war. Finally, theory anticipates. The choice of verb is deliberate. In the physical realm, theory predicts. Newton's theory of gravitation and Kepler's laws of planetary motion, combined with detailed observations of perturbations in the orbit of Uranus and systematic hypothesis testing, allowed Urbain Jean Le Verrier and John Couch Adams independently to predict the location of Neptune in 1845.[12] But action and reaction in the human arena are much less certain, and here we must be content with a less definitive standard. Anticipation, however, can be almost as useful as prediction. In the mid-1930s Mikhail Tukhachevskii and a similarly minded coterie of Soviet officers discovered that they had the technological capacity "not only to exercise pressure directly on the enemy's front line, but to penetrate his dispositions and to attack him simultaneously over the whole depth of his tactical layout."[13] They lacked both the means and the knowledge that would allow them to extend this "deep battle" capability to the level of "deep operations," where the problems of coordination on a large scale would be infinitely more complex. But the underlying conceptual construct, i.e., what was practically feasible on a small level was theoretically achievable on a larger scale, was a powerful notion that informed the actions of the Soviet armed forces in the latter stages of World War II and the American armed forces in the Gulf War of 1991.

But theory also has its limitations. No theory can fully replicate reality. There are simply too many variables in the real world for theory to contemplate them all. Thus, all theories are simplifications. Second, as alluded to earlier, things change. In the realm of military affairs, such change is uneven, varying between apparent stasis and virtual revolution. Therefore, military theory always lags behind the explanatory curve of contemporary developments. Here we can paraphrase Michael Howard's stricture on doctrine, theory's handmaiden, and declare dogmatically that whatever theories exist (at least in the realm of human affairs), they are bound to be wrong—the trick is to keep them from being "too badly wrong."[14]

Thus, although theory is never complete and is always bound to be at least partially invalid, it performs several very useful functions when it defines, categorizes, explains, connects, and anticipates.

And it is primarily of the mind. The formulation of theory demands intense powers of observation, ruthless intellectual honesty, clear thinking, mental stamina of the highest order, gifted imagination, and other qualities that defy easy description.[15] These are not qualities normally associated with the military profession.

Why not? First, war is an intensely practical activity and a draconian auditor of individuals and institutions. The business of controlled violence in the service of political interest demands strict attention to detail and concrete results. Complex organizations of people and equipment must be trained and conditioned to survive under conditions of significant privation and great stress, moved to the right place at the right time, and thrust into action against an adversary determined to kill or maim in frustrating the accomplishment of their goals. Those who cannot succeed in this brutal and unforgiving milieu deservedly fall by the wayside. Second, war demands the disciplined acceptance of lawful orders—even when such orders can lead to one's own death or disablement. A warrior unwilling to follow orders is a contradiction in terms. Thus, there is an inherent bias in military personnel to obey rather than to question. This tendency does more good than harm in the long run, but it does limit theoretical contemplation. Finally, war is episodic. Copernicus could look at the movement of the planets on any clear night and at the sun on any clear day. But war comes and goes, rather like some inexplicable disease; and the resulting discontinuities make it a difficult phenomenon about which to theorize.

Despite these realities, the military profession is not inherently anti-theoretical. There are countervailing tendencies. As both Sun Tzu and Clausewitz cogently observe, the very seriousness of war provides a healthy stimulus to contemplation.[16] Its episodic nature, while restricting opportunity for direct observation, provides opportunity for reflection. Furthermore, the very complexity of war, while limiting the ability of theorists to master it, creates incentives for military practitioners to discover simplifying notions that reduce its seeming intractability.

But the larger point remains: underlying truths about both theory and the military profession make the relationship between the two problematic. To probe this uneasy relationship more deeply requires a dual-track approach—first, to explore the question of what utility theory *should* have for both individuals and military institutions; second, to see what utility it actually *does* have. The former focuses on the opinions of theorists and educators; the latter plumbs empirical evidence. An important caveat is in order—tracing connections between thought and action is intrinsically difficult. When the nature of the thought is conceptual, rather than pragmatic, as theory is bound to be, such sleuthing becomes even more challenging; and one is frequently forced to rely on inferential conjecture and even a bit of imagination to connect the deed to an antecedent proposition.

THE THEORISTS MAKE THEIR CASE

We are fortunate to possess a narrow but rich body of discourse about theory's contribution to individual military judgment, found densely packed in *On War*. The DNA of Clausewitz's brain is cogently revealed in Book Two, "On the Theory of War." He begins this discourse by classifying war into the related but distinct fields of tactics and strategy. He then stingingly critiques the theories of his day, which sought to exclude from war three of its most important characteristics: the action of moral forces, the frustrating power of the enemy's will, and the endemic uncertainty of information. From this, he deduces that "a positive teaching is unattainable."[17] Clausewitz sees two ways out of this difficulty. The first is to admit baldly that whatever theory is developed will have decreasing validity at the higher levels of war where "almost all solutions must be left to imaginative intellect."[18] The second is to argue that theory is a tool to aid the contemplative mind, rather than a guide for action.

This formulation leads to some of the most majestic passages of *On War*: "Theory will have fulfilled its main task when it is used to analyze the constituent elements of war, to distinguish precisely what at first seems fused, to explain in full the properties of the means employed and to show their probable effects, to define clearly the nature of the ends in view, and to illuminate all phases of war through critical inquiry. Theory then becomes a guide to anyone who wants to learn about war from books; it will light his way, ease his progress, train his judgment, and help him avoid pitfalls."[19] He makes it abundantly clear that the cumulative insights derived from theory must ultimately find practical expression: "It [theory] will be sufficient if it helps the commander acquire those insights that, once absorbed into his way of thinking, will smooth and protect his progress, and will never force him to abandon his convictions for the sake of any objective fact."[20] Thus, to paraphrase Carl Becker's argument that every man should be his own historian, Clausewitz implied that every commander should be his own theorist.[21] The essential function of theory is to aid him in his total learning, which synthesizes study, experience, observation, and reflection into a coherent whole, manifested as an ever-alert, refined military judgment.

There is, however, another view of the utility of theory, articulated by Clausewitz's chief competitor in this arena, Antoine Henri de Jomini. Jomini believed in the power of positive teaching. Although he was prepared to admit that war as a whole was an art, strategy, the main subject of his work was "regulated by fixed laws resembling those of the positive sciences."[22] He asserted that "It is true that theories cannot teach men with mathematical precision what they should do in every possible case; but it is also certain that they will always point out the errors which should be avoided; and this is a highly important consideration, for these rules thus become, in the hands of skillful generals commanding brave troops, means of almost certain success."[23] This faith in the efficacy of prescriptive theory led Jomini to formulate his theory much differently than had Clausewitz. At the epicenter of Clausewitz's theory, we find a trinity of the elemental forces of war—violence, chance, and reason—acting in multifarious ways, whose dynamics the statesman and commander must thoroughly consider before deciding whether to go to war and how to do so.[24] Jomini's central proposition consists of a series of four maxims about strategy, which he summarized as "bringing the greatest part of the forces of an army upon the important point of a theater of war or of the zone of operations."[25]

Clausewitz's and Jomini's views of theory were not mutually exclusive. Jomini addressed some of the wider considerations of policy central to Clausewitz, most notably in the opening chapter of *The Art of War.*[26] And Clausewitz occasionally engaged in formulaic statements, perhaps most notably in his observation that "destruction of the enemy force is always the superior, more effective means, with which others cannot compete."[27] Nevertheless, their two approaches—one descriptive, the other prescriptive—represent the two normative poles concerning both the utility of theory and its proper formulation.

We find useful insights into the utility of theory from more modern observers as well. In his 1959 Foreword to Henry E. Eccles's *Logistics in the National Defense,* Henry M. Wriston writes, "Theory is not just dreams or wishful thinking. It is the orderly interpretation of accumulated experience and its formal enunciation as a guide to future intelligent action to better that experience."[28] Wriston captures an important truth: the fundamental social utility of theory is to help realize man's almost universal longing to make his future better than his past. The fact that Eccles offered a theory of military logistics was but a particular manifestation of a general verity. Several years later, J. C. Wylie developed a formulation similar to Wriston's, which described the mechanics of translating theory into action: "Theory serves a useful purpose to the extent that it can collect and organize the experiences and ideas of other men, sort out which of them may have a valid transfer value to a new and different situation, and help the practitioner to enlarge his vision in an orderly, manageable and useful fashion—and then apply it to the reality with which he is faced."[29] Wriston and Wylie provide a useful synthesis and updating of Clausewitz and Jomini, re-articulating the value of theory to the military professional.

But there are also broader institutional implications of military theory that are manifested most prominently in doctrine.[30] Along a scale from the purely abstract to the purely concrete, doctrine occupies a middle ground representing a conceptual link between theory and practice. Doctrine also represents sanctioned theory. Thus, two principal distinctions exist between theory and doctrine: the latter is decidedly more pragmatic; and it is stamped with an institutional imprimatur.

To recapitulate, two broad concepts exist about how theory should affect the individual military professional. In the Clausewitzian view, it educates the judgment; in the Jominian, it provides concrete guides to action. And one would suspect that institutionally theory's influence would be clearly evident in doctrine. But these observations do not address two essential questions: What role *does* theory play in the development of military professionals, and what influence *does* it have on military establishments?

THE ACTUAL ROLE OF THEORY

Any attempt at comprehensiveness in addressing these two questions would be far beyond the scope of this essay. What follows is impressionistic but hopefully instructive. For the question of individuals, we shall examine two extremely successful commanders—George S. Patton Jr. and Ulysses S. Grant. Patton is the archetype of a military commander who consciously used theory, in conjunction with history, as a tool with which to develop a refined military mind. Grant represents the opposite extreme—a man who developed a sound military mind with practically no recourse to theory or any systematic study of military knowledge. On the doctrinal issue, the chapter explores the theoretical underpinnings of the 1982 and 1986 statements of United States Army doctrine and the 1992 articulation of United States Air Force doctrine.

George S. Patton Jr.

Patton's concept of how scholarship contributed to the development of military capability is clearly evident in his 1927 lecture "The Secret of Victory," published in the January 1931 issue of *Infantry Journal* as "Success in War."[31] There were, Patton argued, "three essentials to victory—inspiration, knowledge, and force."[32] Regarding the second element, Patton believed that "spontaneous, untutored inspiration" was a chimera and the responsibilities of defending the nation demanded "thoughtful preparation and studious effort."[33] His argument was somewhat contradictory. In one passage he stated "that no one element . . . is dominant; that a combination of any two of these factors gives a strong presumption of success over an adversary who relies on one alone, while the three in combination are practically invincible against combination of any other two."[34] On the other hand, he argued that America had the resources to match any potential opponent and that in terms of education, its officers had "no superiors and few equals." Therefore, victory lay in the realm of the human spirit: "The fixed determination to acquire the warrior soul, and having acquired it, to conquer or perish with honor," Patton concluded, "is the secret of success in war."[35]

While it is well known that heeding Napoleon's advice to "Read again and again the campaigns of Hannibal, Caesar, Gustavus Adolphus, Turenne, Eugene, and Frederick" was an integral part of Patton's assiduous quest to acquire the warrior's mind and spirit, a close examination of his reading habits indicates that conceptual works were also a major staple.[36] While a cadet at West Point in 1906, Patton's "List of Books I Should Read" included Napoleon's *Maximes de la Guerre*, E. B. Hamley's *The Operations of War*, G. F. R. Henderson's *The Science of War*, and Jomini's *The Art of War*.[37] In 1926 he charted his progress. In the list of works found in the back of W. D. Bird's *The Direction of War: A Study of Strategy*, Patton indicated that he had read Clausewitz, *On War*; Hamley, *The Operations of War*; von der Goltz, *The Conduct of War*; Henderson, *The Science of War*; and Hohenloe-Ingelfingen, *Letters on Strategy*—as well as some twenty other books.[38] Later that year, he decided to study Clausewitz again, having read him in an abbreviated form in 1910.[39] This time he used the three-volume 1918 edition of the J. J. Graham translation, with notes by F. N. Maude. Patton's notes indicate an intense mental engagement with Clausewitz, vehemently disagreeing with all passages that suggested moderation in the conduct of war. But other passages appealed to him. Where the Prussian theorist had written, "Every special calling in life, if it is to be followed with success, requires peculiar qualities of understanding and soul. Where these are of a high order, and manifest themselves by extraordinary achievements the mind to which they belong is termed *genius*," Patton underscored the word "soul" and substituted the word "person" for Clausewitz's "mind."[40] But Patton was even more taken with Ardant du Picq's *Battle Studies,* which had been translated into English in 1921. Here was a practitioner-theorist after Patton's own heart. Although du Picq clearly argued that good arms, sound doctrine, and proper organization were necessary for success in battle, he emphasized the moral dimension of combat effectiveness.[41] Patton typed 138 notes on 26 cards summarizing and commenting upon du Picq's work. Thus, it is clear that Patton studied theory as assiduously as he did history.

But what can we say of Patton's success in war? Three things stand out. First, he knew how to integrate multiple capabilities. Second, contrary to popular opinion and although it deeply offended his instincts, he could be as successful in positional warfare as he could in open-field maneuver. Finally, like all senior commanders, he made mistakes. The integration of diverse capabilities is perhaps best exemplified in his August 1944 drive across France. He artfully blended ground maneuver, intelligence, and air support into a coherent whole that kept the Germans on the defensive, minimized Third Army's casualties, and liberated great swaths of the French countryside.[42] But in his cover letter to the Third Army after-action report for operations in Europe in World War II, Patton made the following observation: "It is noteworthy that while our operations in pursuit or exploitation have at times developed exceptional speed, they have always been preceded by bitter and sometimes prolonged assaults."[43] Perhaps the most bitter of this fighting was the grinding battle of attrition around Bastogne in the days after III Corps had relieved the surrounded soldiers of the 101st Airborne Division but before the back of the German assault had been broken. Shortly after noon on 31 December 1944, the III Corps chief of staff called Patton to update him on the situation. During this conversation, Patton told III Corps that "he didn't care how much ground to the Northeast [*sic*] Bob [Robert W. Grow, Commanding General, 6th Armored Division] gained today—to fan out and kill Germans."[44] This order clearly reveals the flexibility of Patton's mind. Patton was renowned for his desire to gain ground quickly. But in this phase of the war, it became clear to him that breaking out of the Bastogne perimeter meant killing as many German soldiers as possible—even if it took more time.

Patton was not, however, infallible. His move to turn the Third Army ninety degrees and direct it toward Bastogne during the Ardennes counteroffensive is rightly regarded as one of his greatest moments. He listened receptively to his G-2's warning that an offensive was likely; he instructed his staff to prepare contingency plans to deal with such an eventuality; and he set aside personal reservations about the III Corps commander, the un-tested John Millikin, to orchestrate the attack because Millikin's corps was in the best position to do so.[45] But if we pry beneath the surface, we find an army commander whose pride in having promised a speedy relief of Bastogne drove him to over-supervision of his subordinates and poorly considered tactical directives. The most egregious of these was his instruction to Millikin to direct his division commanders to attack in columns of regiments. While such formations would theoretically accelerate the attack, in practice they would have impeded it. The reasons were simple: attacking on a front of roughly twenty-two miles, with eight maneuver regimental equivalents, over cross-compartmented terrain, in terrible weather, against a skillful adversary, three columns of regiments would offer the Germans huge gaps between the American columns that could be exploited both defensively and offensively. The only choice open to Millikin was to allow the division commanders to attack on a broad front. This slowed the advance in the short run but made it more certain in the end. To Patton's credit, he did not enforce his edict, eventually got a fourth division into the line, and narrowed the III Corps attack zone. Millikin made the higher tactical decisions that led to the relief of Bastogne. But Patton's operational moves materially assisted in the bitter fighting immediately following Bastogne's relief. Perhaps, in Clausewitzian terms, Patton recognized that in attempting to dictate an inappropriate scheme of maneuver, he had crossed the line between determination and obstinacy.[46]

"Perhaps" here is used advisedly, for when we attempt to make connections between Patton the student of military theory and Patton the warrior, we can, at best, draw but dotted lines. Intellectually, Patton understood the Clausewitzian connection between war and politics; but at the end of World War II, his suggestions for war between America and the USSR seem totally un-Clausewitzian.[47] Perhaps the strongest positive inference that can be made is between du Picq's emphasis on moral factors in war and Patton's constant resort to the same themes. His papers are replete with instances in which he gave himself the main credit for having stiffened the resolve of subordinates who wanted to cancel or postpone an offensive or withdraw in the face of enemy action.[48] But even here we must exercise caution, for we cannot determine for sure whether du Picq influenced his thinking in these matters or merely gave expression to beliefs already deeply held and strongly formed. The best we can conclude from the available evidence is to hypothesize that Patton used theory as Clausewitz intended it to be used—it was "so absorbed into the mind that it almost ceases to exist in a separate, objective way."[49]

Ulysses S. Grant

If Patton was the astute student of military theory who demonstrated a genius for war, Grant developed the genius without the theory. The curriculum at West Point in the mid-nineteenth century concentrated on mathematics, science, and engineering but did not systematically address the conduct of war.[50] What little instruction there was in military matters was chiefly taught by the Professor of Engineering, Dennis Hart Mahan. Even here the engineering portions of Mahan's course took precedence, and instruction in the science of war was confined to only six lessons.[51] Furthermore, the state of instruction in military strategy at West Point while Grant was a cadet was found by a congressional committee chaired by Senator Jefferson Davis to be in significant disarray.[52] And unlike his contemporaries George B. McClellan and Henry W. Halleck, Grant eschewed involvement in Mahan's Napoleon Club, which allowed a few cadets to pursue the study of war in greater depth.[53] So Grant, bored by the curriculum and disinclined toward military pomp, diverted himself by reading novels. From the vantage point of four decades later, he opined that he "never succeeded in getting squarely at either end of my class, in any one study, during the four years."[54] What was true of the particular was true of the general: Grant graduated nineteenth in a class of thirty-nine.[55] Nor is there any evidence of his doing serious professional reading between his 1843 graduation and his resignation from the Army in 1854.

So, then, how did Grant learn to become a high commander? The story is compellingly told by Arthur L. Conger in *The Rise of U. S. Grant*.[56] Conger's answer is simple: Grant learned on the job. But unlike other men, once Grant internalized a lesson, it never left him. This was perhaps most evident in a small incident that occurred in July 1861 while Grant was commanding a regiment of Illinois volunteers ordered to engage a Confederate force under Colonel Thomas Harris. Grant's account of the operation is revealing. As he approached the enemy's camp, Grant grew increasingly anxious, only to discover upon arrival that his adversary had already departed. Then, "It occurred to me at once that Harris had been as much afraid of me as I had been of him. It was a view of the question I had never taken before; but it was one I never forgot afterwards. From that event to the close of the war, I never experienced trepidation upon confronting an enemy. . . . I never forgot that he had as much reason to fear my forces as I had his. The lesson was valuable."[57]

Sherman also testified that Grant indeed never forgot that lesson. Writing to his friend and compatriot, J. H. Wilson, he put Grant's sang-froid into an important perspective: "I am a damn sight smarter than Grant. . . . But I tell you where he beats me, and where he beats the world. He don't care a damn for what the enemy does out of his sight, but it scares me like hell."[58]

Grant's insight paid great dividends. In February 1862 after an easy victory at Fort Henry on the Tennessee River, he marched across country to attack the much stronger Confederate garrison at Fort Donelson on the Cumberland.[59] After an initial attempt to pound the fortress into submission with a naval bombardment was beaten off, the Confederates attacked Grant's unguarded right flank, pushing one division back and threatening a second. Grant quickly stabilized the situation. He then reasoned that the enemy force would be somewhat demoralized by its failure to lift the siege, so he ordered an attack for the next morning, which forced a Confederate withdrawal and led to General Simon Bolivar Buckner's reluctant acceptance of Grant's terms: unconditional surrender. Similarly, taken unawares by Albert S. Johnston's attack on his encampment at Shiloh on 6 April 1862, Grant again moved to the scene of the action, surveyed the battlefield, ordered up reserves, and staved off disaster.[60] His calm demeanor and organized mind inspired confidence in his subordinates. But his insight into the apprehensions and difficulties that existed on the other side of the hill also paid off. For while Grant had no way of knowing that Johnston had been killed leading a charge in the center of the Confederate line, he sensed late in the afternoon that the impetus of the attack had been broken. Asked by a reporter if the capture of the Union general Benjamin M. Prentiss and over two thousand men made for a very bad situation, Grant replied, "Oh, no. They can't break our lines tonight—it is too late. Tomorrow we shall attack them with fresh troops and drive them, of course."[61] But Conger also illuminates another aspect of Grant's performance at Shiloh—he had by this time recognized the importance of delegating authority to trustworthy subordinates. And this not only included his division commanders, it also included Lieutenant Colonel James B. McPherson, Grant's chief of engineers, who acted as an ex-officio deputy chief of staff during the first, critical hours of the battle, moving about the battlefield, positioning reserves, and maintaining coordination among the division commanders until Grant's arrival at Pittsburg Landing.

Thus, by the time he was appointed as commander of the Union armies, Grant had internalized the mental, psychological, and organizational attributes necessary to win at the level of senior military commander. In this high command, we can detect the underlying attributes of his genius through the eyes of three very different historians. To Conger, Grant's greatest attribute was his ability to see the war whole.[62] He understood that the Union's superior resources must be brought to bear against the main centers of Confederate strength, both economic and military. Although imperfectly executed in 1864, this strategic concept was basically sound, congruent with political reality, and ultimately successful. To Bruce Catton, Grant's genius was in his unwavering determination to succeed and the bond this commitment cemented between the commander and his soldiers. The key moment came on the night of 7 May 1864 when, after two days of horrendous fighting in the Wilderness, Grant decided to break off the attack.[63] As the columns moved east, many of the bone-weary soldiers grew cynical, believing Grant, like all his predecessors, was marching toward Fredericksburg and north across the Rappahannock to safety. But when they took a route southeast toward Spotsylvania Courthouse, they knew that they had a commander who would keep fighting. To J. F. C. Fuller, Grant's genius lay in his instinctive recognition of the realities of modern economic, industrialized warfare. Unlike the European general staffs of the late nineteenth century, which looked upon the American Civil War as an aberration, Fuller, looking back from the post–World War I era, drew a straight line from the American Civil War, through the Franco-Prussian War, to World War I.[64] He called Grant "a man of quite extraordinary vision; a vision which was prophetic."[65]

This description fit with Grant's conception of himself. Conger noted that in the aftermath of Shiloh, Grant found it difficult to consult with his superior, Henry Halleck, because he did not understand Halleck's strategic vocabulary of the formal geometry of eighteenth century warfare.[66] Indeed, Grant said, "I don't underrate the value of military knowledge, but if men make war in slavish observances of rules they will fail. . . . War is progressive, because all the instruments and elements of war are progressive. . . . every war I knew anything about had made laws for itself."[67] To which Clausewitz would reply with a knowing wink, "what genius does is the best rule. . . ."[68]

Like Patton, Grant's generalship at the apogee of his career was not perfect. On the evening of 1 June 1864, he reconnoitered Lee's position at Cold Harbor.[69] There, he believed he saw an opportunity to interpose Meade's army between Lee's and Richmond, and ordered an attack for the next day. But the Army of the Potomac was lethargic and could not attack until the morning of the 3rd. Lee used the intervening time to reinforce his lines. The Union attack, which Meade directed but Grant allowed, was a bloodbath—the Federals lost over seven thousand soldiers to the Confederates' fifteen hundred.[70] Grant later expressed regret that the attack had been made, noting accurately that "no advantage whatever was gained to compensate the heavy losses we sustained."[71] But this was the last time he allowed an attack go forth under such unfavorable conditions, so perhaps he had realized that he had, like Patton was to do eighty years later, crossed the faint line between determination and obstinacy. Thus, Cold Harbor may represent both a blight on Grant's generalship and another step in the maturation of his genius.

In summary, the evidence as to the role of theory in the development of a great commander is mixed. In Patton, we can at best make informed inferences that his assiduous reading, which included classical and modern military theory, biography, campaign studies, and contemporary developments, combined with a warrior spirit to produce a highly competent practitioner of the operational art. In Grant's case, we see the mind of both an effective strategist and campaigner developed through intense powers of observation and reflection, without any semblance of formal study. This leads to the conclusion that for the military professional, the study of theory, while it can be quite useful, is insufficient for the development of military genius and that it in some (probably rare) cases may not even be necessary.

DOCTRINE

If the evidence as to how theory affects individuals is suggestive but inconclusive, what can we discover about how theory influences military institutions? As noted earlier, such influence is most pronounced in the formulation of doctrine.

Normally theory provides general propositions and doctrine assesses the extent to which these strictures apply, fail to apply, or apply with qualifications in particular eras and under particular conditions. In other words, the intellectual influence flows from the general to the particular. But at times the relationship is reversed. This occurs when doctrine seeks to deal with new phenomena for which theory has not yet been well developed, such as for the employment of nuclear weapons in the 1950s, or when doctrine developers themselves formulate new ways of categorizing or new relational propositions. In cases such as these, doctrine preempts theory.

Our first laboratory for exploring these relationships is the United States Army in the aftermath of the Vietnam War. In 1976 it promulgated Field Manual 100-5, *Operations*. This manual was crafted by its architect, William E. DePuy, first commander of the U.S. Army Training and Doctrine Command (TRADOC), to shake the Army out of its post-Vietnam miasma and provide a conceptual framework for defeating a Soviet incursion into Western Europe.[72] It succeeded in the first but failed in the second. DePuy definitely got the Army's attention; but his fundamental concept of piling on in front of Soviet penetrations, which he referred to as "Active Defense," did not find favor. It was seen as reactive, rather than responsive; dealing with the first battle, but not the last; and insufficiently attentive to Soviet formations in the second operational and strategic echelons. Thus, the stage was set for a new manual, a new concept, and a new marketing label.

The new manual was the 1982 edition of FM 100-5; the new concept was to fight the Soviets in depth and hit them at unexpected times from unexpected directions; and the new marketing label was "AirLand Battle." The principal authors were two gifted officers, L. D. "Don" Holder and Huba Wass de Czege. The manual they produced under the general direction of Donn A. Starry, DePuy's successor at TRADOC, was clearly informed by theory as well as history. From Clausewitz came notions such as the manual's opening sentence, "There is no simple formula for winning wars"; a direct quotation to the effect that "The whole of military activity must . . . relate directly or indirectly to the engagement"; "The objective of all operations is to destroy the opposing force"; and another direct citation characterizing the defense as a "shield of [well-directed] blows."[73] But there was also a strong element of indirectness in the manual that one could trace to the ideas of Sun Tzu, who was explicitly mentioned, and Basil Liddell Hart, who was not. Sun Tzu was quoted to the effect that, "Rapidity is the essence of war; take advantage of the enemy's unreadiness, make your way by unexpected routes, and attack unguarded spots"; soldiers were adjured that "our tactics must appear formless to the enemy"; and one of the seven combat imperatives was to "Direct Friendly Strengths Against Enemy Weaknesses."[74] Additionally, the manual's extensive discussion of "Deep Battle," which advocated striking well behind enemy lines to disrupt the commitment of reinforcements and subject the opposing force to piecemeal defeat, drew heavily on the legacy of Mikhail

Tukhachevskii, V. K. Triandafillov, A. A. Svechin, and other Soviet thinkers of the 1920s and 1930s.[75] Although it was politically infeasible to acknowledge this intellectual debt at the height of the Cold War, the apparent reasoning here was that one had to fight fire with fire. A further reflection of this debt was the introduction of a variation of the Soviet term "operational art" into the American military lexicon as the "operational level of war."[76]

The manual was updated four years later. This time, a third author was brought into the work, Richard Hart Sinnreich. Holder, Wass de Czege, and Sinnreich engaged in a collaborative effort that expanded and conceptualized the notion of operational art, which was directly borrowed from the Soviet nomenclature. But rather than associating the term "operational" with large-scale operations, as had been done in the previous edition, the 1986 manual defined operational art as "the employment of military forces to attain strategic goals in a theater of war or theater of operations through the design, organization, and conduct of campaigns and major operations."[77] This depiction of operational art as a conceptual link between tactical events and strategic results significantly broadened the Soviet concept and made it applicable to the wide variety of types of wars that the American army might have to fight. It also harkened back to Clausewitz's definition of strategy as "the use of an engagement for the purpose of the war."[78] The manual then ventured into some theory of its own in requiring the operational commander to address three issues: the condition required to affect the strategic goal, the sequence of actions necessary to produce the condition, and the resources required to generate the sequence of actions. The combination of a new definition of operational art and a framework for connecting resources, actions, and effects gave the manual an underlying coherence that made it a useful document in its day and an admirable example of the genre of doctrinal literature.

Roughly contemporaneously with the publication of the second expression of the Army's AirLand Battle doctrine, a group of airmen with a scholastic bent was assembled at the Airpower Research Institute (ARI) of the U.S. Air Force College of Aerospace Doctrine, Research, and Education (CADRE) to launch a bold experiment in the formulation of Air Force doctrine. This effort was based on an idea put forth by the respected Air Force historian Robert Frank Futrell, who opined that doctrine should be published with footnotes to document the evidence supporting doctrinal statements.[79] The ARI Director, Dennis M. Drew, decided to put Futrell's idea to the test. But he and his team expanded on Futrell's notion. They would publish the doctrine in two volumes. The first, relatively thin, document would contain the bare propositional inventory; the second, more substantial, tome would lay out the evidence upon which the statements in the first were based. The result was a good deal of research and a good deal of argument; but by the eve of the 1991 Gulf War, Drew and his team had produced a workable first draft.

Publication was delayed until 1992 to allow the Air Force to assimilate the experience of the recent war. The result was what Air Force Chief of Staff Merrill A. McPeak called "one of the most important documents published by the United States Air Force."[80] He was arguably correct. No other American armed service had ever mustered the intellectual courage to put its analysis where its propositions were. It was potentially a paradigm for a new, analytically rigorous approach to the articulation of doctrine.[81] The primary influence on the manual was empirical. Historical essays addressed issues such as the environment, capabilities, force composition, roles and missions, and employment of aerospace power as well as the sustainment, training, organizing, and equipping of aerospace forces.[82] But there was a notable conceptual cant as well. The opening pages contained either paraphrases or quotations from Clausewitz: "War is an instrument of political policy"; "the military objective in war is to compel the adversary to do our will"; and "war is characterized by 'fog, friction, and chance.'"[83] And the notion that "An airman, acting as an air component commander, should be responsible for employing all air and space assets in the theater" was right out of Giulio Douhet and Billy Mitchell.[84] There was also a nod in the direction of Sun Tzu and Liddell Hart: "Any enemy with the capacity to be a threat is likely to have strategic vulnerabilities susceptible to air attack; discerning those vulnerabilities is an airman's task."[85] The 1992 statement of Air Force basic doctrine represented a promising new approach to doctrinal formulation and articulation. Given this strong dose of intellectual rigor, it is not surprising that the experiment was short-lived.[86]

CONCLUSIONS

In summing up, it is tempting to find a general parallel with Patton's experience. Military theory *can be* quite valuable as *one* ingredient in the formation of a military mind; it serves best as an *adjunct* to genius. But it is also important to note that in rare cases of natural genius, such as Grant's, it may not be necessary. It is, however, extremely useful in doctrinal development. Furthermore, we must not lose sight of a larger truth. To a mind that artfully combines discipline with intuition, well-founded theory affords the warrior the opportunity to roam freely between the general and the particular. In doing so, it can help him frame issues more broadly, ask questions more concisely, evaluate responses more discriminately, propose alternatives more imaginatively, investigate options more systematically, and arrive at accurate conclusions more rapidly. All these capabilities have powerful transfer value to the real world, and the last one has particular relevance for the military practitioner.

Thus, like the merchant of the New Testament, we should seek, as we would a pearl of great price, a theory that will reveal the fundamental verities of the science of war; and, as America's first commander in chief adjured, we should also strive to develop the theory of the art of war in its most advanced and perfect state. But we must also realize that our reach will always exceed our grasp; for while a good theory is as valuable as a precious stone, all theories, like all jewels, are bound to contain imperfections.

NOTES

1. George Washington, Eighth Annual Address to Congress, December 7, 1796, cited from John C. Fitzpatrick, ed., *The Writings of George Washington from the Original Manuscript Sources* (Washington: United States Government Printing Office, 1940), 35:317.

2. This chapter is derived from a paper of same title given at the May 2004 meeting of the Society for Military History. I am indebted to Colin Gray for his encouragement to seek publication and to James Schneider for suggesting several of the functions of theory herein addressed. It was published in *The Journal of Strategic Studies* 34 (December 2011): 853–77 and is used here with minor emendations by kind permission of the Taylor & Francis Group.

3. *Webster's Encyclopedic Unabridged Dictionary of the English Language* (New York: Gramercy Books, 1996), 1967.

4. Carl von Clausewitz, *On War,* ed. and tr. Michael Howard and Peter Paret (Princeton: Princeton University Press, 1989), 75.

5. Clausewitz, *On War,* 87.

6. Perhaps the most spirited assault on Clausewitz's notion that war is an extension of politics is found in John Keegan, *A History of Warfare* (New York: Alfred A. Knopf, 1993), 3–60. For an equally spirited rejoinder, see Christopher Bassford, "John Keegan and the Grand Tradition of Trashing Clausewitz: A Polemic," *War in History* 1 (November 1994): 319–36.

7. Clausewitz, *On War,* 128.

8. Clausewitz, *On War,* 611–37.

9. For a fascinating description of how Copernicus developed his new view of the universe, see Thomas S. Kuhn, *The Copernican Revolution: Planetary Astronomy in the Development of Western Thought* (1957; reprint, Cambridge: Harvard University Press, 1999), 134–84.

10. The roots and early study of operational art are succinctly described in David M. Glantz, *Soviet Military Operational Art: In Pursuit of Deep Battle* (London: Frank Cass, 1991), 17–38.

11. Albert Einstein's lead essay in the collection *Science et Synthèse* (Paris: Gallimard, 1967), 28, cited in Gerald Holton, *Thematic Origins of Scientific Thought: Kepler to Einstein* (Cambridge: Harvard University Press, 1980), 357.

12. J. J. O'Connor and E. F. Robertson, "Mathematical Discovery of Planets," available from http://www-history.mcs.st-and.ac.uk/HistTopics/Neptune _and_Pluto.html. Accessed 4 October 2010.

13. Mikhail Tukhachevskii, "The Red Army's New (1936) Field Service Regulations," in Richard Simpkin, *Deep Battle: The Brainchild of Marshal Tukhachevskii* (London: Brassey's Defence Publishers, 1987), 170.

14. Michael Howard, "Military Science in an Age of Peace," *Journal of the Royal United Services Institute for Defence Studies* 119 (March 1974): 7.

15. Holton attempts to capture the essential qualities of scientific genius in *Thematic Origins of Scientific Thought,* 353–80. His major focus in this investigation is the genius's ability to work in the mental realm of apparent opposites. Although I am not equating the ability to formulate theory with genius, I am arguing that such formulation requires many of the same qualities that Holton describes.

16. "War is a matter of vital importance to the State; the province of life or death; the road to survival or ruin. It is mandatory that it be thoroughly studied." Sun Tzu, *The Art of War,* tr. Samuel B. Griffith (New York: Oxford University Press, 1963), 63. "War is not pastime; it is no mere joy in daring and winning, no place for irresponsible enthusiasts. It is a serious means to a serious end. . . ." Clausewitz, *On War,* 86.

17. Clausewitz, *On War,* 140. In the Paret-Howard translation, the phrase reads, "A Positive Doctrine is Unattainable." The text comes from a subchapter heading, *"Eine positive Lehre ist unmöglich."* Carl von Clausewitz, *Vom Kriege,* 19th ed., ed. Werner Hahlweg (Bonn: Ferd. Dümmlers Verlag, 1991), 289. The rendering of the German *Lehre* as doctrine is entirely appropriate. However, in light of the very specific military connotation that the term doctrine has developed since the early 1970s as being officially sanctioned principles that guide the actions of armed forces, I have chosen to render *Lehre* as the somewhat more general term, teaching.

18. Clausewitz, *On War,* 140.

19. Clausewitz, *On War,* 141.

20. Clausewitz, *On War,* 146–47.

21. Carl Becker, "Everyman His Own Historian," *American Historical Review* 37 (January, 1932): 221–36; reprinted in Carl L. Becker, *Everyman His Own Historian: Essays on History and Politics* (New York: F. S. Crofts, 1935), 233–55.

22. Baron de Jomini, *The Art of War,* tr. G. H. Mendell and W. P. Craighill (1862; reprint, Westport, Conn.: Greenwood Press, 1971), 321.

23. Jomini, *Art of War,* 323.

24. Clausewitz, *On War,* 89. Clausewitz's description of the three elements provides a strong indication of his lack of dogmatism. "These three tendencies are like three different codes of law, deep-rooted in their subject and yet variable in their relationship to one another. A theory that ignores any one of them or seeks to fix an arbitrary relationship between them would conflict with reality to such an extent that for this reason alone it would be totally useless."

25. Jomini, *Art of War,* 322. The maxims themselves are found on p. 70.

26. Jomini, *Art of War,* 16–39. The chapter is titled, "The Relation of Diplomacy to War."

27. Clausewitz, *On War,* 97.

28. Henry M. Wriston, Foreword to Henry E. Eccles, *Logistics in the National Defense* (1959; reprint, Washington: Headquarters United States Marine Corps, 1989), vii.

29. J. C. Wylie, *Military Strategy: A General Theory of Power Control* (1967; reprint, Annapolis: Naval Institute Press, n.d.), 31.

30. Theory is also an important element of military pedagogy, but discussion of this relationship has been omitted for brevity's sake.

31. Excerpts of the lecture are found in Roger H. Nye, *The Patton Mind: The Professional Development of an Extraordinary Leader* (Garden City, New York: Avery Publishing Group, 1993), 77–78. All quotations are from the published version, George S. Patton Jr., "Success in War," *Infantry Journal* 38 (January 1931): 20–24.

32. Patton, "Success in War," 22.

33. Patton, "Success in War," 22.

34. Patton, "Success in War," 23.

35. Patton, "Success in War," 24.

36. Napoleon's Maxim LXXVIII, cited in *The Military Maxims of Napoleon,* tr. George C. D'Aguilar, introduction and commentary by David Chandler (New York: Macmillan, 1988), 240.

37. Nye, *Patton Mind,* 14–15. Patton, a dyslexic and a notorious misspeller, rendered Hamley as "Hemley."

38. Nye, *Patton Mind,* 67–68.

39. For Patton's initial encounter with Clausewitz, see Nye, *Patton Mind,* 27–28.

40. Nye, *Patton Mind*, 72.

41. Ardant du Picq, "Battle Studies," in *Roots of Strategy, Book 2* (Harrisburg, Pa.: Stackpole Books, 1987), 121–22.

42. For a detailed exposition of this aspect of Patton's genius, see Bradford J. "BJ" Shwedo, *XIX Tactical Air Command and ULTRA: Patton's Force Enhancers in the 1944 Campaign in France* (Maxwell AFB, Ala.: Air University Press, 2001).

43. Cover letter to Third Army After Action Report for Operations in Europe in World War II, 15 May 1945.

44. Harold R. Winton, *Corps Commanders of the Bulge: Six American Generals and Victory in the Ardennes* (Lawrence: University Press of Kansas, 2007), 230.

45. What follows is based on Winton, *Corps Commanders of the Bulge*, 217–26.

46. "Strength of character can degenerate into *obstinacy*. The line between them is often hard to draw in a specific case, but surely it is easy to distinguish them in theory." Clausewitz, *On War*, 108.

47. On Patton's attitude toward the USSR at the end of World War II, see Nye, *Patton Mind*, 149, and Carlo D'Este, *Patton: A Genius for War* (New York: Harper Collins, 1995), 735–36.

48. See, for example, Martin Blumenson, ed., *The Patton Papers 1940–1945* (Boston: Houghton Mifflin, 1974), 559–60, 609–10, and 620.

49. Clausewitz, *On War*, 147.

50. In the years Grant was a cadet, roughly 70 percent of the curriculum was devoted to mathematics, science, and engineering, while roughly thirty percent went to all other subjects. James L. Morrison Jr., *"The Best School in the World": West Point in the Pre-Civil War Years, 1833–1866* (Kent, Ohio: The Kent State University Press, 1986), 91.

51. George Peterson Winton Jr., "Ante-Bellum Military Instruction of West Point Officers and Its Influence upon Confederate Military Organization and Operations," Ph.D. dissertation, University of South Carolina, May 1972, 24, 234.

52. Carol Reardon, *With a Sword in One Hand & Jomini in the Other: The Problem of Military Thought in the Civil War North* (Chapel Hill: University of North Carolina Press, 2012), 8–9.

53. William S. McFeely, *Grant: A Biography* (New York: W. W. Norton, 1981), 15.

54. Ulysses S. Grant, *Personal Memoirs of U. S. Grant* (2 vols.: 1885; reprint, New York: Bonanza Books, n.d.), 1:39.

55. *Register of Graduates and Former Cadets* (West Point: United States Military Academy, 2000), 1198.

56. Arthur L. Conger, *The Rise of U. S. Grant* (1931; reprint, New York: Da Capo Press, 1996). For information on Conger's productive career as a

soldier and military educator, see Carol Reardon, *Soldiers and Scholars: The U.S. Army and the Uses of Military History, 1865–1920* (Lawrence: University Press of Kansas, 1990), 69–75, 78, and 177–79.

57. Grant, *Memoirs,* 1:249–50.

58. T. Harry Williams, *McClellan, Sherman, and Grant,* (1962; reprint, Westport, Conn.: Greenwood Press, 1976), 59.

59. What follows on the Henry-Donelson Campaign is based on Conger, *Rise of U.S. Grant,* 155–77, and Bruce Catton, *Grant Moves South* (Boston: Little, Brown, 1960), 158–78.

60. Unless otherwise noted, this account of Grant at Shiloh is based on Conger, *Rise of U. S. Grant,* 238–56.

61. Catton, *Grant Moves South,* 237–38.

62. What follows is based on Conger, *Rise of U. S. Grant,* 306–27.

63. What follows is based on Bruce Catton, *The Army of the Potomac: A Stillness at Appomattox* (Garden City, New York: Doubleday, 1953), 91–92.

64. On the general tendency of European soldiers to disregard the experience of the American Civil War, see Jay Luvaas, *The Military Legacy of the Civil War: The European Inheritance* (1959; reprint, Lawrence: University Press of Kansas, 1988). The great exception, as Luvaas notes, was the dynamic and prolific soldier-scholar, Colonel G. F. R. Henderson, whose study of Jackson captured the imagination of a generation of British officers.

65. J. F. C. Fuller, *The Generalship of Ulysses S. Grant* (1929; reprint, New York: Da Capo Press, n.d.), 396–97.

66. Conger, *Rise of U. S. Grant,* 273.

67. James Russell Young, *Around the World with General Grant* (2 vols.: New York: 1879), 2:352–53, 615, as cited in Brooks D. Simpson's introduction to Conger, *Rise of U. S. Grant,* x.

68. Clausewitz, *On War,* 136.

69. Unless otherwise indicated, this account of Cold Harbor is based on Bruce Catton, *Grant Takes Command* (Boston: Little, Brown, 1968), 258–74.

70. Casualty figures from Vincent J. Esposito, ed., *The West Point Atlas of American Wars* (2 vols.: New York: Praeger, 1967), 1:136.

71. Grant, *Memoirs,* 2:276.

72. For DePuy's pivotal role in the formulation of the 1976 edition of FM 100-5 and the reaction thereto, see Romie L. Brownlee and William J. Mullen III, *Changing an Army: An Oral History of General William E. DePuy, USA Retired* (Carlisle Barracks, Pa.: United States Military History Institute, n.d.), 187–89, and John L. Romjue, *From Active Defense to Air-Land Battle: The Development of Army Doctrine 1973–1982* (Fort Monroe, Va.: United States Army Training and Doctrine Command, 1984), 3–21.

73. Department of the Army, Field Manual 100-5, *Operations* (Washington, 1982), 1-1, 1-4, 2-1, and 11-1.

74. FM 100-5, *Operations* (1982), 2-1, 2-8, 2-8.

75. FM 100-5, *Operations* (1982), 7-13 through 7-17.

76. FM 100-5, *Operations* (1982), 2-3.

77. Department of the Army, Field Manual 100-5, *Operations* (Washington, 1986), 10.

78. Clausewitz, *On War*, 76. This definition, as the drafters of the manual were well aware, was much more conceptual than Jomini's description of strategy as "the art of making war upon the map. . . ." Jomini, *Art of War*, 69.

79. Interview with Professor Dennis M. Drew, School of Advanced Air and Space Studies, 11 March 2004. In addition to an extremely detailed history of USAF operations in the Korean War, Futrell produced a two-volume compilation titled, *Ideas, Concepts Doctrine: Basic Thinking in the United States Air Force* (Maxwell AFB, Ala.: Air University Press, 1989).

80. Department of the Air Force, Air Force Manual 1-1, *Basic Aerospace Doctrine of the United States Air Force* (2 vols.: Washington, 1992), 1:v.

81. For a detailed assessment of this ground-breaking work, see Harold R. Winton, "Reflections on the Air Force's New Manual," *Military Review* 72 (November 1992): 20–31.

82. AFM 1-1, *Basic Aerospace Doctrine* (1992), 2:i.

83. AFM 1-1, *Basic Aerospace Doctrine* (1992), 1:1–2.

84. AFM 1-1, *Basic Aerospace Doctrine* (1992), 1:9.

85. AFM 1-1, *Basic Aerospace Doctrine* (1992), 1:12.

86. The subsequent statement of Air Force basic doctrine, published in 1997, reverted to the traditional format. See Department of the Air Force, Air Force Doctrine Document 1, *Air Force Basic Doctrine* (Maxwell AFB, Ala.: Headquarters, Air Force Doctrine Center, 1997).

CHAPTER THREE

The Realist as Strategist

A Critique

JAMES WOOD FORSYTH JR.

The perils of weakness are matched by the temptations of power.
—Kenneth N. Waltz

✳

U nlike physics or poetry, strategy does not constitute an academic discipline per se. It is, in every way, an interdisciplinary enterprise. As Everett
Carl Dolman has written, strategy is not a thing to be "poked, prodded,
or probed. . . . It is an idea, a product of the imagination. It is about the future,
and above all it is about change." In a word, it is "alchemy; a method of transmu-
tation from idea into action."[1] Realists would not agree.[2]

When it comes to strategy, realists have a tidy set of notions. Most would
accept Kenneth Waltz's formulation of it: strategy is the means to ensure state survival; it is conceived in the minds of statesmen. In the standard Waltzian account,
international systems are like economic markets, in that both are ones of self-help.
The self-help principle sees to it that states "live, prosper, or die" depending on
their own efforts.[3] In economic markets, firms devise strategies to maximize gains;
in international ones states devise strategies to ensure their survival. In both, survival is the prerequisite to achieving any other goals. Thus, the survival motive is
"taken as the ground for action where the security of states is not assured."[4]

The privileged position afforded to survival leaves statesmen little room for
the consideration of much else: this chapter evaluates the usefulness of that claim.
Taking the realist tradition as a whole, I examine it from the perspective of its

key theoretical premises: states, anarchy, interests, and power.[5] I follow this with discussions of international practices and the mediating role of moral concerns. Laying my cards on the table: realism is a theoretical tradition worth defending, but it is important to stress that a strategy contingent upon the relentless pursuit of survival, with little regard for moral concerns, can be as useless as it would be dangerous.[6]

THE REALIST TRADITION

From the earliest moments of recorded history, realist thought has dominated the study and practice of international politics. Realists tend to see themselves as heirs to Thucydides and write as if his hand were guiding their pens. Waltz sees the relevance of Thucydides in an age of nuclear weapons.[7] Robert Gilpin insists that the "classic history of Thucydides is as meaningful a guide to the behavior of states as when it was written."[8] John Mearsheimer insists that Thucydides' insights into international politics were pertinent long before the modern state system ever existed.[9] Since Thucydides occupies a prominent place within the realist tradition, it is appropriate to begin with his account of human nature, which he captures in his description of events at Corcyra during the Peloponnesian War:

> Then, with the ordinary convention of civilized life thrown into confu-
> sion, human nature, always ready to offend . . . showed itself proudly in
> its true colors, as something incapable of controlling passion, insubordi-
> nate to the idea of justice, the enemy to anything superior to itself. . . .
> [I]n these acts of revenge . . . men take it upon themselves to begin the
> process of repealing those general laws of humanity which are there to
> give a hope of salvation to all who are in distress, instead of leaving those
> laws in existence, remembering that there may come a time when they,
> too, will be in danger and will need their protection.[10]

Human nature drives men to repeal those "general laws of humanity" even when those deeds have the potential to hurt not only the guilty but the innocent as well. Why? People are not led by reason; they are led by reason *and* passion, and it is passion that leads to conflict and war.[11] Thus, it is not enough to con-clude that reason can temper passion. Rather, the issue is that one can never be certain that reason will temper passion *all of the time.*[12] For statesmen, the lesson is simple, the implications enormous: statesmen must be on guard, not because they "are never honorable and peaceful, but because they might at any moment become dishonorable and belligerent."[13]

Philosophically speaking, realism is pessimistic, and modern realists often appeal to "the limitations which the sordid and selfish aspects of human nature place on the conduct of diplomacy."[14] Hans Morgenthau put the problem this way: "Man cannot achieve [justice,] for reasons that are inherent in his nature. The reasons are three: man is too ignorant, man is too selfish, and man is too poor."[15] Reinhold Niebuhr, in *Moral Man and Immoral Society*, concluded that social groups fail to live up to the moral commitments that individuals typically do.[16] Thus, when it comes to refining social or political structures, short-term fixes to society's ills might be achievable but large-scale attempts to cure society of its larger afflictions are destined to fail.

Contemporary realists do not disagree but spend little time on man's nature, preferring to focus on the problems of anarchy and the international system. In what is considered the most important work in the neorealist revival, *Theory of International Politics,* Waltz makes no index entries for ethics, justice, or morality. He is emphatic about how different his realism is from that of Morgenthau and Niebuhr. Man's nature might be grounds for conflict and war, but the anarchic nature of international life remains an inescapable condition that states must contend with.

Since states and anarchy play cardinal roles in contemporary realist thought, it is important to be clear about their meanings. A state is what one ordinarily calls a "country." Costa Rica, Russia, and Finland are good examples. States have at least four essential features: territory, population, government, and sovereignty. The first three are self-explanatory; the latter is in need of clarification. Sovereignty is often confused with freedom of action. Those polities unhindered are thought to be sovereign, those restrained not. But that is not what sovereignty means. Sovereignty merely refers to a state's ability to conduct domestic and foreign policies without undue external interference. No state can do whatever it likes, whenever it chooses. That is to say, while all states enjoy some measure of autonomy, great powers can do more than weak ones, but no state—even one with the greatest of powers—can do all it wants all the time. No matter how powerful, the unequal distribution of power throughout the world constrains what states can do.[17]

Anarchy does not mean chaos. It refers to the absence of rule or of a hierarchical order based on formal subordination and authority. As Hedley Bull made clear, there is considerable order in an anarchic international system but that order is not the hierarchic one characteristic of domestic politics.[18] That being the case, the consequences of anarchy are severe. Because there is no higher authority for states to appeal to, statesmen must think in terms of security first.

In the absence of world government, statesmen must provide for their own protection. To do so means marshaling their power or the power of friends and allies who will support and defend them. However, such self-help actions, even when taken for purely defensive purposes, can appear threatening to others, who will be forced to respond in kind. This *security dilemma* explains why arms races occur and how some wars begin.[19]

Because the potential for violence in the international system is so great, statesmen must prioritize their interests. Interests come in many forms. Peace, prosperity, and freedom are good examples, and while each might be an interest of *most* states, survival is the interest of *all* states.[20] The means to ensure survival is power; yet power is a vexing word. While it might be hard to define, it is not hard to recognize.[21] Most would accept Waltz's conception of it. In the standard Waltzian account, power provides a means to achieve autonomy; permits a wider range of actions; increases margins of safety; and, for the sake of great power, gives its possessors a greater stake in the management of the system.[22]

Thus power plays an important role in Waltzian international politics: it structures things. It provides a positional picture of the world, with strong states occupying dominant positions and weak ones taking subservient ones.[23] Power differentials between states are unambiguous, making differences between states stark. The contrast among them reinforces a harsh, albeit central, reality: the strong can do more than the weak. One of the most important things strong states do is socialize others to the rules of the game.

"Rules of the game" refer to those "imperative principles" that require or authorize states to behave in prescribed ways. Few would deny that states share many beliefs about the "rules of the game, who its players are, what their interests are, what rational behavior is, and so on."[24] In other words, order is maintained in an international system "not merely by a sense of common interests . . . but by rules that spell out the kind of behavior that is orderly."[25]

Socialization refers to a relationship between at least two parties where "*A* influences *B*. *B*, affected by *A*'s influence, then influences *A*." As Waltz put it, "Each is not just influencing the other; both are being influenced by the situation their interactions create." Moreover, the behavior of the pair cannot be "apprehended by taking a unilateral view of either member."[26] Each acts and reacts in accordance with the other. The global teenager provides an example of the socialization process that occurs throughout the world. No one tells all the teenagers in the world to dress alike, but most of them do, most of the time. Likewise, no one tells all the states in the world to behave themselves, but most of them do, most of the time. States are socialized to this idea by interacting with one another. In this regard, socialization is "a process of learning to conform one's behavior to societal expectations"; it is a "process of identity and interest formation."[27] Socialization draws members of a group into conformity with its norms and encourages similarities in behavior.

One need only think of the Cold War to grasp the idea here. What kept the Cold War "cold" was the socialization effect produced by superpower interaction. Although far from a perfect peace—there were several proxy wars and serious crises during this time—"the long peace," as John Gaddis has described it, enabled international life to go on without producing a cataclysmic, nuclear war. From the perspective of socialization, power socialized leaders to the dangers of nuclear war and conditioned their behavior.

Regardless of how power might be conceptualized, it is important to stress that it is fungible and relative. "Fungibility" refers to the ease with which capabilities in one issue area can be used to solve problems in other issue areas. From a realist perspective, military power remains the most fungible of all the instruments of power, including economic, diplomatic, and informational. And indeed, when reviewing the case history, one discovers that force and threats of force have been a common choice for states in times of crisis, which is why realists generally assume that force is the final arbiter in international politics.

"Relative" refers to relative gains, as the term is used in economics. Realists believe that relative gains matter more to states than absolute gains. Why? As Waltz made clear, one can never be sure how a state will use *any gain from any transaction*. States might spend gains—in the form of money—on services to improve life at home for their citizens; they might spend those gains on a large military force capable of threatening others. This is why in games of strategy the question is not "Who gains?" The question is always, "Who gains more?"[28]

Recall the fierce debate in the U.S. Congress on the North American Free Trade Agreement. The debate was not over the issue of "What will America gain?" Rather, the debate—at least on the part of some dissenters—centered on the fear that Canada and Mexico might gain more. Was the United States afraid that

Canada or Mexico might build a large army to threaten it? Of course not, but the mere fact that tensions existed among such close neighbors highlights how difficult international cooperation is to achieve, even on something as relatively benign as free trade among liberal states. In the end, one can think of international politics as a struggle for power and peace, but that struggle is tempered by the notion that state security must never be impaired.

Summing up, realists insist that the international system shapes what statesmen must do by presenting them with overwhelming incentives to pursue self-interest relentlessly. It is further assumed that those states that follow realist maxims grow, while those that ignore the consequences of anarchy decline or lose all influence. In either case, to the extent that survival pressures tightly constrain state behavior, one should not expect moral concerns to affect state conduct seriously. In such a world, strategy can serve no higher purpose than the preservation of the state itself.

INTERNATIONAL PRACTICES

When considering the preservation of the state, realists fall back on arguments about war and intervention. Because the world is anarchic, war is always a possibility, which is why realists present it as a standard, albeit destructive, instrument of statecraft. This can be attributed to Clausewitz, who insisted that war was "not merely an act of policy but a true political instrument, a continuation of political intercourse, carried on by other means."[29] As satisfying as Clausewitz might be, war can require moral justification. Yet realists consistently downplay such concerns, insisting that most wars can be justified in terms of interests or the balance of power. The central premise of the balance of power is stability, not justice. In fact, realists argue that the very idea of a just war is incoherent. If one adopts Robert Tucker's stance on the role of the statesman, a view that presupposes the protection and preservation of the state, there seems to be no escaping the demands of the national interest.[30] It is important to stress that though considerations about justice might be real and important, they are not as important as the demands of stability.[31]

Moral concerns aside, realists believe stability is present in an international system when the system remains anarchic—without a strong central authority—and the principal parties within the system remain unchanged.[32] If one state threatens to achieve a position from which it might be able to dominate the rest, a military coalition of the other great powers will form against it, and a general war will follow. Thus balance of power arguments are not strong arguments for war any more than they are strong arguments for peace. They are antihegemonic, in that a balance of power seeks to prevent, through war if necessary, the rise of any one dominant power.

A related and appropriate concern for this volume is airpower. What is airpower? There are many answers to that question. Philosophically speaking, its theorists can be clumped into two groups: those who think of airpower as something "independently decisive" and those who think of it in terms of "support fires." Generally, both appreciate the usefulness of airpower yet disagree over its presumed strengths and limitations. Realists hold the prudential view that airpower is power projected through the air; they put the emphasis on power. For them, it is an empirical question, not a philosophical one. If we accept the idea that power "gives its possessors a greater stake in the management of the system," one can deduce that "airpowers" are states with considerable material capabilities. An air-going nation requires sound governmental structures, a skilled labor force, the ability for technological innovation, the infrastructure to support such a broad endeavor, and the ability to pay for it. Thus material capabilities are central to airpower, which is why realists are, in the language of air strategy, denial strategists. Since military contests are essentially "power games," reducing the enemy's material capabilities is a vital concern when considering threats or use of military force.

Although many states have intervened in the affairs of other states, contemporary realist authors have surprisingly little to say about *intervention*. When they do address it, it is usually under the heading of nonintervention. Again, this is because realists tend to think of intervention as an empirical question. That being the case, those who do tackle it fall back on ideas regarding self-determination and sovereignty.

Michael Walzer, in *Just and Unjust Wars*, examines the argument put forth by John Stuart Mill.[33] To paraphrase, we are to treat states as self-determining communities, whether or not they are free, because self-determination and freedom are not the same. Citizens have the right to fight for their freedom, and even when they struggle and fail, they are self-determining.[34] This view of self-determination sets people up for the right to become free by their own efforts, and it cuts against the grain of intervention in general. Sovereignty, which legally defines a state's ability to conduct domestic and foreign policies without undue external interference, is the arena in which self-determining communities fight and sometimes win their freedom.[35] It goes without saying that there are things the international community cannot do for states, even for their own good. By this measure, the intervening state must make the case that its interference in someone else's liberty is best served by something other than moral support.[36]

During the 1990s the United States was involved in numerous interventions, some of which challenged traditional views of sovereignty. In the face of the ethnic killings and displacement in Yugoslavia, Rwanda, and Kosovo, the idea of saving strangers came to the fore. Coupled with the attacks of 11th September, 2001, the question of intervention posed new problems for realists as strategies of preemption took hold of American policy. In some measure, there has always been a tension between those who wish to see the United States play an active interventionist role and others who seek to back away from such a role. In framing the future of intervention strategy, realism has something to offer statesmen. Waltz put it this way: "One may notice that intervention, even for worthy ends, often brings more harm than good. The vice to which great powers easily succumb in a multipolar world is inattention; in a bipolar world, overreaction; in a unipolar world, overextension."[37]

THE MEDIATING ROLE OF MORAL CONCERNS

Up to now, I have focused on description and analysis, in an attempt to clarify the realist tradition. In this section I want to evaluate the usefulness of realism or, more specifically, ascertain the utility of the survival motive as it pertains to strategy. In the standard realist account, strategy is the means to ensure state survival; it is conceived in the minds of statesmen. Moreover, because the international system is one of self-help, the survival motive is (in a phrase I have already quoted and cited) "taken as the ground for action where the security of states is not assured." In some measure, this line of reasoning stems from an interpretation of Thucydides, but while Thucydides does stress the importance of survival, it is not the only motive states have, nor is it their most pressing concern all of the time. Let us return to Corcyra.

Once civilized life had thrown itself into confusion, "human nature [as we have also seen], always ready to offend . . . showed itself proudly in its true colors, as something incapable of controlling passion, insubordinate to the idea of justice, the enemy to anything superior to itself." Since human nature *always* stands "ready to offend," the prudent strategist cannot place faith in reason alone. Statesmen must be on guard, not because, again, they are never "honorable and peaceful but because they might, at any moment, become dishonorable and belligerent." This prudential logic was to be reinforced at Melos.

The debate at Melos is about rights: Do communities have a right to neutrality? The stakes are high. Facing certain destruction from a larger Athenian force, the Melians make their case for neutrality by claiming that one should not "destroy a principle that is to the general good of all men," with the general good being "such a thing as fair play and just dealing." The Athenians respond by claiming that one should "not be led astray by a false sense of honor—a thing which often brings men to ruin when they are faced with an obvious danger that somehow affects their pride." It is not the hostility of the Melian request for neutrality that affects the Athenians' calculations but what that neutrality might mean for others. If the Athenians were on friendlier terms with Melos, "our subjects would regard that as a sign of weakness . . . whereas your hatred is evidence of our power." So it is with power politics: the standard of justice "depends on the equality of power to compel and that in fact the strong do what they have the power to do and the weak suffer what they have to accept."[38]

Ever since Melos, realists have insisted that statesmen must assume the worst about each other, even if they prefer not to. Given the inequalities of power and the dangers of misplaced trust, there seems to be no logical way to escape the necessity. Hans Morgenthau took it one step farther by asserting that statesmen set moral considerations aside. "I stick to the fundamental principle that lying is immoral. But I realize that when you are dealing in the context of foreign policy, lying is inevitable." He concluded, "The moral dilemma of foreign policy is but a special and—it is true—particularly flagrant case of the moral dilemma which faces man on all levels of social action."[39] Philosophers have long acknowledged the tensions between justice and necessity, but what makes realism so distinctive is its solution: "When the demands of statecraft and demands for justice cannot be reconciled, statesmen must choose injustice, even if it means war."[40]

Yet, to claim that statesmen must "choose injustice" is not the same as concluding that moral concerns have no place in strategy at all. Presumably, a strategy based solely on survival would be as absurd as one based exclusively on moral concerns. Realists insist that such absurdities can be avoided by stressing the importance of self-interest. George Kennan made it plain when he wrote, "Our own national interest is all that we are really capable of knowing and understanding."[41] But what happens to states that pursue self-interest relentlessly? Do they thrive and prosper, as realists might have it? To the extent survival pressures constrain state behavior, one should not expect moral considerations to affect state conduct seriously. Yet throughout Thucydides' history they do—profoundly at times.

Thucydides tells his readers that three things motivate states: fear, honor, and interest. Fear and interest fit neatly within the realist arsenal of ideas; honor does not. This begs the question: What role does honor play in the formulation of Athenian strategy? Pericles appeals to it as he begins his funeral oration, "I shall begin speaking about our ancestors, since it is only right and proper . . . to pay them the honor of recalling what they did." In this way, the Athenian "government does not copy the institutions of our neighbors. It is more the case of our being a model to others . . . this is a peculiarity of ours: we do not say that a man who takes no interest in politics is a man who minds his own business; we say he has no business here at all." During the plague, honor is on the defensive. For "what is called honor, no one showed himself willing to abide by its laws. . . . [I]t was generally agreed that what was both honorable and valuable was the pleasure of the moment and everything that might conceivably contribute to that pleasure." Finally, honor is hard pressed at Mytilene, where Cleon reminds the Athenians that "to feel pity, to be carried away by the pleasures of hearing a clever argument, to listen to the claims of decency are three things that are entirely against the interest of an imperial power." Yet that is precisely what the Athenians choose to do by siding with Diodotus, who reminds them that the "good citizen" does not deprive others of "honor they already enjoy."[42]

In fact, in all three instances, Athenian policy is an amalgam of interests *and* honor, with honor holding its own under severe pressure.[43] It is not until Melos that matters of policy are guided singularly by concerns over survival. And what comes of it? In a dramatic turn of events, the men of Melos reject Athenian demands to form an alliance and go to their deaths believing that it is more *honorable* to live a life of one's own than to live under the flag of another. Contrary to realist assertions, survival can be trumped by other concerns—honor being one.[44]

As this brief examination illustrates, the honor motive poses challenges to the ordinary realist narrative. Certainly survival, while an interest of states, is not the only one states have, nor is it their most pressing concern all of the time. If it was, states would never fight wars at all, because they are "such risky endeavors!"[45] Moreover, the survival motive does not clarify state interests, as realists might have it. Instead, as Athenian power grew, obsessive concerns regarding state interest gave way to desire.[46] This is most evident in events running up to the invasion of Sicily.

On the eve of the Sicilian expedition, Nicias attempts to ward it off, arguing that "to deal with a power [Sicily] of this kind we shall need something more than a fleet with an inconsiderable army. . . . We must have in addition a large army of infantry to sail with us . . . and are not to be restricted in our movements by the numbers of their cavalry." What interests were to be served by this enormous undertaking? The best Alcibiades can offer is that the city "will wear out of its own accord if it remains at rest." The sheer size of the undertaking was not lost on the citizens of Athens, but instead of tempering their desires, it inflamed them. Thucydides writes: "And what made this expedition so famous was not only the brilliant show that it made, but also its great preponderance of strength over those against whom it set out, and the fact that this voyage, the longest ever made by an expedition from Athens, was being undertaken with hopes for the future, when compared with the present position, of the most far-reaching kind."[47]

In the end, the fall of Athens can be described in terms of realism, but not as realists might wish. As Jack Donnelly makes clear, "The statesmen, rather than abdicate to desire, must temper fear and interest with a sense of public purpose and a certain respect for justice and honor."[48] It was, in fact, the growing realism of Athenian strategy that led to its downfall, not the other way around. Thus, contrary to the dictates of realism, statesmen who pursue survival relentlessly, without regard for moral concerns, can wind up destroying themselves as well as others. That is another way of saying that there is a moral purpose to strategy, and we lose sight of that at our peril.

CONCLUSIONS

Suppose that as the result of a cataclysm all of our scientific knowledge about international politics were lost except for one sentence that could be written down and passed on to the next generation. What would you write? If you were a realist you might write: *States, regardless of their internal composition, goals, or desires, pursue interests in ways they deem best.* There is wisdom in those words, and with a little imagination one could teach an undergraduate course around its central themes. Thus realism, in spite of its wrinkles, has much to offer the budding strategist. But as I have attempted to argue here, the dogged pursuit of survival can lead to a bad end, and therein lies the rub: it is not enough to claim that "states act with interests in mind." Rather, what strategists need to ascertain is, "What kind of interests do statesmen have in mind when they act?" Survival is but one, honor another. No doubt there are more. In the spirit of this volume and in the name of good strategy, let us work to uncover them all.

NOTES

1. Everett Carl Dolman, *Pure Strategy: Power and Principle in the Space and Information Age* (New York: Frank Cass, 2005), 1.
2. Portions of this article previously appeared in *Strategic Studies Quarterly.* See "The Past as Prologue: Realist Thought and the Future of American Security Policy" (Fall 2011).
3. Kenneth N. Waltz, *Theory of International Politics* (New York: McGraw-Hill, 1979), 91.
4. Ibid., 92.
5. There are many realist authors and many forms of realism. The classical argument begins with Thucydides, Thomas Hobbes, and Niccolò Machiavelli. The theological argument is found in the works of Reinhold Niebuhr and Herbert Butterfield. Nicholas Spykman and A. T. Mahan represent the geopolitics school. The modern account begins with Hans Morgenthau, E. H. Carr, and George Kennan. The English school is best represented in the work of Martin Wight, Hedley Bull, and Adam Watson. The contemporary argument is found in Kenneth Waltz, John Herz, Robert Tucker, Robert Osgood, and John Mearsheimer. Although they differ, the contemporary realist argument orbits around states, anarchy, interests, and power.
6. I was fortunate to study international politics with Jack Donnelly at the University of Denver. While there, I was educated in and attracted to his line of reasoning and critique. Thus, I make no claims of originality and rely on Donnelly throughout. For a full account of how Donnelly approaches the realist tradition and its relation to moral and ethical concerns see Jack Donnelly, *Realism and International Relations* (London: Cambridge University Press, 2000).
7. Waltz, *Theory of International Politics,* 66.
8. Robert Gilpin, *War and Change in World Politics* (New York: Cambridge University Press, 1981), 7.
9. John Mearsheimer, *The Tragedy of Great Power Politics* (New York: W. W. Norton, 2001), 365.
10. Thucydides, *History of the Peloponnesian War,* trans. Rex Warner (London: Penguin Books, 1972), 245.
11. Kenneth Waltz, *Man, the State, and War* (New York: Columbia University Press, 1959), 24.
12. Ibid., chap. 2.
13. Ibid., 25.
14. Kenneth W. Thompson, *Moralism and Morality in Politics and Diplomacy* (Lanham, Md.: University Press of America, 1985), 20. Also in Donnelly, *Realism and International Relations,* 161.

15. Hans J. Morgenthau, *Truth and Power: Essays of a Decade, 1960–1970* (New York: Praeger, 1970), 63.

16. Reinhold Niebuhr, *Moral Man and Immoral Society: A Study in Ethics and Politics* (New York: Charles Scribner's Sons, 1932).

17. This is an essential Waltzian claim, one that has produced a cottage industry of scholarship. The recent debate among defensive and offensive realists turns, in part, on this notion. Waltz represents defensive realism, John Mearsheimer offensive realism.

18. Hedley Bull, *The Anarchical Society* (New York: Columbia University Press, 1977).

19. The idea is sketched out in Waltz's *Man, the State, and War.* His work outlines the basic argument around which studies of war and peace still take place.

20. Waltz makes this point time and again, and it reverberates throughout his writings. In *Theory of International Politics,* he writes, "I built structural theory on the assumption that survival is the goal of states"; "The survival motive is taken as the ground of action"; "By assumption, economic actors seek to maximize expected returns, and states strive to secure their survival"; and, "I assume that states seek to ensure their survival" (respectively 91, 92, 134, 91).

21. Joseph S. Nye Jr., *The Future of Power* (New York: PublicAffairs, 2011), 5.

22. Waltz, *Theory of International Politics,* 194–95.

23. Ibid., chap. 7.

24. Although wildly different in their approaches, some variants of constructivism and realism share several assumptions; see Alexander Wendt, *Social Theory of International Politics* (New York: Cambridge University Press, 1999), 190.

25. Bull, *Anarchical Society,* 52.

26. Waltz, *Theory of International Politics,* 74–75.

27. Wendt, *Social Theory of International Politics,* 170.

28. Waltz, *Theory of International Politics,* chap. 7.

29. Carl Von Clausewitz, *On War,* trans. Michael Howard and Peter Paret (Princeton, N.J.: Princeton University Press, 1976), 87.

30. Robert Osgood and Robert Tucker, *Force, Order, and Justice* (Baltimore, Md.: Johns Hopkins University Press, 1967), 304n171.

31. Jack Donnelly "Twentieth Century Realism," in *Traditions of International Ethics,* ed. Terry Nardin and David Mapel (London: Cambridge University Press, 1992).

32. Waltz, *Theory of International Politics,* 65–73.

33. Though hardly a realist, Walzer does provide a strong, realist-like defense of nonintervention. See Michael Walzer, *Just and Unjust Wars* (New York: Basic Books, 1977), chap. 6.

34. Ibid., 87.
35. Ibid., 89.
36. Ibid., 90–91.
37. Kenneth N. Waltz, "Structural Realism after the Cold War," *International Security* 25, no. 1 (Summer 2000): 13.
38. See the Melian Dialogue in Thucydides, *History of the Peloponnesian War,* 400–408.
39. Hans Morgenthau, *Human Rights and Foreign Policy* (New York: Council on Religion and International Affairs, 1979), 10–11.
40. Donnelly, "Twentieth Century Realism," in Nardin and Mapel, *Traditions of International Ethics,* 101.
41. George F. Kennan, *Realities of American Foreign Policy* (Princeton, N.J.: Princeton University Press, 1954), 103.
42. See Pericles' funeral oration in Thucydides, *History of the Peloponnesian War,* 143–51.
43. Donnelly, *Realism and International Relations,* 184–85.
44. This is a central theme of Donnelly's account. See Donnelly, *Realism and International Relations,* chap. 6.
45. Indeed, this would be the world Randall Schweller describes as "all cops and no robbers." See Randall Schweller, "Neorealism's Status-quo Bias: What Security Dilemma," *Security Studies* 5 (Spring 1996): 90–121.
46. Donnelly, *Realism and International Relations,* 184.
47. See the launching of the Sicilian expedition in Thucydides, *History of the Peloponnesian War,* 414–43.
48. Donnelly, *Realism and International Relations,* 184.

CHAPTER FOUR

Classical Strategy

A Socratic Dialogue

JAMES M. TUCCI

STRANGER: When a person supposes that he knows, and does not know, this appears to be the great source of all errors of the intellect.

THEAETETUS: True.

STRANGER: And this, if I am not mistaken, is the kind of ignorance which specially earns the title of stupidity.

THEAETETUS: True.

STRANGER: What name, then, shall be given to the sort of instruction which gets rid of this?

THEAETETUS: The instruction which you mean, Stranger, is, I should imagine, not the teaching of handicraft arts, but what, thanks to us, has been termed education in this part of the world.

STRANGER: Yes, Theaetetus, and by nearly all the Hellenes. But we still have to consider whether education admits of any further division deserving a name.

THEAETETUS: We have.

STRANGER: Of education, one method appears to be rougher, and another smoother.

THEAETETUS: How are we to distinguish the two?

STRANGER: There is the time-honored mode which our fathers commonly practiced toward their sons, and which is still adopted by many—either of roughly reproving their errors, or of gently advising them—which varieties may be correctly included under the general term of admonition.

THEAETETUS: *True.*

STRANGER: *But whereas some appear to have arrived at the conclusion that all ignorance is involuntary, and that no one who thinks himself wise is willing to learn any of those things in which he is conscious of his own cleverness, and that the admonitory sort of education gives much trouble and does little good . . .*

THEAETETUS: *There they are quite right.*

STRANGER: *Accordingly, they set to work to eradicate the spirit of conceit in another way.*

THEAETETUS: *In what way?*

STRANGER: *They cross-examine a man's words, when he thinks that he is saying something and is really saying nothing, and easily convict him of inconsistencies in his opinions; these they can then collect by the dialectic process, and placing them side by side, show that they contradict one another about the same things, in relation to the same things, and in the same respect. He, seeing this, is angry with himself, and grows gentle towards others, and thus is entirely delivered from great prejudices and harsh notions, in a way which is most amusing to the hearer, and produces the most lasting good effect on the person who is the subject of the operation. For as the physician considers that the body will receive no benefit from taking food until the internal obstacles have been removed, so the purifier of the soul is conscious that his patient will receive no benefit from the application of knowledge until he is refuted, and from refutation learns modesty; he must be purged of his prejudices first and made to think that he knows only what he knows, and no more.*

—Plato, *Sophist*, 229c–231d

✳

Polemon, a schoolmaster.
Polystratus, a teacher.
Hermarchus, a teacher.
Strato, a teacher.

POLEMON: Colleagues, let us consider the mission of teaching strategy and attempt to determine how a strategist should be educated. To begin, I think we do need to decide what is meant by the word "strategist" in our context.

POLYSTRATUS: One who practices strategy.

POLEMON: Simple enough. But that begs a far more complicated question: What is strategy?

POLYSTRATUS: A method for seeking out continual advantage.

HERMARCHUS: No, it's not. It's the analysis of ways and means in order to achieve ends.

STRATO: You're both wrong. Strategy is thinking critically about . . .

POLEMON: We seem to be in a state of *aporia* on the definition of strategy. In fact, I suggest that we accept this condition and refuse to offer a textbook definition of strategy, allowing each student, based on the combination of their personal background, experiences, and academic studies, to come up with his or her own vision of strategy.

ALL: Agreed.

POLEMON: Since our students will not devise their own definition of strategy until after they complete our course of study, it seems most practical to proceed by educating them all in the same manner—that is, by learning the same subjects and using the same method.

STRATO: That seems reasonable.

HERMARCHUS: I accept that our goal is to produce strategists, but where do we find our students? Whom shall we teach?

POLEMON: For our discussion, let's assume our students are a group of midlevel military officers, individuals who have demonstrated both intelligence and the potential for senior command.

HERMARCHUS: But surely you are not suggesting that strategy should be confined to just military action? Economics and diplomacy are also useful instruments as part of strategy.

POLEMON: I do not advocate tailoring any strategy to just military options. I am suggesting that given that our students are to be military officers preparing for staff and command positions, we ought to focus on strategy as it relates to warfare. You are quite correct to suggest that even military strategy may very well include these other instruments you're proposing.

STRATO: I agree. Since a significant portion of our theoretical group of graduates may rise to the rank of general, perhaps it is a good idea to focus on strategy as it relates to the conduct of warfare.

POLEMON: Plato teaches that the role of a general is to decide how to fight wars and that the role of a statesman is to decide whether to fight wars. The former is the art of war and military strategy, the latter the art of statesmanship.[1] So for our discussion today, let's follow Plato and focus on a strategist's role once the state has decided upon the use of the military instrument as part of its grand strategy. We will discuss the mission of teaching strategy to a student body of midcareer military officers. Does this seem a reasonable framework for our discussion?

ALL: It does.

POLEMON: Since we are all professors devoted to this mission, we can agree that education, for our purposes, means a graduate-school program consisting of courses wherein students read scholarly works and discuss the ideas and concepts in graduate seminars. But what should we teach? What should our students read? What subjects should our program offer toward educating a strategist?

HERMARCHUS: Clearly any understanding of strategy must be founded upon an extensive study of history.

POLEMON: Clearly.

POLYSTRATUS: I also think that the study of international relations is essential for a strategist.

POLEMON: I agree.

STRATO: In modern warfare, an understanding of the impact technology has on strategy and warfare is essential.

POLEMON: Indeed it is.

POLYSTRATUS: Our students should also study civil-military relations.

POLEMON: For today, let's focus on the seminars and what our students should study in preparation for discussion, what subjects and topics we should focus on, and what our students should read. Am I correct that we are all agreed that the seminar is the cornerstone of our program? And by "seminar," I mean a faculty-led student discussion in which we critically evaluate the ideas and concepts argued in scholarly works from a variety of academic fields.

POLEMON: There is much debate among educators on the best way to teach.

POLYSTRATUS: Indeed. There are many theories and approaches as to the best method of education.

STRATO: There are scientific principles in education that must be mastered.

HERMARCHUS: There is a vast body of literature on education, too.

STRATO: In addition to seminars, wouldn't it be useful for experts in various subjects related to strategy to give lectures to our students? And isn't the use of the latest communications technology, like phones, tablets, and computers, an important means for education?

POLEMON: *Suum cuique.* Perhaps on a limited basis, but the reason the seminar should remain the focus of our institution's educational methodology is a very sound one. As some of our colleagues said recently, "Socrates came up with a very good method of teaching that has proven successful for over 2,000 years."[2]

HERMARCHUS: Socrates, again? I am not sure an ancient Greek's viewpoint is appropriate for students of modern strategy. Studying modern history, certainly, but ancient history is not terribly useful. History is immensely valuable, but only the last century or so offers relevant examples.

POLYSTRATUS: I agree. Developing theory as a way to analyze and understand the complexities of how the world interacts is a modern science, not an ancient one.

STRATO: Yes, and today's advanced science and technology have made the battlefield, and thus any military strategy, a very different environment than that faced by soldiers wielding swords and shields.

POLEMON: So are you all in agreement that the study of the ancient world, and specifically the classical world, ancient Greek and Roman civilization, is not suitable for the education of a strategist?

POLYSTRATUS: Strategists should study what is current and relevant in order to learn examples of good strategy.

POLEMON: Would the methods used by another great power to educate their strategists, a state that achieved strategic success in the modern era, be worth considering?

POLYSTRATUS: I believe so.

POLEMON: So then, the British Empire as a case study would be acceptable?

POLYSTRATUS: Yes, certainly.

POLEMON: Then, I offer the British Empire as an example in support of the value of classical study for a strategist. The classics, to include the study of ancient Greek and Latin literature, formed the basis of education for most upper-class Englishmen for centuries, and the British have been one of the best practitioners of strategy in history. A number of scholars have explored the connection between the classics and the British Empire.[3]

STRATO: I think British mastery of superior naval technology was the key to their success, not reading Caesar and Xenophon in grammar school.

HERMARCHUS: Yes, and when the U.S. Navy's technology surpassed the Royal Navy's, the baton of world hegemony was figuratively passed from Horatio Nelson to "Bull" Halsey.

POLEMON: I leave aside how other European states have also studied the classics in their education,[4] or even how their study formerly formed an important part of the education of Americans in the past,[5] but let's look at the issue from another perspective.

POLYSTRATUS: What do you mean?

POLEMON: You have stated that contemporary, or at least modern, subjects should be the focus of our strategists' studies. Why is that?

POLYSTRATUS: Modern analysts offer superior scholarship on strategy and theories of war.

POLEMON: Well, perhaps you can name some modern writers whose works are worthy of study.

STRATO: What about Clausewitz's *On War*?

POLYSTRATUS: Yes, well, that is a very important, indeed even foundational, work for a strategist to read. In fact, I don't believe ancient writers were as sophisticated in their consideration of war as modern theorists. For example, Clausewitz's connection of war to politics is fundamental to strategy. It is a modern conception of warfare.

POLEMON: Plato made this connection, subordinating the conduct of warfare to politics.[6]

POLYSTRATUS: Ah, but Clausewitz is the first theorist to account for the role chance plays in warfare. Further, he claims that the only way to mitigate the impact of chance in war is to place the campaign in the control of a well-educated general.

POLEMON: Plato also states that strategy is a product of chance and that human skill, like the helmsman of a ship at the rudder, can help to guide it.[7]

POLYSTRATUS: I see.

POLEMON: Now to return to the discussion point at hand, Clausewitz wrote nearly two hundred years ago. Since studying Clausewitz is important for studying strategy, would studying history back to the Napoleonic era then make sense?

HERMARCHUS: That is logical.

POLEMON: As you said earlier, reading Clausewitz is important for the study of strategy. Clausewitz states that there are two means of studying the art of war: personal experience and the experience of previous generals—that is, the study of military history.

STRATO: Yes, but Clausewitz himself says the study of ancient history is not helpful.

POLEMON: I'll grant you that, and yet he does cite ancient examples repeatedly in *On War*. Furthermore, whom does Clausewitz regard as a true genius in the art of war?

HERMARCHUS: Napoleon Bonaparte.

POLEMON: And what was Napoleon's advice on the study of military history?

HERMARCHUS: "Peruse again and again the campaigns of Alexander, Hannibal, Caesar, Gustavus Adolphus, Turenne, Eugene, and Frederick. Model yourself upon them. This is the only means of becoming a great captain, and of acquiring the secret of the art of war. Your own genius will be enlightened and improved by this study, and you will learn to reject all maxims foreign to the principles of these great commanders."[8]

POLEMON: So if Clausewitz regards Napoleon as a military genius and Napoleon regarded the study of ancient military commanders important, there seems to be a justification for considering the classics as part of a strategist's education.

POLYSTRATUS: It would seem so.

HERMARCHUS: Yes, but more recent generals are certainly not advocates for studying the classics.

POLEMON: In the late nineteenth century, the German strategist Alfred von Schlieffen wrote a staff college paper on the battle of Cannae that demonstrated how maneuver could be tactically decisive. His work on Cannae was translated and distributed among the U.S. Army's officer corps, too.[9]

STRATO: Cannae?

POLEMON: Cannae was the battle at the beginning of the Second Punic War in which the Carthaginian general Hannibal Barca, despite being outnumbered, executed a double envelopment of the Roman army and annihilated it. More Romans were killed at Cannae than Britons on the first day of the Somme.[10]

HERMARCHUS: As I recall, Schlieffen hoped to do the same in his plans for war against France in World War I; a quick decisive victory in the West would allow Germany to then pivot east and tackle the Russians.

POLEMON: Yes, although Schlieffen's plan failed to be the decisive battle for which he'd hoped. It's a pity the Germans didn't take their study of the Punic Wars a bit farther. Cannae was the tactical model for the perfect battle, and its architect, Hannibal, was victorious. The wily Carthaginian, in fact, won nearly every battle his army fought, but in the end Carthage lost the Second Punic War and was nearly destroyed by the struggle.

HERMARCHUS: The Confederacy would have benefited from the strategic lessons of Hannibal.

STRATO: The United States also should have remembered the example of Hannibal in its conduct of the Vietnam War.

POLEMON: The Second Punic War also offers a case, perhaps *the* case, of a classic asymmetric strategy against an opponent who is superior in conventional warfare, a strategy in which one avoids a pitched battle between armies but instead uses hit-and-run, guerilla-style attacks to wear down an opponent by attrition.

POLYSTRATUS: You mean Fabian tactics or strategy?

POLEMON: Yes, named for Quintus Fabius Maximus, the Roman general who first proposed the strategy against Carthage during the Second Punic War. When the Romans engaged Hannibal at Cannae, they were rejecting Fabius' proposed strategy. After the disastrous defeat at Cannae, they adopted it and refused battle with Hannibal whenever possible.[11]

HERMARCHUS: So the Romans' reaction to Punic superiority on the battlefield was to change their strategy and avoid a pitched fight with the Carthaginians, at least when Hannibal was in command.

POLEMON: Yes. The Romans did seek to engage Punic armies that were not under Hannibal's command, as when Scipio landed a Roman expedition at New Carthage, the main Punic base of operations in Spain. They did so again when Hannibal's brother, Hasdrubal, attempted to march an army into Italy from Spain to reinforce Hannibal. Hasdrubal was defeated and decapitated; the Romans tossed his head over the ramparts of Hannibal's camp as a message signifying their resolve.[12]

POLYSTRATUS: Didn't Hannibal himself identify Alexander as the greatest commander in history?

POLEMON: That is true. And Napoleon also mentioned Alexander the Great. What do you think about studying his life?

STRATO: I'll admit Alexander was a great commander and strategist, but I see no connection between him and modern warfare, which utilizes advanced weaponry like aircraft. What does Alexander have to do with airpower?

POLEMON: John Warden, the modern airpower theorist, envisioned an air campaign concept that was the foundation for the bombing campaign in Operation Desert Storm. Some would argue that his ideas resurrected airpower theory from its nuclear doldrums. His strategy used airpower to target the enemy's leadership as a center of gravity. He was inspired in his thinking by his study of Alexander the Great's strategy against Persia, especially his tactics at the battle of Gaugamela.[13]

STRATO: Well, Warden always was the scholarly type.

POLEMON: The modern theorist J. F. C. Fuller wrote about Alexander's generalship,[14] because he believed that Alexander's excellence in tactics, logistics, intelligence, strategy, and leadership was exemplary for modern commanders.

HERMARCHUS: What other modern figures come to mind who were advocates of the classics?

POLEMON: George Marshall was the senior military officer and adviser to President Franklin Roosevelt in World War II and also secretary of state and secretary of defense in the Truman administration. I believe the Marshall Plan is one of the nation's most successful strategic accomplishments. Marshall argued that contemporary officers should carefully read Thucydides' *Peloponnesian War.*[15]

POLYSTRATUS: Now, Thucydides is an ancient author that I do believe modern strategists need to read. His analysis of power politics in the Peloponnesian War is poignant. His ideas are often cited as the foundation of the study of political science and of international relations theory.

POLEMON: Can you be more specific about theory?

POLYSTRATUS: Thucydides' account demonstrates concepts foundational to power politics and classical realism. For example, the Athenians' conduct leading up to the war, as in the Corcyra crisis, and their actions during the conflict, as in their dispute with Melos, demonstrate the foundational precepts of realism.

POLEMON: And so realpolitik?

POLYSTRATUS: Indeed. But I don't believe Thucydides really discusses strategy in the modern sense. He's fine for military power but light on economics. And do you think his discussion of strategic decision making is worthwhile for a modern audience?

POLEMON: Thucydides focuses on several examples of strategic decision making. King Archidamus of Sparta's speech against declaring war in the first book is a superb example of a leader laying out a strategic argument in much the same way strategists today should. A powerful aspect of his speech is his effort to analyze what kind of war a conflict with Athens and its allies would be. He warns that any war with Athens will be a long, and thus expensive, conflict. Then he lays out how much wealthier Athens is than Sparta. He also explains how different war with Athens will be from Sparta's experience in recent conflicts, due to its superior naval power and empire, strategic advantages which were nearly impervious to Spartan land power.[16]

HERMARCHUS: I've always considered Pericles' Funeral Oration, given to commemorate the conflict's casualties, to be one of the masterpieces of political oratory.[17] However, I wouldn't call it strategy.

POLEMON: Reflect that Pericles, the leader of democratic Athens, advocated an asymmetric strategy against Sparta, avoiding its powerful army and utilizing Athenian naval power, economic might, and superior fortifications. But Pericles' strategy required the citizens of Athens to stay within the walls around their city, avoiding pitched battle with Sparta and using their fleet to harass and attack Sparta's allies. As the Spartan army ravaged the countryside, destroying much Athenian property, Pericles' strategy was producing anger and frustration among the citizenry. In a democracy, leaders must persuade the people of the merits of a chosen strategy, a lesson American presidents know all too well.

POLYSTRATUS: I agree politics is particularly well handled by Thucydides. He strives to show how political assemblies and executives make strategic decisions. Much of the first book in Thucydides' history is devoted to the decision by all parties to go to war. This is most illuminating.[18]

POLEMON: In his *Life of Demetrius,* Plutarch states that just as he would teach a person to play the flute by showing them both good and bad flautists, he intends to offer both good and bad examples of leadership in his *Lives of the Noble Greeks and Romans.*[19] Several of the biographies in this work offer excellent parallels with Thucydides' account of the war between Athens and Sparta, and the lives of Alcibiades and Nicias pointedly exemplify a very bad strategic decision taken by a democracy.

POLYSTRATUS: Are democracies better at strategy than other forms of government?

POLEMON: That's an excellent question. Thucydides' account of the decision by Athens, overconfident after their success in bringing Sparta to the peace table, to invade Sicily and attack a fellow democracy, Syracuse, is fascinating. Thucydides' account of how a democracy decides to use military force is riveting. The way in which Alcibiades and Nicias use rhetorical tactics to win votes for their respective arguments is quite revealing of the dependence of a democracy on political oratory as part of any strategy.[20]

HERMARCHUS: Well, I suppose studying the ancient Greeks offers lessons in strategy, but what about the Romans?

POLEMON: In much the same way in which Thucydides discusses strategic decision making, the two best historians of the Punic Wars, Polybius and Livy, discuss the deliberations of Rome and Carthage. The Roman republic's making of strategy is illuminating. Most of the members of its senior assembly, the Senate, were men who had a decade of military experience.

HERMARCHUS: Imagine a legislature making decisions about war whose members actually have military experience!

POLEMON: We mentioned the battle of Cannae, earlier. In that defeat, eighty Roman senators were killed, yet neither the Roman Senate nor the Roman people considered surrender.

POLYSTRATUS: Do any Roman senators stand out as adept strategists?

POLEMON: Basil Liddell Hart, the prominent interwar military theorist, wrote a biography of one of the survivors of Cannae, Rome's most successful general in the Second Punic War. His book was called *Scipio Africanus: Greater than Napoleon.*[21]

HERMARCHUS: Greater than Napoleon?

POLEMON: Yes. Liddell Hart felt that since Scipio served in the Roman Senate, as a field commander in the army, and as the planner and leader of the campaign that eventually defeated Hannibal, his life was particularly worthy of study. Since Scipio had to serve in a republic, a government of the peoples' representatives who argue and think about issues of war and peace, his generalship is particularly useful for study by contemporary strategists. Napoleon, admittedly a great general, was, after all, a despot.

POLYSTRATUS: The subject of democracies and strategy is of particular interest to me. I am attempting to understand how a body of individuals makes decisions.

POLEMON: Rome's Senate, like the Athenian assembly, is an interesting example of democracy in action. Pyrrhus of Epirus, the only general to win battles against the three great military powers of the ancient world— Macedonia, Carthage, and Rome—encountered the Roman Senate's war-making skills. During his early third-century BC invasion of the Roman republic, he defeated the Roman army in a closely fought battle, taking heavy casualties, so heavy that he feared more fighting would overwhelm him—hence the phrase "Pyrrhic victory." Figuring that after their defeat in battle the Romans would be ready to negotiate a treaty, he sent his adviser Cineas, a great orator, to offer Rome most generous terms. Cineas observed the Roman Senate debate the issue with great intensity; finally it rejected Pyrrhus' offer and drafted a new army to continue the war. Cineas returned to Pyrrhus and reported that Rome was ruled not by a king but by a council of kings and that fighting Rome would be like fighting a hydra: cut off one head, and two more replace it.[22]

POLYSTRATUS: Fascinating. Democratic governments, or at least some democracies, are great hedges against despotic power.

HERMARCHUS: We did suggest that civil-military relations were important for strategists in a democracy to consider.

POLEMON: It is worth noting as well that a profound lesson in civil-military relations is offered by the Roman republic. There was a provision in the Roman political system to appoint a dictator as the sole executive in the government, whereas executive power was normally shared by two elected consuls. A dictator's term was supposed to last only six months, unless his term was extended by vote. This system worked well—think of Cincinnatus—until Roman generals began to enrich themselves with the plunder of war and to arrogate to themselves authority granted by the legislatures. This decay and failure to check the power of generals culminated in a half-century of civil wars, Julius Caesar's being appointed dictator for life, and the end of the republic.

POLYSTRATUS: I fear that today overreliance on our very capable and effective military and the rise of privatized military forces, unfettered by any constitutional controls, will move America closer to despotism.

POLEMON: How would you caution the current generation of officers about this danger?

POLYSTRATUS: I would include among our assigned texts readings on the Constitution and civil-military relations.

POLEMON: Would that include any classical accounts?

POLYSTRATUS: Perhaps.

POLEMON: Reading about how the rise in Rome's military capabilities and ability to project power produced a crisis and a coup d'état would be important, especially given that James Madison and other early Americans instituted checks and balances in our government in order to prevent a repeat of the past.

HERMARCHUS: That's true. Caesar is a fascinating figure, a great general but a political tyrant.

POLEMON: J. F. C. Fuller also wrote a military biography of Julius Caesar, along the lines of his work on Alexander the Great. Clearly, Caesar's own account of the conquest of Gaul and the Civil Wars offer many examples of strategic thinking, but more important is the story of the most famous dictator to emerge from an election.

STRATO: Now wait a second. All these points are well and good, but I still maintain that modern technology renders much of ancient thought on strategy irrelevant.

POLEMON: Perhaps you are correct. Let's consider this issue. What role does technology play in strategy?

STRATO: The U.S. superiority in military technology has been an essential element of its national strategy. Nuclear deterrence began with our atomic monopoly, and then, once both the East and West had hydrogen bombs, the advanced technology required to deliver nuclear weapons was critical to effective deterrence. After the Cold War, we demonstrated our technological superiority again, by our rapid victory in the Gulf War. Today, our superior weaponry continues to give us a great advantage over our rivals.

POLYSTRATUS: Yes, but hasn't that superiority also produced two strategic threats to the United States, an asymmetric response, like the irregular warfare Iraq used after our initial successes in Operation Iraqi Freedom, and a symmetric response, as in China's decision to seek more advanced military technology?

STRATO: That is true, and I am happy to debate the merits of technological superiority with you, but the issue at hand is whether technology affects strategy. You've just given two examples to support the notion that our recent technological advances in military weaponry have had a profound strategic effect.

POLEMON: Is technology only a modern phenomenon, then?

STRATO: Well, our current technology is. Certainly the airplane is a modern development, as well as the employment of airpower.

POLEMON: I mean technology as a concept affecting war. Presumably, if technology has had the impact you suggest, this characteristic of impacting strategy has always been a part of it.

STRATO: I think I've shown that currently our technological advances are having a significant impact on strategy.

POLEMON: Yes, but is technology's ability to impact the art of war and strategy restricted to the current era?

STRATO: The latest and greatest weaponry has the greatest impact. Consider what typically happens when our military is opposed by outdated weapons. We achieve swift victory.

POLEMON: Too true, but haven't technological innovations and advancements in warfare been a part of war throughout history?

STRATO: Technology is as old as humankind, but its greatest impact is really a modern phenomenon.

POLEMON: Would developments in superior naval technology affect strategy?

STRATO: Of course. Why do you think China is in the process of modernizing its naval forces?

POLYSTRATUS: China is an interesting case. One of the most difficult strategic problems in considering war is how to deal with an opponent's military superiority when your strength relies on land power and your opponent is a sea power.

STRATO: I agree. China's response to America's ability to project power via naval and air forces into regions of strategic significance has been to improve its naval and air power.

POLEMON: Didn't the Spartans face the same dilemma in the Peloponnesian War? And wasn't the Spartans' decision also to improve their naval power?

And wasn't the exorbitant cost of building technologically advanced naval vessels a critical factor?

STRATO: I suppose that is true.

POLEMON: Rome faced a similar dilemma in the First Punic War, the first military conflict in which Rome operated military forces outside of the Italian Peninsula. The Carthaginians and the Romans had a dispute over territory on the island of Sicily. Carthage was a great sea power and had been so for centuries. The Romans had no fleet. First the Romans used a captured Punic warship as a template to mass-produce enough vessels for their own fleet.[23]

STRATO: Mass production is a modern industrial phenomenon.

POLEMON: Doesn't mass production involve the manufacture of a complex product via a streamlined process, an assembly line?

STRATO: Yes.

POLEMON: Well, that's what the Romans did. They disassembled the Carthaginian ship piece by piece, carefully labeling each piece so it would be simple to reassemble. They created hundreds of new ship pieces modeled after each of the examples. Then they used an assembly line to produce several hundred warships, each modeled after the captured one.

STRATO: I see.

POLEMON: Now despite having a new fleet of vessels nearly identical to their Punic opponents, the Romans were still at a huge disadvantage, because they had no experience wielding naval power or fighting with naval tactics and equipment. Their solution was to play to their strength in land warfare and build a mechanical device, called a *corvus,* a sort of drawbridge with a large spike on the end, and attach one to each of their ships. When a Roman and a Punic ship engaged in battle, the Roman would drop its corvus. The corvus' spike would plunge through the opponent's deck, locking the two ships together, and then Roman troops would run across the resulting bridge into the Punic vessels and attack their crews.

STRATO: I see. So by means of reverse engineering, assembly-line production, and technological innovation, the Romans were able to match Carthage's naval power.

POLEMON: There are many examples of the impact technology has had on strategy in the classical world. Artillery was invented in Sicily in the early fourth century BC, and as it improved in size and power, it revolutionized fortifications and siege warfare. In the Second Punic War, the great engineer Archimedes, assigned to assist in the defense of his city against Roman attack, used a variety of machines and artillery to thwart repeated assaults on Syracuse.[24] The Byzantine Empire—in effect the later Roman Empire—also used a technological innovation, Greek fire, to achieve naval superiority and protect their capitals from repeated assaults by foes with much larger fleets.

STRATO: Well, I suppose the impact of technology is a relative phenomenon. Anything that improves a military force's capabilities has an impact. Some technological advances have had tremendous strategic significance throughout history.

POLEMON: So would you agree that the impact of technology on strategy is not just a modern phenomenon but in fact is a constant throughout military history?

STRATO: Yes.

POLEMON: So reading about early innovations, like the development of the stirrup or the torsion catapult, might prove useful in the education of a strategist?

STRATO: I do think reading some ancient accounts of technology's impact might prove useful to a strategist. I am struck by the rapid Roman development of naval technology from essentially zero capability. Perhaps I need to read more about the Punic Wars.

POLEMON: There are a number of modern analyses of the Punic Wars,[25] but I'd recommend starting with the ancient authors. The best account of the First Punic War is Polybius' *Histories.* Polybius' account is really only one section of his overall work. The Punic Wars are only one stage in the process of Roman expansion, and it is the growth of Roman power that Polybius finds so worthy of study. In the opening of his history, Polybius writes "Is there anyone on earth who is so narrow-minded or uninquisitive that he could fail to want to know how and thanks to what kind of political system almost the entire known world was conquered and brought under a single empire, that of the Romans, in less than fifty-three years?"[26]

POLYSTRATUS: Come to think of it, I remember reading bits of Polybius in a Classical Political Thought course in grad school.

POLEMON: I find Polybius' analysis of the Roman political system particularly interesting. His theory of *anacyclosis* has had a profound impact on political science. Machiavelli discusses a similar notion in *The Discourses,* and of course, our Founding Fathers put elements of both democracy and aristocracy, via a republic, into our Constitution in an effort to stabilize the cyclical nature of politics. Jefferson provided James Madison with a number of books to assist in drafting the Constitution, among which were several works on Roman history.

HERMARCHUS: It does seem like the Greeks and Romans offer examples of strategy and warfare worthy of examination. But weren't all their wars conventional, force-on-force conflicts? What about counterinsurgency operations, the type of war we've faced over the last decade? It seems to me that this type of war is uniquely modern. Alexander was indomitable on a conventional battlefield, but he never had to deal with guerilla operations.

POLEMON: Alexander did win four major battles during his invasion of the Persian Empire, three against the Persian army (Granicus, Issus, and Gaugamela) and one against an Indian army (Indus).

HERMARCHUS: See what I mean?

POLEMON: Alexander was also successful in fighting smaller engagements with insurgents and mobile troops. He took his army deep into Central Asia on a preventive campaign against the Scythians, the nomadic people north of the Persian Empire. Alexander succeeded in devising a tactical scheme for success against the Scythians' highly mobile army and its hit-and-run tactics. He also was successful in subduing a tenacious rebellion in occupied territory, centered in what is modern Afghanistan. Here his opponents used guerilla tactics, against which the Macedonians eventually prevailed. His flexible thinking in the conduct of war was unparalleled.[27]

STRATO: Impressive. He won victories in the region that embraces today Iraq, Iran, and Afghanistan, locations all too familiar to our students.

HERMARCHUS: I still maintain that insurgency, guerilla warfare, and terrorism are all exclusively modern phenomena of irregular warfare.

POLEMON: The Romans faced a number of insurgencies, the longest in Spain. Sertorius was a Roman general who took up arms in an insurgency against Rome. He was addressing a large group of rebels when a man asked him how they could possibly defeat Rome, the most powerful military in the world. Sertorius asked that a large stallion and a small pony be brought forward. He selected one of the strongest and largest of the Spanish warriors and asked him to pull out the pony's tail. Despite his immense strength, the soldier could not yank out the tail. Next, Sertorius selected a small, thin boy to come forward and told him to pull out one hair from the large stallion's tail. The boy grasped a single hair and yanked it out. Sertorius turned to his questioner and responded that this was how they could defeat Rome, by hitting the Roman army one soldier at a time.[28]

HERMARCHUS: It would seem that insurgency is an old method of war, but the use of terror against a population as a weapon to undermine the confidence people have in the ruling power is a modern strategy. Middle Eastern terrorism is a unique strategic problem.

POLEMON: Josephus has written a detailed account of the Jewish War, a rebellion by the Jews against Roman rule in the late first-century BC Near East. He describes how Jewish rebels would surreptitiously murder civilians in crowds, so no one could discern how the attack occurred. The sole purpose of these acts of random violence was to strike terror into the population and undermine their belief in the Romans' ability to protect them.[29]

STRATO: I thought the Romans won that war.

POLEMON: They did. Rome realized that the Jewish rebels were divided into several factions, so they laid siege to Jerusalem, the capital, and let the rebel groups fight each other, weakening the rebels' strength, and then moved in to finish off the survivors. Additionally, when a group of fanatic zealots holed up in Masada, an impregnable mountain fortress in the midst of a desert, the Romans besieged the mountain for two years and captured the stronghold. As part of their operation, they tore down a neighboring mountain and used the dirt and stones to build an assault ramp onto Masada. The operation was very long and tremendously expensive, and Masada itself did not have much strategic value, but its symbolism was powerful. The Romans took their army deep into harsh terrain—a logistical nightmare—conducted a lengthy campaign, and took a fortress hitherto never captured. As a demonstration of Roman military might and as a deterrent against future rebellions, taking Masada proved invaluable. It would be over sixty years before the Jews attempted a major uprising again.[30]

STRATO: I can see an analogy with the long campaigns the United States has been fighting in Iraq and Afghanistan.

POLYSTRATUS: Except that we don't conquer territory as part of expanding or holding an empire.

STRATO: This is all well and good, but doesn't the advent of Islam profoundly change the strategic equation in the Near and Middle East?

POLEMON: How so?

HERMARCHUS: The Romans never had to contend with the religious aspects of today's wars. There were no Muslims in the time of the Romans.

POLEMON: Well, the Romans dealt with a myriad of religions in their empire, and as I mentioned before, their difficulty in controlling Palestine was partly due to this problem. As far as Islam goes, the Roman Empire, also known in its later incarnation as the Byzantine Empire, lasted for fifteen centuries and faced Islamic rivals for more than half that time. Although they lost much of their territory to Arab conquests, the Romans held out successfully against repeated Arab assaults, and then against the Turks, until their capital finally fell in the fifteenth century. Many historians attribute the development of European civilization to the bulwark the later Roman Empire provided against Islamic expansion.

POLYSTRATUS: What you say about the Roman Empire is of interest. Are there more strategic examples from the Roman Empire?

POLEMON: Were you to read Tacitus, you'd have a good idea of the strategic challenges facing the early empire. He wrote an account of the first century of imperial rule, an examination of the Germans, and a biography of the commander in charge of subduing a revolt in Britain.[31] And reading Suetonius' *Lives of the Caesars* reveals the character and leadership of the rulers of the empire, men whose decision-making process was a far cry from that of the Republican Senate.

POLYSTRATUS: How adept at strategy was the empire?

POLEMON: The modern strategist Edward Luttwak has written impressive works on the strategies employed by both the Roman Empire and the Byzantine Empire. He goes far toward illuminating the scope of the difficulties facing Rome and the effective way in which it dealt with crises.[32]

HERMARCHUS: It seems that there is some merit to studying the classics.

POLEMON: Let's return to the earlier suggestion, that the study of classical civilization is not helpful for a strategist. Is our original statement true?

POLYSTRATUS: No, I was mistaken about classical strategy. Thucydides is valuable for understanding how societies interact with one another. And there are a number of examples, like Polybius' analysis of the Roman system of government, that could be of value.

STRATO: Thucydides, for sure, is important. There also appear to be a number of early examples of the impact of technology on strategy. I'd be curious to learn what impact the development of the catapult had on strategy.

HERMARCHUS: I was overly hasty in my disregard for ancient history. Accounts of how a republic or a democracy faces strategic challenges are very useful. And reading the biographies of important leaders faced with difficult strategic decisions is of immense value. Reading the lives of great captains, leaders from throughout history, is a vital part of the education of a strategist.

POLYSTRATUS: But between the ancient and modern worlds, there are no strategic lessons worthy of study. Religion dominated thinking after the Roman Empire fell, and so strategy didn't exist.

POLEMON: Really? Didn't you hear what we said earlier about the Byzantine Empire, which lasted until 1453? What about Charlemagne, the Crusades, the Normans, feudalism, castles, transatlantic power projection, and Maurice's *Strategikon,* to name but a few medieval topics? Do you think that they are without any strategic significance?

POLYSTRATUS: Well, perhaps I was a bit quick to condemn an entire millennium of human experience.

HERMARCHUS: There probably isn't a period of history whose study would not benefit a strategist.

POLEMON: Perhaps you are correct. Nevertheless, in the end, regardless of what our students read, discussing texts in seminar, submitting arguments to rigorous critical analysis, and understanding the ideas within the context of one's education and experiences are the most useful skills a strategist will ever acquire.

STRATO: Well put.

POLEMON: So let's return to our main question, then, of considering how to educate strategists. Plato's discernment between the roles generals and statesmen play in military strategy launched our excursus into the classical world. As we had agreed, we use critical reading and discussion in seminar as a means for education.

POLYSTRATUS: True. I also believe that written communication, developing a cogent argument in an essay, is a very important skill for a strategist.

POLEMON: You are correct, but writing an essay cannot duplicate the extraordinary educational experience of the seminar. A true dialogue in seminar is a living conversation. There are countless interactions, ideas, and questions flowing between students, as well as between students and the professor. Socrates thought that any attempt to capture this type of intellectual dynamic in written form was futile, freezing a fluid experience into a rigid format. The essence of a written argument runs counter to the give-and-take of a discussion. Plato's attempt to capture at least some of that experience in writing may have disappointed his teacher, but it is the closest one can get to the seminar experience in written form.

NOTES

1. Plato, *Statesman,* 304d–305a. The first epigraph taken from Plato, *Sophist,* trans. F. M. Cornford, in *Plato: The Collected Dialogues,* ed. Edith Hamilton and Huntington Cairns (Princeton, N.J.: Princeton University Press, 1989).
2. James Woods Forsyth Jr. and Richard Muller, "We Were Deans Once and Young" (presentation at the 2011 Air Education and Training Command Symposium, San Antonio, Tex.); Plato, *Sophist,* 230b–d.
3. Mark Bradley, ed., *Classics and Imperialism in the British Empire* (New York: Oxford University Press, 2010); Christopher Hagerman, *Britain's Imperial Muse: The Classics, Imperialism, and the Indian Empire, 1784–1914* (New York: Palgrave Macmillan, 2013).
4. Theodor Mommsen was a German scholar and legislator regarded as the nineteenth century's greatest classicist. His monumental history of ancient Rome, *Römische Geschichte,* inspired Mahan's thinking and won Mommsen the Nobel Prize for literature.
5. "I have given up newspapers for Tacitus and Thucydides. . . .", Thomas Jefferson to John Adams, 21 January 1812.
6. Plato, *Statesman,* 304d–305a; *Protagoras,* 322b.
7. Plato, *Laws,* 709b.
8. Napoleon's Maxim LXXVIII, cited in *The Military Maxims of Napoleon,* tr. George C. D'Aguilar, introduction and commentary by David Chandler (New York: Macmillan, 1988), 240.
9. The Leavenworth version is still available at United States Army Combined Arms Center, http://usacac.army.mil/cac2/cgsc/carl/download/csipubs/cannae.pdf.
10. Adrian Goldsworthy, *The Punic Wars* (London: Cassell, 2000), 213.
11. Polybius, *The Histories,* 3.87–94.
12. Livy, *Ab Urbe Condita Libri,* 27.49–51.

13. John Olsen, *John Warden and the Renaissance of American Air Power* (Washington, D.C.: Potomac Books, 2007), 14.
14. J. F. C. Fuller, *The Generalship of Alexander the Great* (New Brunswick, N.J.: Rutgers University Press, 1960).
15. George C. Marshall, 1947 speech at Princeton University, cited in W. R. Connor, *Thucydides* (Princeton, N.J.: Princeton University Press, 1984), 3.
16. Thucydides, 1.80–85.
17. Ibid., 2.35–46.
18. Ibid., 1.23–45, 67–88, 118–28, 139–73.
19. Plutarch, *Life of Demetrius,* 1.3.
20. Thucydides, 6.9–26.
21. B. H. Liddell Hart, *Scipio Africanus: Greater than Napoleon* (New York: Da Capo, 1994).
22. Plutarch, *Life of Pyrrhus,* 19.
23. Polybius, *Histories,* 1.19–20.
24. Plutarch, *Life of Marcellus,* 14–19.
25. Several of the best are Goldsworthy, *Punic Wars;* J. F. Lazenby, *The First Punic War* (Stanford, Calif.: Stanford University Press, 1996); Lazenby, *Hannibal's War* (Norman: Oklahoma University Press, 1978).
26. Polybius, *Histories,* 1.1.
27. The best account of Alexander's campaigns is Arrian's *The Anabasis of Alexander.* Plutarch's *Life of Alexander* is also worth a read.
28. Frontinus, *Strategemata,* 1.10.1.
29. Josephus, *The Jewish War,* 7.71.
30. Ibid., 23.19–50.
31. See Tacitus' extant works, *The Annals, The Histories, Germania,* and *Agricola.*
32. Edward Luttwak, *The Grand Strategy of the Roman Empire* (Baltimore, Md.: Johns Hopkins University Press, 1976); Luttwak, *The Grand Strategy of the Byzantine Empire* (Cambridge, Mass.: Harvard University Press, 2009).

CHAPTER FIVE

Technology and Strategy
A Symbiosis of Sorts

Stephen D. Chiabotti

S trategy appears to have as many definitions as people trying to define it. I prefer "the management of context for continuing advantage." The first part comes from a former student named Mark Davis, who returned from the battle of Fallujah in Iraq saying, "Strategy is all about managing context." The second part comes from colleague Everett Carl Dolman, whose *Pure Strategy* emphasizes the objective of continuing relative advantage in the management of ways, means, and ends.[1]

Technology also sports a variety of definitions. Some would, with chronological and sociological ignorance, define it as "applied science." While many modern technologies speak to the application of science, many do not; as one goes back in time, the frequency of technology being perceived as a "craft tradition" increases. In fact, prior to the late nineteenth century military technology exhibited precious little of what Robert Boyle succinctly described as "investigation by hypothesis subjected to rigorous experimental cross examination."[2] Yet, throughout most of history, technology in the form of tools and techniques has purposely altered the environment.

In other words, while technology is part of the context the strategist must manage, it also serves the same purpose. Hence, the notion of symbiosis. Technologies can transform context and, by inference, strategy itself. Similarly, strategy can transform technologies. One need look only as far as nuclear weapons to confirm this contention. The United States deliberately, as a strategy, enlisted scientific talent and spent billions of dollars to create nuclear weapons. These, in turn, changed the context of strategy, at least for the seven decades since and perhaps forever.

Context is also forever changing: biologically, environmentally, socially, and technologically. Each of these factors has its own rate of progression or change. But of the four, technology changes most rapidly, followed by sociology, then environment, and (perhaps in reaction to environmental changes) biology. Consequently, the strategist, while not ignoring the other factors, would do well to pay close attention to the least stable variable in a universe of possibilities. "Unstable, but somewhat predictable, and very impactful" would most closely describe technological development. Or, as Henry Adams so succinctly quipped on the acceleration of history, "Bombs educate vigorously."[3]

So how do game-changing, war-winning technologies enter military arsenals? Herein lies a dichotomy nested in the technostrategic symbiosis. Technology is an agent of change, and organizations, military ones included, tend to resist change. They are most likely to seek change when expanding, having suffered a reversal, or pressured from without.[4] But then how does the winning military organization subsequently undergoing contraction in peacetime ensure that it is technologically prepared to win the next war? On the surface, it would appear that technological innovation plays the same role as the National Football League draft, in ensuring that the weak will grow stronger and the strong weaker by conferring advantage in the selection of talent to losers over winners. But then, in that league winners tend to be richer and can apply that advantage to the free-agent market, providing they are willing to accept the changes marquee players will make to team chemistry.

Sports analogies aside, the problem of technological innovation in the military is important, complex, and fraught with dramatic strategic implications. In fact, innovation is the central problem in the relationship between strategy and technology. Although David Edgerton contends that innovation is overplayed in the history of technology, one would be hard-pressed to ignore the impact of new devices and methods of employment on strategy.[5] From the Schwiepwald, outside Königgrätz, where prone, rail-borne Prussian riflemen used their new breechloaders to cut down the aspirations of the Austrian empire, to the deserts of Iraq, where Americans used new, stealthy precision weapons to end the reign of both Saddam Hussein and the Soviet empire, technological innovation has mattered strategically. So how does it occur? How does the opportunity—nay, the imperative—presented by new technologies overcome the inertia of military organizations?

To ask such a question is to pit technological determinism against social constructivism in explaining the diffusion of tools and techniques for warfare. As Lynn White so elegantly phrased it, "A new device merely opens a door; it does not compel one to enter."[6] What does? Determinists like Ray Kurzweil speak of the inexorable pressure and innate humanity of the exponential curve of technical progression.[7] Yet constructivists like Trevor Pinch and Wiebe Bijker point to the "empirical program of relativism" in science and how it corresponds to the "social construction of technology," where "artifacts" are shaped by social forces until they reach "closure."[8] Between these poles of argument lie systems thinkers like Thomas Parke Hughes and John Law. Hughes perceives a "technological momentum" that borrows some fury from the determinist argument in the early stages of technological development but then yields to social forces as technologies mature.[9] Law introduces the notion of heterogeneous engineering in technological systems, wherein agency is ascribed to people, technology, and environment.[10] Hughes and Law probably come closest to the truth in contending that technical and social forces have about equal weight in the equation of change and that both must be managed by strategists seeking advantage. Examples will illustrate the argument.

Throughout most of history, technology mattered little to strategic calculation. That is not to say that technology was not important to the conduct of war but rather that there was little advantage to be gained by manipulating technology. The weapons of war advanced, but they did so very slowly. The musket used by British soldiers under Wellington at Waterloo was little changed from that used by those under Marlborough at Blenheim over a century before. Nelson's *Victory* was over forty years old at Trafalgar. This slow rate of technical progression was complemented by the osmotic nature of cultures with regard to technology in general and, specifically, of military cultures to successful weaponry. Once something worked, it was adopted by others. The French advantage in mobile field artillery that Jean Baptiste Vaquette de Gribeauval had pioneered in the late eighteenth century served Napoleon well in early campaigns and up through the battles of Jena and Auerstadt in 1806. By the time of Leipzig in 1814, however, others had caught up, and the galloping guns of the French conferred little advantage. Things began to change, however, in middle of the nineteenth century.

While it is difficult to pinpoint a cause of this technical one-upsmanship, Douglass North leans heavily on property rights. By the early nineteenth century, American patent law had ensured that people could own not only land and structures but also ideas. Patent offices soon proliferated to other nations, and self-interested parties had financial incentives to invent and innovate.[11] This development served to warm the relationship of two strange kinds of bedfellows: military men and merchants. One class was rooted in land and loyalty, the other in markets and money. Throughout most of history, they had little trust in or use for each other. But that began to change with the founding of cannon by private entrepreneurs in the middle of the eighteenth century. It turns out that Louis XIV could get the best guns only from the makers in Liege, where his reign held little sway. As William McNeill so eloquently asserts, "private efforts to maximize profits tended to reward economies in the use of all the factors of production. Market behavior, in short, induced a level of efficiency compulsion rarely could match."[12] This simple truth underwrites the alliance of merchants and military that has persisted to this day.

In attempting to explain the emergence of technical advantage in strategic planning, one could also speculate on the confluence of the political, industrial, and managerial revolutions. Walter Millis used this construct to explain the migration from limited to total wars.[13] The political revolution started in the American colonies and reached full fury in France. By setting the social conditions for the mass army, it greatly multiplied the effect of any technical improvements. The industrial revolution was rooted in the British textile industry and provided the wherewithal to equip the issue of the *levée en masse*. The managerial revolution was rooted in the Prussian general staff as an institutional response to the genius of Napoleon. Among the charters of the Generalstab was to remain abreast of changes in technology and, when appropriate, to procure them for the army.

The General Staff had aged two generations by the middle of the nineteenth century, and by then a number of technologies were presenting opportunities for strategic innovation. Principal among these was the steam-powered railroad. From antiquity to roughly 1860, the sea presented the most efficient line of communication, and command of the sea conferred great advantages in both freedom of action and economy of force. Ferdinand Foch maintained that these two principles circumscribed all others in the military art.[14] Needless to say, A. T. Mahan, in his Spencerian polemic for American sea power, based his entire theory on the logistic efficiency of maritime commerce. Ironically, Mahan published *The Influence of Seapower upon History: 1660–1783* at precisely the moment another form of transportation began to matter more in the equation.[15] And that was the railroad. In fairness to Mahan, sea power and command of the sea still mattered, but in the vast reaches of Eurasia the railroad showed considerable promise for those who wished to project power to the outer reaches of a "heartland" that stretched from the Bay of Biscay to Port Arthur and from Archangel to the Sea of Azov.[16] Although nearly every nation built railroads, it was the Prussian and later German General Staff that seized upon the strategic opportunities that inhered in the new form of transport for a nation gifted with a central position in the Eurasian landmass and with limited opportunities for maritime power. While the railroad appeared at first to be the ideal defensive technology, since nations could change gauges at their borders, the Germans realized the offensive capability of a rapidly mobilized army carried to the frontier ahead of the enemy's mobilization schedule. An army on the strategic offensive could be carried by train to the border, disembark fresh for the march, and surround the opposing force, thus fighting from the tactical defensive. The bullet-stopping power of dirt conferred a considerable advantage to the tactical defender from the mid-nineteenth century until well into the twentieth.

Notably, it was also the Prussian General Staff that embarked in 1841 on a twenty-year program to equip its soldiers with breechloading rifles. As Dennis Showalter has noted, the unification of principalities into the German nation was largely a story of *Railroads and Rifles*.[17] The third *R* of German unification, artillery, in the form of cast-steel breechloaders manufactured by Alfred Krupp, was documented by Michael Howard in *The Franco-Prussian War*.[18] One could argue that lack of organizational inertia and a complementary spirit of free inquiry that typified the German General Staff in this period were instrumental in fomenting the technical changes that led to strategic innovation. But we would be remiss to discount the genius of Helmuth Moltke the Elder in engineering the changes and employing them in succession against the Danes, Austrians, and French. In so doing, Moltke not only provided the military complement to Bismarck's diplomacy in unifying Germany; he also set, in mobilization schedules tied to rail transport, the strategic parameters for the epochal event of history—World War I.

The contrast to Moltke's genius in employing new technologies is perhaps best demonstrated by the example of the French *mitrailleuse,* a large, wheeled prototype of the Gatling gun that had tremendous potential for overcoming German advantages in both population and mobilization. But the French employed it as artillery, far from the front lines and without much use in an indirect-fire role.[19] The French were more successful in reequipping their army—with the Chassepot breechloader, superior to the German Dreyse needle gun—in the scant four years between the Austro-Prussian and Franco-Prussian wars. At Metz, Sedan, and later Paris, however, they suffered greatly from the indirect fire of Krupp's artillery, developed and deployed in exactly the same period of time as the Chassepot rifle. Krupp's artillery brought a new development to the practice of war. A century and a half later, American airmen coined the term "parallel warfare" in reference to their ability to destroy targets throughout a theater of operations and thereby produce a systemic paralysis in the enemy. By 1870, the Germans, using long-range artillery, had achieved the same effect in a radius of action that we would term "tactical." By 1940, using tanks, motorized transport, and aircraft, they had widened the effect of "parallel" attack to a radius more "operational" in scope. In retrospect, the antecedents of technical imperatives for strategic innovation are clear in the German Wars of Unification. While, as mentioned earlier, bombs may indeed educate vigorously, the converse is also true; the German General Staff stands as testament to the fact that military practitioners must engage in education that they might bomb with vigor.

Lest the reader find the author Germanophilic, by the middle of the twentieth century the Teutons had gotten it wrong. The technical imperatives for strategic innovation were perhaps even stronger, but they were mismanaged in the event, and fortunes suffered accordingly. Rather, in the case of jet propulsion and rocketry, good fortune was to be bequeathed in posterity to Germany's enemies.

The Messerschmitt 262 Schwable represents one of the most dramatic aviation developments of World War II. The twin-engine turbojet had both the speed and firepower to disrupt Allied bomber formations and gain air superiority for the Luftwaffe, despite the decided advantages the Allies had in aircraft production. The 262 was the aerial analog to the German *Ostkampfer* fighting four-to-one odds on the Eastern Front. Yet the program foundered in design changes and production delays. Some would later blame Hitler's infatuation with using the plane as a bomber, while others cite the ridiculously short life of its engines. Nonetheless, properly managed, the jet fighter might have turned the tables in the air war—and thereby the ground war, which so often depended upon aerial capability.[20] Why did the grandsons of the men who brought us the Dreyse needle gun, clockwork rail mobilization, and cast-steel, breechloading artillery not seize upon the dire need for this air-superiority jet and engineer its success?

The answer probably lies in the incompatibility of Nazi ideology with "defensive" weapons and the subsequent absence of a champion who could overcome the friction that inhered in German bureaucratic and command structures. These frictions exist in all bureaucracies and commands, representing what John Law termed "dissociative" forces with regard to systemic success.[21] They are overcome by blending what Clausewitz termed "iron will" and "genius."[22] Neither Willy Messerschmitt, Hermann Goering, nor Erhard Milch appears to have possessed the requisite combination of brute force and finesse necessary to field a revolutionary weapon system in numbers sufficient to impact the outcome of a war. But one could also argue that the Nazis had other things on their minds.

The V-2 was an offensive weapon system and, in form as well as function, a near perfect match to Nazi ideology. From its Buck Rogers shape to its indefensible hypersonic approach, it was the perfect *Vergeltungswaffe,* or "vengeance weapon." Also, the rocket was manufactured by slave labor, in horrific conditions at the Dora concentration camp near Sachsenhausen, again exhibiting a macabre congruence to the neo-feudal Weltanschauung of Hitler's regime. In contrast to Milch and Messerschmitt, Werner von Braun and his military counterpart in the development of the V-2, Walther Dornberger, were men of considerable talent who knew how to get things done in the bizarre culture of the Third Reich. (Isaac Asimov once quipped that von Braun had aimed at the stars and hit London.) Yet it was the strategic aim of the Germans that needed refinement. What did they hope to accomplish with a development program nearly as expensive as the Manhattan Project? Certainly more than killing 5,200 British citizens—yet such was the final tally, along with a minor disruption of Allied logistics in the invasion port of Antwerp. (Now, had they wished to colonize the moon . . .) The point taken here is that technological development may require at times both finesse and brute force, but it also requires vision. And lacking that, the other two don't matter much.

Imagine a V-2 with an explosive payload powerful enough to destroy London. This is precisely the image formed by Bernard Schriever upon taking a briefing from noted physicist and mathematician Johnny von Neumann on the possibilities of thermonuclear weapons. Just as Moltke's railroads were complemented by breechloading rifles and artillery, so was von Braun's rocket in need of a nuclear weapon to be effective. Moreover, to be effective over intercontinental distances, in addition to a payload several thousand times more powerful per weight than TNT, it needed a better guidance system and a way of reentering the atmosphere without burning up. By the middle of the 1950s all three of these problems were teetering on the cusp of solutions. The guidance problem was solved by Stark Draper in the Lincoln Lab at MIT using a pendulum-induced, gyrostabilized accelerometer that would provide inertial guidance for terminal accuracy of less than three thousand feet over a distance of five thousand miles.[23] The reentry problem found the counterintuitive solution of ablative shielding—presenting a blunt surface designed to burn up in the atmospheric friction encountered in the missile's descent.

Thermonuclear explosives culminated a research program started at the turn of the century by Ernest Rutherford, when he discovered the atomic nucleus by firing beta particles (ionized helium) at gold foil and noting that some of them bounced back. Atomic nuclei are held together by a curve of binding energy.[24] Lighter elements, such as helium, give up energy when their nuclei are fused. This is the process that powers the universe. At the other end of the binding curve, heavier elements, such as uranium, produce energy when their nuclei are broken apart in fission. Both processes occur in nature. Fusion, however, requires the tremendous heat generated by the gravitational collapse of hydrogen gas; this is how the sun powers our solar system. Fission occurs naturally through the radioactive decay of certain heavy isotopes but to produce energy requires a readily available source of thermal neutrons to destabilize the nuclei of heavy elements. It also requires the presence of other heavy nuclei to sustain a chain reaction. In other words, fission is unlikely to produce significant amounts of energy unless we take pains to assemble a substantial amount of heavy metal, confine it, and provide a bevy of neutrons to start the reaction. Hence, the Manhattan Project, perhaps the greatest technological achievement in history. Many of the scientists who worked in Los Alamos, most notably Hungarian expatriate Edward Teller, realized the complementary nature of fission and fusion: if one could fission heavy nuclei, one could generate enough heat to fuse lighter nuclei. Teller, only mildly interested in the fission bomb, went to New Mexico to work on "the Super."[25] And it was the super—a fusion bomb with a fission trigger—that excited Bennie Schriever's imagination.

Von Neumann told Schriever that fusion weapons with yields of several hundred kilotons were possible in a warhead that weighed less than half a ton—a payload within the capability of a V-2-like rocket. Schriever realized almost immediately the strategic implications of such a device. It could hold cities—nay, nations—hostage to the intentions of its possessor. The pressure to produce a reliable intercontinental ballistic missile (ICBM) came from knowing that the Soviet Union had detonated a fission device in 1949 and was thus capable of producing a thermonuclear fusion device. The Soviets were also familiar with rocketry, by virtue of having expropriated several members of von Braun's team at the end of the war. Hence, Schriever set about forming the Western Development Corporation in Los Angeles for the express purpose of building ICBMs. By so doing he avoided the bureaucratic politics of the Pentagon, while securing the support of Undersecretary of Defense Trevor Gardner to keep Curtis LeMay and the bomber barons of the Strategic Air Command at bay. Schriever was tall, handsome, and a consummate golfer. All three attributes aided his cause in the heterogeneous engineering of the Atlas and Minuteman missile systems.[26]

The notion of "systems" is vitally important to technical imperatives for strategic innovation. Absent an efficient steam engine, the railroad is not possible. Without cartridges, breechloading rifles and artillery are much less efficient. Absent fission, fusion is not possible. Absent fusion, guidance systems, and ablative shielding, the ICBM is not possible. Strategic innovators must command a sense of context and of what is possible. Thermonuclear weapons were nine years, an ocean, and ideological light-years removed from the Third Reich. (Fifty percent of the key scientists working on the Manhattan Project were Jews.) Fusion weapons were, however, well within the grasp of Joseph Stalin, as were ICBMs, as was painfully demonstrated to the West by Sputnik in 1957. It turns out that the guidance system required to put a satellite in orbit is of the same caliber as that necessary to hit a city at intercontinental distances. (If von Braun had missed the stars for London, Stalin had missed by even more, aiming for New York and hitting outer space.)

Regardless of aim, strategists must seize upon the advantages of complementary technologies. In the end, it was the killing power of the breechloading rifle that consummated the strategic conveyance of the railroad in German unification. Similarly, it was the light and powerful thermonuclear device, the killing power of which is derived from lithium deuteride, a relatively common salt, that energized missiles as the dominant coercive force of the Cold War.

But thermonuclear weapons presented a threshold of violence that even the most ideologically strident leaders chose to avoid. And beneath this thermonuclear umbrella, limited conventional wars, often fought by proxies of the superpowers and under the scrutiny of mass media, continued. The wars that occurred in Korea and Vietnam, as well as twice in Afghanistan, Iraq, and Yugoslavia, required the complement of mass destruction. They demanded precision and its somewhat unlikely partner, stealth. Gene Roddenberry in *Star Trek* recognized the potential that lay in a Klingon "bird of prey" equipped with the Romulan cloaking device. The real trick was firing phasers while cloaked. By the late 1980s, the Americans had made Roddenberry's fiction real. They had developed laser-guided bombs to take out bridges during the Vietnam conflict, but these had demanded a steady platform to lase the target while the bomb was guided home. This need gave rise to the impetus for a stealthy platform that could evade detection and attack by the enemy's integrated air-defense system. The F-117 and B-2 were designed for this purpose and were made more lethal by the development of satellite guidance for their bombs via the Global Positioning System.[27] By the end of the twentieth century, American airmen had developed a set of complementary technologies that made them nearly invincible in conventional warfare, providing the opponent had no recourse to nuclear weapons. Often missing, however, was the strategic vision that rationalized the use of these clever weapons.

The wars in Yugoslavia, first Bosnia and later Kosovo, could be labeled as qualified successes. They were short and decisive, and they carried with them a clearly humanitarian imperative that played well to the media-savvy audiences of the information age. The first Gulf War was also a qualified success, but much like World War I it left the problem of dynamism in the region to be solved by a second. Both the second Iraq war and its partner in Afghanistan came in response to imaginative airborne attacks by jihadist terrorists on New York and Washington. Both also took on additional agendas of unfinished business in the Middle East region. Moreover, they represented reprehensible strategic thinking. The global Salafi jihadist movement was a symptom of the war within Islam. But neither the symptom of terrorist acts nor the disease of Islamic radicalism was likely to be cured by invading Muslim countries. Stealth, precision, rapid movement, and information dominance can afford a dramatic operational edge in the employment of military force, but no amount of technological proclivity can overcome bad strategy. If it hasn't already, I suspect that the passage of time will confirm this for the most recent American military operations in Afghanistan and Iraq.

Nonetheless, we can agree that a great deal of technical innovation has occurred in the military art since we started this discussion in the middle of the nineteenth century. Scholars differ, however, on the causes and methods of this innovation. Barry Posen has studied *The Sources of Military Doctrine* in European militaries during the interwar period. In his study, he pitted the assumed inertia of military organizations against imperatives for change stimulated by concerns over the balance of power. In Posen's representation, these changes in the security environment of a nation were better sensed by politicians than generals. Civil leaders, however, lacked the knowledge—better, the language—of military organizations necessary to effect change. They consequently, according to Posen, had to rely on "mavericks" within the military to do their bidding. While the maverick with outside political support might fit the persona of William Mitchell in developing aviation for the U.S. Army, or Heinz Guderian in creating armored forces for the German Wehrmacht, the depiction works less well with figures like Hugh Dowding in building the integrated air-defense system for England in the late 1930s or William Moffett in building American carrier aviation during the same time period. Since Schriever married into the aristocracy of American airpower and had the patronage of Gen. "Hap" Arnold throughout much of his career, he could hardly be labeled a maverick. Hyman Rickover, who had much to do with the nuclear navy, comes closer to Posen's depiction, since he would likely have never made flag rank without congressional help. Both he and Schriever recognized, however, that innovation in the form of nuclear-powered submarines and ships and of ICBMs, respectively, was unlikely to occur in the bureaucratic setting of the Pentagon and its specialized research-and-development organizations. Both Rickover and Schriever formed new organizations with built-in counters to the stifling influence of tradition and bureaucracy, and they ensured that their "development corporations" were supported by civil leaders with stakes in national security—to wit, the president, the Congress, and the secretary of defense. So Posen's notion of civil influence is important but perhaps slightly miscast.[28]

His one-time student Stephen Rosen offers a refinement. In Rosen's representation of military innovation it is military leaders, not politicians, who sense changes in the security environment and react to them by innovating doctrinally. Although Rosen chooses to deal with "technological innovation" separately, here he is talking about research-and-development programs. Most of his doctrinal innovation—and he offers a multitude of cases—occurs in response to technological stimuli. Rosen's most important contribution is the realization of what is important to military men and women and their organizations: promotion (particularly, for individuals, to flag and general rank). Hence, Rosen contends, the success or failure of military innovations is played out as much in the arena of personnel as on the battlefield. Successful innovations may take a generation to mature, and a notable characteristic of their success is that the new way of doing business affords mainstream practitioners progression through the ranks to the grade of general or admiral. Rosen suggests that "seeding" new forms of endeavor with officers who are "fast movers" in other branches is yet another way of sustaining viability. In other words, the proper management of people is what assures the success of a new military technology.[29]

While it is possible to view Posen and Rosen as polar opposites in the way they represent military innovation, "complementary" may be the more applicable adjective. Posen appears to view the military in the manner of Samuel Huntington, as a bunch of hidebound men separated from American society as much by their own desires as by the norms of their profession.[30] Eliot Cohen exhibits a similar view in *Supreme Command,* where military men, to be effective, need continual supervision and intervention by their civil masters. While Cohen admits to a civil-military dialogue, it is very unequal, with both power and knowledge slanted to the civil side.[31] This Ivy League, ivory-tower view of the military is perhaps deserved on occasion, but it ignores the sensitivities, education, and imagination of military practitioners. Although the men and women on both sides of the Potomac are specialists, I will hazard to say that soldiers, sailors, and airmen are more aware of political affairs than are politicians of military art. That imbalance in knowledge and experience should serve to even out the dialogue a bit. There are indeed times when military people "stuck in old ways of doing business" need civil intervention to right their ships, dress their ranks, and trim their aircraft.[32] But instances also exist when military people have sensed changes in the security environment and set about making the changes necessary for national defense.

So where does this leave us, and what does the future hold? Almost certain is the prospect that technology will continue to present opportunities for change. But will history treat twenty-first-century Americans with the same disdain it has for twentieth-century Germans? Will it view the United States as an unfortunate victim of its own technically induced hubris? Will the bankruptcy of ideas lead to the economic ruin some are so willing to forecast? I think not.

The same things that make Americans technologically savvy will make them politically wise. American technology grew from the scarcity of labor on the frontier. A scarcity of resources in the global economy will incentivize both technical and political ingenuity. Democracies are learning organisms, and ours will learn from its mistakes. To encourage both technical innovation and political moxie, we must address both of what C. P. Snow termed "the Two Cultures"—and we must do it through education.[33] We need an efficient photovoltaic cell and a better way of placing payloads in orbit. Education in science, engineering, and mathematics will lead to solutions for these problems. We need better linkage between our foreign and domestic policies and better mechanisms for distributing wealth and stimulating economic growth—at the same time. Education in history, politics, and economics will lead to solutions here. Finally, we need better strategists, with one foot planted firmly in each culture, to orchestrate a second century of American leadership in the world.

Our strategists must understand the technical imperatives for strategic innovation, but they must also understand the political ramifications of using military force in the context of globalization. Our strategists must be "heterogenius engineers." They must combine the grey art of systems engineering with the black art of military genius. They must at times possess iron will and use brute force in assembling relative advantage. They must understand the incentives of the merchant class and the role of private property, particularly as applied to ideas, in creating new and improved weapons. But they must also have the vision to foresee socioeconomic consequences and mitigate ill effects. They must, moreover, deal effectively with a conundrum that stems from the very definition of strategy employed here.

That is, nearly every advantage carries with it a disadvantage. Strategy exploits, and there is almost always a bill to pay for exploitation. No one enjoys being exploited, and payback runs the gamut from resentment to revolution. After the Prussians had won the battle of Königgrätz, Moltke wanted to parade his army through the streets of Vienna. But Bismarck, knowing he might need the Austrians to remain neutral in a potential fight with France, expressly forbade the insult. It was enough for him to know that the four southern German provinces would now form a defensive alliance with Prussia instead of with Austria.[34] George H. W. Bush and his team of strategists viewed Iraq as an effective counterpoise to Iran in the Gulf and forbade the enlargement of coalition aims to take down the regime of Saddam Hussein after blitzing his forces out of Kuwait. Bismarck and Bush were both moderate in the advantages they sought, and this may be sound advice to all strategists: accrue only the advantage necessary in the moment. Long-term arrangements, no matter how easily secured with superior technology, must appear advantageous to both sides. American strategy must be good for not only the United States but also the rest of the world. One could argue that this was true in the twentieth century; keeping it true for the remainder of this century will be a tall order.

Some of the early historians of technology postulated *Homo habilis*—man the toolmaker. They contended it was technology that made us human. We know

now that this is not true. What makes us human is sentience in the moment and the ability to move our minds in space and time—to foresee, to imagine, to dream, to plan. Technology merely makes us *more* human. It seeks a better way of managing the context we inhabit. If we are to succeed as a species, then, we must make technology humane. This includes the technology of making war. That was the idea held by Giulio Douhet and many of the early theorists of airpower, who were reacting to the dehumanizing carnage of World War I. Unfortunately, things did not work out as they planned—at least initially. The people of Guernica, Rotterdam, Coventry, Hamburg, Dresden, Tokyo, Hiroshima, and all the other "dead cities" of World War II would be unlikely to testify to the humanity of the new aerial weapon, any more than World War II residents of Kharkov and Budapest would extol the lifesaving virtues of invading armies. More recently, however, the inhabitants of Baghdad and Belgrade might have a different take on the issue. Modern conventional weapons can be employed with diminished collateral effects, and the impact of mass media and networked populations makes it imperative that they be so employed. Robotic developments also place combatants farther from harm's way. So, elements of modern warfare point toward greater humanity. But others don't. Thermonuclear weapons are still a significant threat, one that could possibly destroy the ecosphere that sustains human life on this planet, or at least the threads of social fabric that bind us together. The good news is that numbers are coming down, and with that reduction at least the environmental threat is somewhat diminished.

The desideratum of the twenty-first century may indeed then be a strategy problem. How well have we harmonized the resources of this planet and the objective of a flourishing species through the aegis of a plan? The problem is complex, perhaps even chaotic, and has a strong technological component, but it has a solution. And, as an educator, I can only hope our students will find it.

NOTES

1. Everett C. Dolman, *Pure Strategy: Power and Principle in the Information Age* (New York: Frank Cass, 2005), 6.

2. Robert Boyle, *The Sceptical Chymist or Chymico-Physical Doubts and Paradoxes* (London: F. Caldwell, 1661), 4.

3. Henry Adams, *The Education of Henry Adams* (Boston: Houghton Mifflin, 1918), 34.

4. Barry R. Posen, *The Sources of Military Doctrine: France, Britain, and Germany between the Wars* (Ithaca, N.Y.: Cornell University Press, 1984), 47.

5. David Edgerton, *The Shock of the Old: Technology and Global History since 1900* (Oxford: Oxford University Press, 2007).

6. Lynn White Jr., *Medieval Technology and Social Change* (Oxford: Oxford University Press, 1962), 28.

7. Ray Kurzweil, *The Age of Spiritual Machines: When Computers Exceed Human Intelligence* (New York: Penguin Books, 1999).

8. Wiebe E. Bijker, Thomas P. Hughes, and Trevor Pinch, eds., *The Social Construction of Technological Systems: New Directions in the Sociology and History of Technology* (Cambridge, Mass.: MIT Press, 1987), 12.

9. Ibid., 51–82.

10. Ibid., 111–34.

11. Douglass North, *Structure and Change in Economic History* (New York: W. W. Norton, 1981)

12. William H. McNeill, *Technology, Armed Force, and Society since A.D. 1000* (Chicago: University of Chicago Press, 1982), 156.

13. Walter Millis, *Arms and Men: A Study in American Military History* (New Brunswick, N.J.: Rutgers University Press, 1956).

14. Ferdinand Foch, *The Principles of War,* trans. Hilaire Belloc (New York: Henry Holt, 1920). See also Andre Beaufre, *An Introduction to Strategy* (New York: Praeger, 1965), 21–50.

15. Alfred T. Mahan, *The Influence of Sea Power upon History: 1660–1873* (Mineola, N.Y.: Dover, 1890).

16. Halford Mackinder, "The Geographical Pivot of History" (reprint of 1904 article), *Geographical Journal* 170, no. 4 (2004): 298–321.

17. Dennis Showalter, *Railroads and Rifles: Soldiers, Technology, and the Unification of Germany* (Hamden, Conn.: Archon Books, 1975).

18. Michael Howard, *The Franco-Prussian War: The German Invasion of France, 1870–1871* (London: Rupert Hart-Davis, 1961).

19. Bernard Brodie and Fawn M. Brodie, *From Crossbow to H-Bomb: The Evolution of the Weapons and Tactics of Warfare* (Bloomington: Indiana University Press, 1973), 145.

20. William Green, *Warplanes of the Third Reich* (New York: Galahad Books, 1986), 619–38.

21. John Law, "Technology and Heterogeneous Engineering: The Case of Portuguese Expansion," in Bijker, Hughes, and Pinch, *Social Construction of Technological Systems,* 111–34.

22. Carl von Clausewitz, *On War,* ed. and trans. Michael Howard and Peter Paret (Princeton, N.J.: Princeton University Press, 1976), 110–12.

23. Donald MacKenzie, *Inventing Accuracy: A Historical Sociology of Nuclear Missile Guidance* (Cambridge, Mass.: MIT Press, 1990).

24. John McPhee, *The Curve of Binding Energy: A Journey into the Awesome and Alarming World of Theodore B. Taylor* (New York: Farrar, Straus, and Giroux, 1974).

25. Richard Rhodes, *The Making of the Atomic Bomb* (New York: Simon and Schuster, 1986), 418–22.

26. Neil Sheehan, *A Fiery Peace in a Cold War: Bernard Schriever and the Ultimate Weapon* (New York: Random House, 2009).

27. Michael Russell Rip and James M. Hasik, *The Precision Revolution: GPS and the Future of Aerial Warfare* (Annapolis, Md.: Naval Institute Press, 2002); Paul G. Gillespie, *Weapons of Choice: The Development of Precision Guided Munitions* (Tuscaloosa: University of Alabama Press, 2006).

28. Posen, *Sources of Military Doctrine*.

29. Stephen P. Rosen, *Winning the Next War: Innovation and the Modern Military* (Ithaca, N.Y.: Cornell University Press, 1991).

30. Samuel P. Huntington, *The Soldier and the State: The Theory and Politics of Civil-Military Relations* (Boston: Belknap, 1957).

31. Eliot A. Cohen, *Supreme Command: Soldiers, Statesmen, and Leadership in Wartime* (New York: Free Press, 2002).

32. The reference here is to a speech made by Secretary of Defense Robert Gates at Maxwell-Gunter Air Force Base on 21 April 2008, just prior to sacking the Air Force Chief of Staff and the Secretary of the Air Force.

33. C. P. Snow, *The Two Cultures and a Second Look* (London: Cambridge University Press, 1964).

34. Otto Pflanze, *Bismarck and the Development of Germany: The Period of Unification, 1815–1871* (Princeton, N.J.: Princeton University Press, 1971), 200–208.

CHAPTER SIX

The Airpower Historian and the Education of Strategists

RICHARD R. MULLER

The formal use of military history as an aid to professional officer education and the development of military strategists began with the nineteenth-century Prussian tradition of Gerhard von Scharnhorst and Helmuth von Moltke. Alfred Thayer Mahan based his theories of navalism and the linkage between sea power and the rise of empires on a rigorous if selective study of British naval history, and his ideas helped shape generations of U.S. strategy making. Yet as a rule air forces have not embraced historical study to the same extent as have their army or navy counterparts. While many of the air arms of the great powers, including the Royal Air Force (RAF), the German Luftwaffe, and the U.S. Air Force and its predecessors have used official history as a means of "telling the Air Force story" and cementing demands for institutional autonomy, these most modern and technology-dependent military forces have been reluctant to emphasize historical study as an essential part of the education of strategists. They have instead stressed their discontinuity with the past, their future-looking orientation, and their freedom from the established principles of war. To this day, the U.S. Air Force (USAF) follows the lead of airpower prophet Gen. William Mitchell, who in 1925 argued, "In the development of air power, one has to look ahead and not backward to figure out what is going to happen, not too much what has happened."[1]

This chapter examines the use of military history by the U.S. Air Force in its efforts to produce educated air strategists, from the 1930s to the present. It concentrates on midcareer officer education, first at the Air Corps Tactical School

(ACTS) at Maxwell Field, Alabama, in the 1930s, through the creation of Air University in 1946, particularly at the Air Command and Staff School (ACSS) and its successor Air Command and Staff College (ACSC), and the School of Advanced Air and Space Studies (SAASS), where the author presently teaches.[2] The investigation suggests that the USAF has been reluctant to emphasize historical study in its midcareer officer education until the last twenty-five years, preferring to concentrate on current international affairs, staff and managerial skills, and tactical and technological development. In this, it is little different from most of the great air arms of the twentieth century. What one historian called "the Air Force's chronic impatience with history" is equally evident in the general neglect of strategy education at all levels.[3]

This chapter also makes a case for the value of historical study in the education of officers and the development of strategists. It is based upon the official records preserved at the USAF Historical Research Agency, including actual curriculum materials and course catalogs; half-forgotten unit histories (completed annually and in great detail, then filed away at Air University), as well as interviews and correspondence with faculty and students from some of the periods under discussion. Published works include Robert T. Finney's and Peter Faber's published scholarship on the Air Corps Tactical School, Gen. Haywood Hansell's memoirs of his time there as a student and faculty member, and several recent publications on the history of Air University and Maxwell Air Force Base. The published material has its limitations. Air Force professional education has not caught the fancy of many scholars outside the organization, so much of the source material has a distinctly "inside" flavor. I have also drawn heavily on my own experiences as a faculty member, department chair, and dean at ACSC, and faculty member and dean of academics at SAASS, over the past twenty-four years. Finally, and to put, in the Air Force tradition, the "bottom line up front," the study of military and airpower history can—and does—play a unique and invaluable role in the development of effective strategists.

THE BEGINNINGS: THE AIR CORPS TACTICAL SCHOOL ERA

What eventually became the Air Corps Tactical School was established at Langley Field, Virginia, in 1920 as the professional school for the air service, in an acknowledgment that aviation had reached parity with the cavalry, the artillery, the infantry, chemical weapons service, and other branches. The school relocated to "the colonies," specifically Maxwell Field, Alabama, in 1931. It was at Maxwell that the school achieved either fame or notoriety as the fount of daylight precision strategic bombardment doctrine, played out in the skies over occupied Europe from 1942 to 1945.[4] This story is well known; less studied is the actual role of military historical study in the Tactical School's curriculum.

An inkling of that role may be gleaned from the school's motto: *Proficimus More Irretenti* (We Progress Unhindered by Tradition). Interwar advocates of air-power were keenly aware that while aviation's baptism of fire in World War I contained a wealth of historical experience, relatively little of that experience sup-ported an independent or strategic role for airpower in a future conflict. While the Attack and Pursuit Aviation courses at ACTS contained a fair measure of historical material (mainly tactical illustrations and battle studies) from World War I, the all-important Bombardment course (which later came to dominate the intellectual life of the school) eschewed historical analysis almost completely. It is not surprising that the ACTS faculty were drawn to the airpower writings of the Italian general Giulio Douhet. Douhet explicitly argued that prior historical expe-rience was irrelevant to practitioners of the new art of aerial warfare and strategy making in the third dimension. Douhet went on to define "aerial strategy" as "the selection of objectives, the grouping of [target] zones, and determining the order in which they are to be destroyed."[5] Douhet regarded this as the most "difficult and delicate" task facing the airman, and he insisted that the study of history offered no guidance.[6]

This is not to say that intellectual activity was nonexistent; the course fea-tured a sophisticated ongoing research effort into the strengths and vulnerabilities of the U.S. economy, complete with guest speakers drawn from industry and city planning.[7] Indeed, the early lectures of faculty stalwarts Harold George and Haywood Hansell (which established the intellectual foundation for the school) contain frequent references to Clausewitzian theory and concepts.[8] The ACTS faculty on the whole remained convinced that the study of the past was an impedi-ment to forward progress as they attempted to educate the student-officers in the art of air strategy. Indeed, as airmen sought to distance themselves from the constraints of the army doctrine of the day, their desire to advocate airpower's emancipation from historical lessons is perhaps more understandable. One com-mentator noted,

While developing [their] one-of-a-kind theory, the ACTS Bomber Mafia acted, in the candid words of Donald Wilson "on no firmer basis than reasoned logical thinking bolstered by a grasp of fundamentals of the application of military force and the reactions of human beings." In other words, they relied on deductive reasoning, analogies, and metaphors to develop their working propositions into a pseudo-scientific theory of strategic bombardment.[9]

Such a theory did not depend on any rigorous examination of the past practice of warfare. Individual faculty members incorporated historical material into the curriculum on their own initiative, yet the school's avowed goal of espousing a new doctrine of strategic bombardment usually discouraged such efforts. One faculty member, Capt. Ralph F. Stearley, added material dealing with the U.S. Marine Corps' experience with close air support during the "banana wars" in Haiti and Nicaragua only because of his personal friendship with several of the Marine aviators who had taken part in these operations.[10] Likewise, the desire to focus on hypothetical future strategic air operations against modern industrial powers stifled any attempts to draw relevant lessons from the use of airpower by the Japanese in Manchuria and China in the 1930s or the European powers in Spain.[11] The lessons of the "banana wars," China, and Spain seemed of little relevance. Still, lest we judge the American airmen too harshly, it is worth underlining that British and German airmen of the interwar era likewise believed the experiences of Manchuria, colonial air policing, and even the Spanish Civil War offered limited insight into future air wars.

THE ADVENT OF AIR UNIVERSITY

With a global war looming, the Air Corps Tactical School effectively closed down for academic year 1939–40, although a series of accelerated short courses, emphasizing air tactics and other practical subjects, took place.[12] Not until the postwar establishment of Air University (AU) on 12 March 1946 did a systematic educational program return to Maxwell Field. Both Billy Mitchell and the Army Air Forces chief, Gen. Henry H. "Hap" Arnold, had envisioned a unique airpower education system, an "air institution of learning," or a "University of the Air." While to this day every school on AU's Academic Circle claims to be the direct descendant of the Air Corps Tactical School, truthfully the main activities of the old ACTS were spread among two or three institutions as part of the new Air University, most notably ACSS and Air War College (AWC).[13] One historian of ACTS has noted,

The air experience of World War II presented instructors at the Air University with more definite ground on which to base their judgments of the employment of the air weapon than their counterparts of the Air Corps Tactical School had enjoyed, yet when the time came to resume the process of theorizing and of determining doctrine for air force employment, the value of that experience diminished before the impact of new types of aircraft and new weapons. Thus, the faculty at Air University has had to be just as much concerned with the theory of war, the problems of bomber versus fighter, the effectiveness of bombs, and the question of air superiority as were instructors at ACTS.[14]

The pace of technological change overshadowed even the dedication ceremonies of the new AU. The presence of a static display of German "miracle weapons" (including a V-2 ballistic missile) and a lecture by the new AWC commandant, Maj. Gen. Orvil Anderson, on the strategy implications of atomic weapons (he was later fired for his candor) served to focus attention on the future, rather than the past.[15] A review of the curriculum material for the 1949 academic year at Air Command and Staff School reveals only the most cursory introductory historical materials, mere stage setting for discussions of current and future capabilities.[16] In fairness, the initial course of study was overwhelmingly influenced by recent wartime experience (the first several classes were made up largely of experienced aviators awaiting assignment to the newly created post–World War II operational commands). The school's first commandant, Maj. Gen. Earl W. Barnes, had commanded XIII Fighter Group in the Southwest Pacific during World War II; one of the new school's first students was Paul W. Tibbets, who had ushered in the atomic age as the commander of the B-29 *Enola Gay* during the strike on Hiroshima on 6 August 1945. Recent and relevant war experience was an almost universal characteristic of these first classes; lengthy analysis of historical experience therefore seemed unnecessary. The selection of courses instead reflected the march of aviation technology, the presumed primacy of strategic (read atomic) air operations, and the need for staff and management skills as the USAAF moved toward independence. The 1946 curriculum mission statement spoke of the need not only to prepare officers for "command of groups, wings, and for staff duties" but also to "stimulate constructive thought" about the employment of military aviation, impart an awareness of the "capabilities and limitations" of ground and naval forces, and "to acquaint officers with world affairs which may influence military thought." There was no explicit reference to strategy. With only cosmetic modifications, this staff college mission statement has remained essentially unchanged through the decades.

From 1950 to 1954, the ACSS curriculum changed drastically as part of the USAF's response to the exigencies of the Korean War. ACSS took responsibility for two shorter staff courses, as well as a number of specialized courses, taken by (for example) intelligence or logistics officers in lieu of the general Field Officer Course. It was not until 1954 that the school returned to a more generalist approach to professional military education (PME)—a single comprehensive course for handpicked midcareer officers.

From 1954 to 1963, the curriculum emphasized the bipolar world of the intensifying Cold War. Two broad curriculum phases, Air Power Fundamentals and USAF Operations, contained blocks of instruction such as "The Enemy," "The Free World," "Military Doctrine," and "Technological Developments." While occasionally introductory historical material kicked off these courses, the focus was on mastering the current international situation and comprehending the latest operational doctrine—not discussing or debating its historical origins or evolution or its relationship to overall U.S. strategy in any but the most cursory fashion. Missing were any examinations of the French experience in Indochina, the British use of airpower in Malaya, or even the USAF's actions in the Korean War, despite these conflicts' rich legacy of valuable historical airpower insights. Though the USAF commissioned a comprehensive historical study of the war in Korea, representing a wealth of detail and analysis, the study was classified for many years and in any case maintained that the conflict had been an aberration. The study's impact on education at Maxwell seems to have been minimal.[17]

Indeed, without much exaggeration it can be asserted that in the 1961–62 academic year the most visible manifestation of airpower history in the course involved multiple screenings of the classic film *Twelve O'Clock High* (1949), which was the focus of many leadership seminars. An Army officer attending the course described a single "week in the life" of a staff college student during the early 1960s:

> On Monday morning, we met in the large auditorium with the entire class and watched the film "Twelve O'Clock High." That afternoon was a fitness afternoon, so I went out and played golf. Tuesday morning, we met in seminar and discussed "Leadership Lessons Learned from Twelve O'Clock High." Tuesday afternoon was a flying afternoon. [In

those days Air University kept a fleet of T-33 trainers at Maxwell so rated officers could remain jet qualified.] I wasn't a pilot, so I went out and played golf. Wednesday morning, we met in seminar and prepared a group briefing on "Leadership Lessons Learned from Twelve O'Clock High." Wednesday afternoon was our other fitness afternoon, so I went out and played golf. Thursday morning, we rehearsed our briefings on "Leadership Lessons Learned from Twelve O'Clock High." Thursday afternoon, like Tuesday, was also a flying afternoon, so I went out and played golf. On Friday morning we met in the large auditorium. Selected seminars presented their briefings on "Leadership Lessons Learned from Twelve O'Clock High." On Friday afternoon we never had classes, so I went out and played golf.[18]

Other portions of the course with some historical or strategy content included Unit II, "International Conflict," in which officers were encouraged to "summarize man's varying beliefs concerning his relationship to other men. Emphasis is placed upon the origin of the current world ideological conflict."[19] A later course in that year, "The Military Instrument of Power," ostensibly focused on "the nature of war and the application of the classical principles of war to modern warfare," yet the bulk of the course again dealt with current military capabilities rather than any critical examination of their evolution or relevance.[20]

As with much of the U.S. military establishment, the American experience in Southeast Asia provided a catalyst for a reinvigoration of the staff colleges and the use of historical and critical approaches. Many accounts rightly emphasize the postwar changes wrought by the Vietnam experience, but at Air University an interesting though short-lived attempt to apply historical analysis techniques to current operations in Vietnam took place at the height of that conflict.[21] This was Corona Harvest, a 1967–71 Air Staff initiative that took advantage of the fact that most students at Air University had recently completed operational tours in Southeast Asia, were en route to such tours, or both. Students at Air War College set to work analyzing strategic problems associated with that conflict, while ACSC seminars toiled over analyses of the effectiveness of B-52 Arclight strikes on North Vietnamese Army positions and other operational-level issues relating to the use of airpower in Southeast Asia.[22] The goal was to incorporate these lessons into the next iteration of Air Force basic and operational doctrine, and indeed Corona Harvest actually came up with many salient conclusions, some of which would have to be rediscovered by historians years or decades later. ACSC students, for example, identified flaws in the Air Force's method of using "truck kills" (the airpower equivalent of the notorious "body count") to measure the success of its interdiction operations against the Ho Chi Minh trail. However, Air Staff interest in the project waned as the U.S. commitment to Southeast Asia wound down, and most of the Corona Harvest studies wound up as highly classified documents in the Air Force archives.

The years following the end of the Vietnam War witnessed something of an intellectual renaissance at the staff and war colleges. Clausewitz was rediscovered and made required reading, to the chagrin of generations of majors and lieutenant colonels. Service chiefs (most notably the Commandant of the Marine Corps) developed professional reading lists, heavily laced with military history works. The Army Command and General Staff College boasted a rigorous military history program, the Combat Studies Institute, backed up by an excellent series of faculty publications. Yet the Air Force, in part because of a tendency to view Vietnam as somehow a political rather than a service failure, lagged behind. There was virtually no military or airpower history in the curriculum through most of the 1970s. Review of the course catalogs and interviews with graduates of the program during those times confirm that historical study of airpower was confined to a single day—a lecture on the Principles of War (a hardy perennial), a lecture on the historical evolution of the Air Corps Tactical School's doctrine of precision daylight bombardment, and a seminar in which students compared current Air Force (AF) doctrine to the writings of Douhet and Mitchell.[23]

It was not until 1979 that some faculty members at ACSC, largely on their own initiative, began to redesign the curriculum to include historical study. The course entitled "The Military Environment" was renamed "Warfare Studies."[24] This grassroots curriculum reform was driven by midcareer Air Force officers who had endured the Vietnam years; had acquired advanced degrees in history, political science, and international relations at civilian universities; and were aware of developments at other PME schools. One faculty member recalled,

> How else does one study strategy and doctrine than through the eyes of military and airpower history? The first big change was to inject as much history as we could into the curriculum. It wasn't easy. True story— I happened to pass the ACSC commandant in the hallway and in an exchange of greetings I mentioned our plans to teach a good deal of

military and airpower history in the following year. His only comment was, "Why would you want to do that?" The question spoke volumes about the problems of the school, and about AF PME in general during those years. [That particular commandant], by the way, came to ACSC from the Air Force Academy. His first act as the ACSC/CC was to put up posters all over the building with pictures illustrating the proper way to render a military salute—this to a command composed of nothing but field grade officers. Amazing![25]

Despite (or perhaps because of) this evident lack of high-level support, those believers in the value of historical and theoretical study persevered and put together a challenging academic program. Yet results were mixed. The ACSC history for 1979 reports,

> The Phase Manager made a valiant effort to stimulate the creative juices of the student body during their study of strategy and doctrine. The curriculum was a mixture of theory and fact, liberally sprinkled with controversy. Students were exposed to not only Air Doctrine and strategy, but also to naval and land theories of warfare.
>
> The most general negative comment was that the level of abstraction of the speakers was too high. Many students felt that although the issues were challenging, their basic knowledge was insufficient. One comment overheard was, "I understand the issue, but I don't understand strategy. What is it?"[26]

In spite of such formidable obstacles, the new program gained some ground. Course and graduation objectives began to reflect the new emphasis on the need to "value the role of historical military experience."[27] A greater sophistication in the topics examined was evident; including a "closer analysis of the USSR's contribution to victory in World War II." In 1984 a panel of outside evaluators (several drawn from history faculties of civilian universities), conducted an informal review of the military history, strategy, and theory curriculum. They gave it overall positive marks, but the one that gave the ACSC faculty the most pride was "better than Air War College." (Then, as now, professional rivalry among the schools on Academic Circle is marked.) Progress aside, the history and doctrine course was still an ungraded part of the curriculum; it would not be testable until 1986.

The next few years of curriculum evolution at ACSC demonstrated clearly how fragile the gains of the previous years really were. Although these years saw the introduction of visiting civilian history professors (there would be no full-time civilian historians on the faculty until 1991), as well as the introduction of popular elective courses on the Civil War, the Vietnam War (which only two years previously had been canceled due to lack of enrollment), History of Air Power, and War through the Ages, lack of support for historical study by the ACSC commandant hampered further growth in the core curriculum. That particular commandant noted, "You don't need to teach history at ACSC. You've got at least ten air force officers in each seminar, with an average of twelve years' active-duty experience each. That's 120 years of history right there!"[28]

Yet several trends both within and outside of the USAF were converging that would ultimately improve the status of historical inquiry in—as well as the overall quality of—professional officer education. Several critics of ACSC consistently cited a failure to study the lessons of the Vietnam War and earlier conflicts. Many saw the Air Force's evident failure to craft a strategy appropriate for that war and its reliance on such questionable measures of success as "sortie generation" and "bombs on target" as stemming in part from an internal overemphasis on "managerial" values.[29] Even commentators who were not sympathetic to this particular line of reasoning noted a need to "put the 'war' back into the war colleges." Air University underwent congressional scrutiny in the late 1980s from a House subcommittee headed by Representative Ike Skelton (D-Mo.). The Skelton Report offered a blistering critique of Air Force PME;[30] it recommended a general raising of academic standards, an increased study of military history and classical theory (as well as the aforementioned Clausewitz, Skelton insisted that Thucydides' masterpiece *History of the Peloponnesian War* be added to the ACSC reading list), and an improvement in military and civilian faculty credentials. The Skelton Panel also led directly to the establishment of SAASS, discussed in a later section. The Air University commander from 1989 to 1993, Lt. Gen. Charles Boyd, a former Vietnam F-105 "driver" and prisoner of war, not only supported these efforts but perhaps more notably protected officers and civilian academics who were working on books and articles critical of Air Force policy. At ACSC, internal reforms, initially by two successive commandants, Brig. Gen. Charles D. Link (1989–90) and Brig. Gen. Phillip J. Ford (1990–91) aided this critical spirit. General Ford invited RAND Corporation analyst Carl Builder to ACSC in early 1991 to launch a study investigating why Air Force officers seemed to have lost their theoretical and historical moorings.[31] These leaders initiated and institutionalized significant changes to the ACSC curriculum, including a renewed emphasis on military history and airpower theory. Perhaps most importantly, their combined tenure allowed the reforms to become ingrained into the school's program.

The coalition air operations against Iraq during Operations Desert Shield and Desert Storm in 1990–91 indirectly touched off another major curriculum revision. The catalyst was the arrival as commandant in summer 1992 of Col. John A. Warden III, the architect of the Gulf War air campaign plan.[32] Warden, a keen (though largely self-taught) student of military history, had a mandate from the Vice Chief of Staff of the Air Force to redesign completely the ACSC program for the post–Cold War age, emphasizing strategy, the operational art, campaign planning, and the lavish use of historical analysis and case studies. He also greatly increased the reading load, adding many historical works to the ACSC required student list. While some students (and faculty) bitterly resented the demise of "Air Command and Golf," and while the curricular reforms remain a subject for lively debate,[33] virtually every one of ACSC's nine academic courses gained academic rigor and significant historical content.

FOUR REASONS WHY AIRMEN SHOULD STUDY HISTORY

What should be the place of historical education in the development of air strategists? There are many possible answers to this question. Within the U.S. Air Force, there are four broad reasons why historical material relates to the development of strategic sensibility and has found its way into the curricula of its professional schools. Some of these reasons may at first seem suspect to academically trained historians, yet collectively they work to broaden and deepen that strategic sensibility. The first is simply to instill corporate spirit and foster awareness of airpower's rich heritage. Examining airpower's contribution to victory in previous wars or hearing lectures from (or about) aviation pioneers helps effectively, if occasionally uncritically, connect students to their service's historical foundations. This can have a powerful effect in what educators refer to as the "affective domain" of learning. ACSC's annual "Gathering of Eagles" aviation history symposium and visits by World War II or Vietnam veterans to elective classes are always highlights of the academic year. A group of SAASS students recently developed and presented a program on the 1942 Doolittle Raid, emphasizing its second- and third-order strategic impact but also including a toast with Hennessy cognac, to an audience that included the Air University commander. Academics scoff at such events at their peril; anything that sparks an interest in historical study and reflection is to be encouraged and can open doors and minds to more systematic and rigorous explorations of historical material.

A second function of history has been to illustrate or even legitimize current doctrine, operational concepts, organizational reforms, or weapons systems. Examples of this tendency include the invocation of Gen. George C. Kenney's Fifth Air Force in the Southwest Pacific as an early manifestation of the Combined Forces Air Component Commander (CFACC) concept and the presence of short, perhaps oversimplified historical vignettes in recent iterations of core USAF doctrine manuals. The Air Force Doctrine Center has created a "Historical Evidence Database" containing concise "nuggets" of historical information to support specific points of USAF doctrine. During the Cold War, such legitimizing examples drawn from the history of World War II on the Eastern Front were rife within the U.S. Army, but the USAF also weighed in. Advocates of the A-10 tank-busting attack aircraft looked to the successful use of German armored anti-tank aircraft in order to validate their position.[34] The author vividly remembers an Air Staff project in which AU historians were asked to provide evidence that being part of the Army had actually benefited the Air Corps in the interwar period, as a means of deflecting the idea of creating an independent space service. Some of these uses of history are rigorous and convincing; others are devoid of context and smack of special pleading. The omnipresent use of Clausewitz, Douhet, or Mitchell quotes—some applicable, most not—is another manifestation of the latter tendency. Of late, USAF leadership has turned to historical arguments in efforts to refute criticism of the service in the mass media. Recent op-eds in respected media outlets and academic journals (or their associated blogs) calling for the abolition of the Air Force as a separate service have been met with calls to "mobilize the historians" in rebuttal.[35] Again, Air Force historians who balk at participating in such efforts need to remember who is paying the bills. A well-crafted historical argument can be a powerful corrective to some of the foolish ideas ("Strategic bombing never works, so we should abolish the USAF") that sometimes seem to rage unchecked.

There are two somewhat more sophisticated uses of military history in officer education and strategist development with which academic historians might feel more comfortable. One is a more rigorous search for "lessons," or, in USAF parlance, "takeaways"—a systematic attempt to extract useful insights from a thorough examination of previous wars, campaigns, or other historical events. Though many scholars shy away from the very idea that history offers exportable "lessons," most would agree that historical study has the potential to improve current practice by establishing a common vocabulary, providing a basis for analogical reasoning, or identifying broad patterns of development. This form of analysis can involve use of the case-study method, in-depth campaign studies, and consulting primary sources such as after-action reports. Such inquiries seek the historical roots of everything from service organization to operational doctrine through successful and relevant examples of innovation, adaptation, revolutions in military affairs, or (to use a more recent buzzword) "transformation." Historians working for the military services need to be able and willing to connect practitioners to the "usable past" or else cease complaining when those practitioners ignore their insights.

Finally, there is a more holistic reason for including military history as part of midcareer officer education, and this is the one perhaps most relevant to teachers and students of strategy. How better to inculcate the ability to think in terms of cause and effect or to work through complex interactions of personalities, contextual factors, "friction," and so on than through historical study? Such study, in the words of one of my colleagues, instills "habits of mind" and fosters "patterns of inquiry" among military professionals who, though masters of their particular crafts, have usually not had the opportunity or inclination for sustained academic study. Although some pragmatists may complain that this seems like doing "history for history's sake," it is one of the richest opportunities for truly educating future strategists. Use of varied teaching methods, including assigning a canon of readings (including military biographies, scholarly monographs, and interdisciplinary works), taking the students on historical staff rides (even the USAF makes some use of this teaching technique), and even historical war gaming can equip future strategists with enhanced critical and analytical skills. Of course, this takes time; education remains a somewhat inefficient exercise. But it is this approach to teaching the subject, largely free of a need to extract specific, concrete "lessons," with which academic historians are most comfortable and to which they have the most to offer.

One final thought: one of the greatest payoffs of a historical education is the resulting sense of humility. Too many new AF programs are hailed as "revolutionary" or "path-breaking." The Air Expeditionary Force (AEF) of the 1990s owed much to the Composite Air Strike Force (CASF) of the 1950s; the "unprecedented" use of heavy bombers for close air support in Afghanistan in fact had precedents reaching back to World War II. Airmen have grappled with the implications of unmanned aircraft for many decades. A historical sensibility can equip today's professionals with a means of avoiding costly reinvention of the wheel. Likewise, historical study inculcates respect for what our predecessors achieved without the benefits of hindsight and leaves us with the sobering thought that future generations will examine how well we did when faced with similar challenges.

TWO APPROACHES: THE STAFF COLLEGE

The state of military history education at ACSC today has come a long way since the grim days of the post-Vietnam era or even the beginning of the 1990s. The core curriculum consists of a ten-month master's-level program, designed to expose students to the operational level of war, the role of force in statecraft, and the practice of employing joint military forces in pursuit of national objectives. Since the late 1990s, the program has been composed of courses that deal with both context and application. A major curriculum revision in academic year 2000 produced a two-semester program, the first dealing with international security, the nature of war, and the evolution of the air weapon. The spring semester was devoted to contemporary warfighting subjects. Currently, the program is delivered through a modular approach, with two courses running simultaneously throughout the year. Several of the current courses, notably "Warfare Studies" and "Airpower Studies I and II," possess significant historical content. These are taught by a mixture of civilian academics and military officers, many with advanced degrees in military history, international relations, and political science. Some of the military officers are sent by the Air Force to obtain PhDs at such schools as Indiana University, Southern Mississippi, Ohio State, and Duke. "Warfare Studies" is similar to many overview courses in military thought taught at civilian universities, in that students are exposed to the classical thinkers (Jomini, Clausewitz, Sun Tzu, etc.) as well as to typologies and taxonomies useful for studying the profession of arms. "Airpower Studies" is a critical historical examination of the development of the air weapon, emphasizing the translation of airpower theory into practice in the wars of the twentieth and early twenty-first centuries. Collectively, the program is designed to foster an ability to draw meaningful conclusions from past experience and to prepare strategists for an uncertain and ambiguous future.

While all five hundred–plus students take the core curriculum, they also each enroll in up to four elective courses. These are small graduate seminars (eight to fourteen students) taught by single faculty members. PhD faculty are expected to design and offer courses in their subject areas, as long as they relate in some fashion to warfare at the operational level. These courses—many addressing historical topics—are virtually indistinguishable from their counterparts in civilian graduate programs.

What then distinguishes teaching history at a staff college from teaching at a civilian university? While the course outlines, reading lists, thematic approaches, and subject matter seem remarkably similar, there are a number of key differences. First of all, the students (and the leadership of the institution) quite naturally expect to reap some utilitarian benefit from studying the past. There is an explicit desire for lessons learned or easily digestible bottom lines to emerge from a study of a particular war, campaign, or battle. Some instructors might recoil at the idea of reducing the sublime complexity of their particular subject areas to "sound bites," yet it is certainly possible to do justice to the craft while still providing the students with useful professional insights. For example, a detailed and rigorous examination of the battle of Leyte Gulf will go down much better with the target audience if it is introduced as a case where an enemy force, demonstrably inferior in technology, training, intelligence preparation, and command and control, was still able to surprise and threaten a U.S. air and naval force at the peak of its power.[36] Use of primary documents, such as Ultra decrypts, and contemporary situation maps allows students to gain insight into operational decisions made by their predecessors, often on the basis of incomplete or conflicting information. If set up in this fashion, it probably won't be necessary for the instructor to draw parallels to current events; the students will quickly make the connections. Drawing students' attention toward contrasting styles of leadership and other human factors, examples of the inevitable friction that occurs in military operations, or innovative staff planning techniques not only makes the lessons more palatable but allows the students to relate the historical account to their own considerable military experience.

As with all educational endeavors, successful teaching at a staff college requires the instructor to analyze the audience. Midcareer majors selected for resident attendance are from the very top of their year groups. Most can expect promotion and joint tours or important command or staff assignments following graduation. In terms of raw intelligence and ability, they match (and in some cases exceed) their counterparts in civilian graduate programs. Moreover, they have ten to fifteen years of practical military and life experience on which to draw. A large number are veterans of recent deployments, although many come from career fields that, by their own admission, are not at "the pointy end of the spear" (although as cyberspace operations become more important the traditional definition of "warfighter" is beginning to blur). Some are avid military history buffs, with large personal libraries, televisions always tuned to The History Channel, and a tremendous knowledge of operational detail. Each seminar of fourteen students contains at least one Army, one sea service, one Guard/reserve/civilian representative, and two international officers. The intellectual and cultural diversity in each seminar is far greater than many outsiders imagine.

That being said, many of the students will not have recently dealt with the broad conceptual issues raised by historical inquiry. Even basic knowledge of the wars of the twentieth century should not be assumed. Service-academy graduates may not have taken any military history classes since their undergraduate days; those from Officer Training School or Reserve Officers Training Corps commissioning sources may not have had any. I was particularly intrigued when a Luftwaffe lieutenant colonel signed up for my World War II elective, explaining that in Germany "this material is left out of the lesson plan."

Students' tolerance for ambiguity may be low. ACSC students are particularly impatient with conflicting historical interpretations. (To cite only one example, presenting divergent views of the reasons for the failure of the Schlieffen Plan often leads to a cry for "the right answer.") Of note, some recent ACSC students seem to have concluded that strategic bombing "failed" in World War II, as if winning the war single-handedly was the only relevant criterion for success. Assigning complex works such as Clausewitz's *On War*, Thucydides' *History of the Peloponnesian War*, and others often meets with initial resistance. Sun Tzu is widely preferred, to quote one of my former students, "because he's short." Getting the benefit out of such study demands that the instructor spend long, patient hours in seminar discussions guiding the students through the difficult concepts and drawing them into the analysis. As with all education, it is a war of small and steady gains.[37]

Two Approaches: SAASS

In the halls of the SAASS building hang a number of *Mad Men*–inspired advertising placards. They read:

TALENT VISION INTEREST

Between 6 October and 19 November 1987, Representative Ike Skelton (D-MO) made a series of speeches on the floor of the U.S. House of Representatives decrying America's lack of strategists and castigating the military establishment for not doing anything about it.

In June 1988, then–Air Force Chief of Staff (CSAF) General Larry E. Welch testified before a panel chaired by Skelton. He outlined a number of initiatives to enhance Air Force education, one of which was the formation of an institution to allow those officers with "the talent, vision, and interest to pursue strategic studies" the opportunity to do so.

That institution became the School of Advanced Air and Space Studies, where you now stand.

This "foundation legend" remains a source of great pride at the school. From a practical standpoint, addressing Representative Skelton's critique involved creating a small institution with an all-volunteer, board-selected student body, a highly qualified faculty, and uncompromising academic standards. This meant small seminars, few if any traditional lectures, frequent writing opportunities with extensive faculty critiques, and a significant reading load.

The new school took as its motto "From the Past, the Future." This choice of motto, seeming to stand the old ACTS slogan on its head, is not surprising: the vast majority of the "plank owner" (that is, original) faculty in 1991 were historians. As the school evolved, a healthy balance emerged as both the faculty and the curriculum became more interdisciplinary. Currently (2015) of the eleven courses that make up the program, two might explicitly be described as "historical" in orientation. Of the remainder, one focuses on works of classical military theory, while others emphasize international relations or decision making or deal with specific topics such as space, cyberspace, or irregular warfare. Some are explicitly interdisciplinary in character. Students of strategy are encouraged to view the subject through as many "lenses" as practicable: economic, theoretical, scientific, psychological, and behavioral, as well as historical.

As the program and faculty have become more interdisciplinary, some things have not changed. SAASS remains an explicitly book-based program; there is no formal page limit for the day's assigned reading. A normal SAASS seminar orbits around the consideration of a single book, connecting that book to previous readings and the ongoing conversation about strategy. Selection of the correct books, it is often said, is the task for which SAASS course directors really earn their pay. There are far more worthy books than there are available curriculum days. So the search goes on for the books that are, in a word, "SAASSable"—those that most effectively provoke discussion and illuminate the larger questions of strategy. Two books currently used in the SAASS program are representative.

Today's USAF is a product of its entire historical experience, yet the impact of World War II and the Vietnam War perhaps loom largest. World War II represented the maturation of airpower, and particularly strategic bombing, as a distinct method of waging war. Accordingly, considerations of the development, execution, and effectiveness of the Combined Bomber Offensive have occupied a significant place in the SAASS curriculum since its inception. Yet too often the discussion devolves into a simple debate over whether strategic bombing "worked" or not. The SAASS faculty sought a means of addressing a deeper and more complex question: What is the role of airpower in terms of both economic planning and strategic decision making as well as the impact of airpower upon a target state? In 2008, economic historian Adam Tooze published his *The Wages of Destruction: The Making and Breaking of the Nazi Economy*.[38] This book received not only universal acclaim from the academic community but has proven to be a most valuable tool in the education of strategists.

Tooze's book is neither light nor breezy. It is a seven-hundred-page tome that does not offer simple conclusions. It is well and forcefully written, and some of its findings are startling. Tooze, for example, concludes on the basis of rigorous analysis of production targets and output that RAF Bomber Command's assault on the Ruhr industrial region in 1943 "stopped [Nazi Minister of Armaments and War Production Albert] Speer's armaments miracle in its tracks." His work allows for a consideration of German decision making regarding the role of air armament in national economic and strategic planning and how that economy responded to the ever-growing Allied bomber offensive as well as to the demands of a multifront war. He gives full attention to the roles of personalities, ideology, and organizational dynamics in the Third Reich, allowing students to consider strategy and decision making in the broadest sense. And in the four years it has been in use at SAASS, it has ranked at or near the top of students' lists of "most valuable" readings for the year. This is proof that officer-students, when challenged with complex and meaningful works, will rise to the occasion.

The rigor and forthrightness of the USAF's study of airpower in the Vietnam War, as noted earlier, has waxed and waned over the years. At times, the comfortable myth that the USAF won the war in the eleven days of Linebacker II over Hanoi in December 1972 substituted for any real analysis of that conflict. By the 1990s, however, at both ACSC and SAASS, works such as Mark Clodfelter's *The Limits of Air Power* had largely displaced such myth making.[39] Clodfelter argues that the changing nature of the conflict, as well as the USAF's unwillingness or inability to adapt its strategy to the war at hand, had at least as much to do with failure in Vietnam as did President Lyndon Johnson's untutored meddling in military affairs.

A recent book by historian and retired USAF officer Stephen Randolph has proven to be a most effective means of unpacking the type of strategic issues we seek to address at SAASS.[40] For those who think that President Richard Nixon had a much smoother relationship with his senior military than his predecessor, *Powerful and Brutal Weapons* provides a needed corrective. Randolph develops three thematic and narrative arcs—"presidential leadership in wartime . . . the dynamics of military effectiveness . . . and the action-reaction cycle" between the adversaries.[41] The book places our students at the nexus of political-military decision making and within the difficult process of interpreting presidential guidance and "operationalizing" it into coherent war plans, all the while dealing with capricious and idiosyncratic leadership, recalcitrant allies, and a tenacious enemy. This was taking place not in the context of pursuing traditional victory but rather in the process of extricating the nation from an unpopular war. One of my students e-mailed me after six months in Afghanistan that he was carefully rereading Randolph's book. "It's happening again," he said.

CONCLUSION

Ironically, the perceived airpower successes in Operation Allied Force in Kosovo in 1999, in the routing of the Taliban regime in Afghanistan in 2001–2002, and the three-week "major combat operations" phase in Iraq in 2003 have to an extent worked against the efforts to ground AF education in historical context. Senior leadership has noted explicitly that "the recent past [is] more lesson filled than the distant past."[42] The last few revisions of the Air Force Chief of Staff's Professional Reading List appear to deemphasize historical studies and classical treatments of war and strategy (which were the basis of some of the previous CSAF lists and remain the bread and butter of the current U.S. Navy, U.S. Army, and USMC reading lists) in favor of examinations of recent operations, management concepts, and current events. To be sure, the latest (2015) list manages to strike a reasonable balance between critical treatments of history and strategy and works that focus on the latest trends or offer inspirational messages.[43] Other recent lists favored heroism, comradeship, and the latest management fads over works offering historical or strategic insights. As a rule, critical self-assessments such as Robin Higham's *Why Air Forces Fail* were outnumbered by uplifting works such as Laura Hillenbrand's *Unbroken* and discussions of popularized management techniques. A healthy trend is the inclusion of novels such as Joseph Heller's *Catch-22* and James Salter's *The Hunters*. Of course, professional reading lists target a wide audience and are intended to do much more than foster strategic acumen. Valuable as it is for advanced students of strategy, Tooze's masterwork on the German war economy would probably not be a good fit. Nevertheless, examination of the changing tone of the list since it first appeared in 1996 is instructive. Ever since 9/11, numerous articles and public statements by senior AF and Department of Defense leaders have stressed that "it's a whole new world out there" and have implicitly and explicitly decoupled current events from past experience. The current "pivot" to the Pacific and rising concerns about an aggressive China have, however, led to calls from USAF leadership for renewed study of the history of major conventional air operations.

The fact that military and airpower history is currently valued at Air Force institutions of higher learning should give both historians and practitioners some satisfaction. Willingness to subject oneself to historical scrutiny and to confront and thereby learn from one's failures, even while hailing the successes, is a sign of institutional maturity. Yet it would be wise to remember that this commendable attitude toward historical self-examination by the U.S. Air Force is barely three decades old. It began as a grassroots effort by relatively few individuals, most now long retired after rising not terribly high in the Air Force. If a few commandants and other senior leaders nurtured the growth of historical education programs, others viewed them with indifference or incomprehension, or at best as opportunities to celebrate the service's heritage.

All that being said, it must be remembered that these students are military professionals and strategists in training studying military history as part of their professional development. They are not aspiring to become practicing military historians. Their "comprehensive exams" will take place in the field or on staffs, possibly several assignments down the road. While some of my colleagues regret not having traditional graduate students to mentor and to carry on in the profession, others take pride in the fact that our instruction may very well prepare our graduates to shape campaigns and operations yet to come.

The motto of Air University to this day remains "We Progress Unhindered by Tradition," though the motto is rarely used. A recent straw poll of my SAASS students failed to find a single one who could recite it. Perhaps it's just as well.

NOTES

1. William Mitchell, *Winged Defense: The Development and Possibilities of Modern Air Power, Economic and Military* (New York: Dover, 1988), 20–21.

2. This essay concentrates on midcareer officer education, though it is worth underlining that historical study has long been a part of the curriculum at the USAF's senior school, the Air War College, and that the Air War College currently offers a Grand Strategy Program with substantial historical content.

3. Donald J. Mrozek, *Air Power and the Ground War in Vietnam* (Maxwell Air Force Base, Ala.: Air University Press, 1988), 8. Mrozek was a civilian academic brought to Maxwell's Airpower Research Institute to offer an outside perspective.

4. Among the best treatments of ACTS's role is Tami Davis Biddle, *Rhetoric and Reality in Air Warfare* (Princeton, N.J.: Princeton University Press, 2002), esp. chaps. 3 and 5.

5. Giulio Douhet, *The Command of the Air* (New York: Coward-McCann, 1942), 50.

6. Bernard Brodie, *Strategy in the Missile Age* (Princeton, N.J.: Princeton University Press, 1959), 90–91.

7. H. Dwight Griffin, *Air Corps Tactical School: The Untold Story* (Maxwell Air Force Base, Ala.: Air Command and Staff College, 1995), 21ff.

8. Haywood S. Hansell, *The Air Plan That Defeated Hitler* (Atlanta, Ga.: Higgins-MacArthur, 1972), 32ff.

9. Peter Faber, "Interwar US Army Aviation and the Air Corps Tactical School: Incubators of American Airpower," in *The Paths of Heaven,* ed. Philip Meilinger (Maxwell Air Force Base, Ala.: Air University Press, 1996), 218.

10. Air Corps Tactical School, *Attack Aviation Course 1937* (Maxwell Air Force Base, Ala.: USAF Historical Research Agency 168.7045-30), 6.

11. Griffin, *Air Corps Tactical School,* 12–14.

12. Robert T. Finney, *History of the Air Corps Tactical School, 1920–1940* (Washington, D.C.: Center for Air Force History, 1992), 79–81.

13. SAASS, established in 1991, also claims the mantle of ACTS.

14. Finney, *Air Corps Tactical School,* 85.

15. Jerome Ennels and Wesley P. Newton, *The Wisdom of Eagles: A History of Maxwell Air Force Base* (Montgomery, Ala.: Black Belt, 1997), 118–26.

16. Course books, Air Command and Staff School, 1949, in author's possession.

17. This was eventually published as Robert Frank Futrell, *The United States Air Force in Korea* (Washington, D.C.: Air Force History and Museums Program, 2000).

18. Story related to me by Lt. Col. Herbert Frandsen, U.S. Army (Ret.).

19. Air Command and Staff College History, Academic Year 1961–1962. Every unit in the USAF is required to submit an annual history, and ACSC was no exception. The most complete collection of these histories is maintained in the ACSC building; copies are also available at the USAF Historical Research Agency (HRA) and the Air University Historian's Office (AU/HO), also located at Maxwell.

20. A valuable resource for the early years of ACSC is *History of the Air Command and Staff College: Twentieth Anniversary Command Edition,* Air University History, AUOI Series no. 18 (Maxwell Air Force Base, Ala., 15 February 1966) [hereafter cited as ACSC History (academic years)]. Copy on file at ACSC.

21. Ibid., 1967–68.

22. Robert Frank Futrell, *Ideas, Concepts, Doctrine: Basic Thinking in the United States Air Force,* vol. 2, *1961–1984* (Maxwell Air Force Base, Ala.: Air University Press, 1989), 322.

23. ACSC Histories, academic years 1970–71, 1971–72, 1972–73.

24. One former faculty member noted that the course title, "The Military Environment," "sounded like we were educating the students to go out and hug trees."

25. Interview with Dennis M. Drew, Col., USAF (Ret.), May 1999.

26. ACSC History, academic year 1979.

27. Ibid., academic year 1984.

28. This anecdote related to me by Dr. Earl H. Tilford Jr., now professor emeritus at Grove City College, Grove City, Ohio. Dr. Tilford was a visiting professor of military history at ACSC during those years.

29. For perhaps the most forceful expression of this viewpoint, see Earl H. Tilford, *Setup: What the Air Force Did in Vietnam and Why* (Maxwell Air Force Base, Ala.: Air University Press, 1991), 286.

30. John Andreas Olsen, *John Warden and the Renaissance of American Air Power* (Washington, D.C.: Potomac Books, 2007), 117.

31. That study eventually grew into Builder's influential book *The Icarus Syndrome: The Role of Air Power Theory in the Evolution and Fate of the U.S. Air Force* (New Brunswick, N.J.: Transaction, 1994).

32. On Warden's role in the planning process, see Richard G. Davis, *On Target: Organizing and Executing the Strategic Air Campaign against Iraq* (Washington, D.C.: Air Force History and Museums Program, 2002).

33. Some critics noted that the Warden curriculum overemphasized the success of airpower in Desert Storm. Others pointed out that the famous "Five

Rings" targeting construct associated with Warden might drive planners into a dogmatic and mechanical application of airpower against the "leadership ring," ignoring cultural differences among potential adversaries. Supporters of the reforms retorted that for the first time in decades, serious thinking about airpower was at the heart of the program. For two views of the "Warden revolution," see Olsen, *John Warden and the Renaissance of American Air Power,* chap. 11, and Joel Hayward and Tamir Libel, "Reflections on the Maxwell 'Revolution': John Warden and Reforms in Professional Military Education," *Royal Air Force Air Power Review* 14 (Spring 2011): 11–33. Warden's "revolution" was one of the rare academic events at AU that caught the attention of scholars outside of the USAF.

34. Capt. Lonnie O. Ratley III, "Air Power at Kursk: A Lesson for Today?," *Military Review* 62 (April 1978): 54–62.

35. See, among a number of possible examples, Robert Farley, "Ground the Air Force: Revising the Future of Flight," *Foreign Affairs* (18 December 2013), http://www.foreignaffairs.com/articles/140574/robert-farley/ground-the-air-force (accessed 3 January 2014).

36. I am grateful to my friend John Prados for this particular insight.

37. For some views on the education of today's air force students, see James W. Forsyth Jr. and Richard R. Muller, "'We Were Deans Once, and Young': Veteran PME Educators Look Back," *Air & Space Power Journal* 25, no. 3 (Fall 2011): 91–99.

38. Adam Tooze, *The Wages of Destruction: The Making and Breaking of the Nazi Economy* (New York: Penguin Books, 2008).

39. Mark Clodfelter, *The Limits of Air Power: The American Bombing of North Vietnam* (New York: Free Press, 1989).

40. Stephen Randolph, *Powerful and Brutal Weapons: Nixon, Kissinger, and the Easter Offensive* (Cambridge, Mass.: Harvard University Press, 2007).

41. Ibid., 2–3.

42. Gen. John P. Jumper, "Chief's Sight Picture: CSAF's Reading List," July 2002.

43. See the latest list at "Air Force Chief of Staff: Reading List 2015," CSAF Reading List, http://static.dma.mil/usaf/csafreadinglist/index.html.

CHAPTER SEVEN

Beyond the Horizon

Developing Future Airpower Strategy

JEFFREY J. SMITH

T he strategic imperatives of military airpower have been widely debated
since the beginnings of airpower itself. At the heart of these debates has
been the idea of an airpower theory: a description, explanation, and even
prediction for how and why airpower can provide advantage in military operations. This debate centers on the recognition that one must create desirable parameters of an airpower theory before developing a feasible airpower strategy. The
key to success in this endeavor lies in correctly recognizing and promptly incor-
porating contextual realities into both concepts. This chapter offers a critique of
current airpower strategy, presenting a foundational account of how airpower
theory and strategy emerged and painfully adapted to changing contexts through
the years, and concludes with a predictive assessment of why and how airpower
strategy must embrace contextual realities in the years ahead.[1]

FOUNDATIONS OF AIRPOWER THEORY AND STRATEGY

In its early years, airpower was just another tool for advancing the long-standing
land power theory that required both taking and holding real estate to limit or
remove enemy options. The U.S. Army saw the airplane as an ancillary capability
to existing land power, while the advent of flight afforded ground commanders
the first real look "beyond the horizon." They quickly realized airpower could
spot and track enemy positions and movement, rapidly provide communication
between ground forces often separated by impassable terrain, and eventually provide some level of air-to-ground attack against selected targets. However, during

World War I, it became clear airpower had the potential to be much more than ancillary to Army ground operations. Many of the earliest airpower pioneers, having flown during World War I, recognized and understood that airpower provided extensive advantage to a wider spectrum of warfare beyond land power. Perhaps the most outspoken of those new "airmen" was Brig. Gen. Billy Mitchell. Mitchell is often misquoted and taken out of context in regards to what he so powerfully argued in the years between the world wars. Although much acclaim has been given to his advocacy for an independent air force, Mitchell's argument was actually much more refined. His position rested on the clear understanding that airpower provided an opportunity to bypass and overfly the traditional strengths of an enemy's ground forces and target those areas the belligerent held dear (usually targets well beyond enemy frontlines). This capability, as Mitchell recognized it, afforded a new theory of warfare—airpower theory.[2] The theory rested on the axioms that taking and controlling the high ground, bypassing enemy strong points, and operating at a speed unmatched in traditional ground force-on-force warfare provided extensive, game-changing capabilities. Early attributes of airpower theory rested on the empirical evidence airpower provided: access and speed to areas inside enemy territory that had previously not been accessible without considerable ground combat and the associated cost in blood and treasure. This access and speed enabled an additional element to the new and emerging airpower theory—strategic strike.

Early airpower theory described the airplane as the means to the grander ends of military advantage. This new theory, according to Mitchell, held such significant implications for the nature and outcome of war that he believed airpower must be considered a national security imperative.[3] Given his forceful belief that the future security of the United States would require significant and deliberate attention to the development of airpower, he rationally concluded that to fulfill such an important requirement, airpower must be organized, resourced, and led by air-minded thinkers (airmen). Furthermore, Mitchell's experience working under the shadow of the U.S. Army led him to believe airpower was neither appreciated nor given its rightful place as an instrument of national security. He concluded airpower should not only be led by airmen, but it should also be independent from the U.S. Army. The vital historical narrative is that Mitchell effectively connected the means of airpower (the airplane) with the ends of national security. The importance of this recognition further suggested airpower should be led by air-minded thinkers within the organizational construct of an independent air force. As long as the fundamental axioms of this new airpower theory (access, speed, and strategic strike) remained an empirical reality, then airpower could be built on its own independent military foundation.

Along the same lines of reasoning, the Air Corps Tactical School (ACTS) developed and refined these early airpower attributes. Over thousands of hours of study, debate, and speculation prior to World War II, airmen at the ACTS concluded that given the right type of bomber airplane with the appropriate self-defending capabilities, airpower could target the industrial base of enemy vital centers.[4] This was one of the first airpower strategies created from the emerging new airpower theory. Drawing upon the airpower theory axioms of access, speed, and strategic strike, airmen at the ACTS developed a bombing strategy they believed would quickly and most certainly end the possibility of an enemy being able to continue hostilities. Their confidence in airpower capabilities led them to add "decisive" to existing airpower theory, suggesting airpower had the potential to produce war-ending strategic effects.[5] The expanded decisive airpower theory informed and encouraged the development of an airpower strategy for World War II that suggested airpower's fundamental ability to overfly traditional ground positions and target vital centers of production, transportation, and military-specific commerce would so cripple a belligerent's capability to wage war that capitulation would most surely follow. It is important to understand the evolutionary process in the development of an airpower strategy. Airpower theory rested on the axioms of access, speed, strategic strike, and now, the yet-to-be-proven attribute of decisiveness. This airpower theory led to development of a strategy that further reified how and why airpower would be used to meet the strategic ends of military advantage and ultimately victory. As long as the fundamental axioms of the theory could be supported by empirical evidence, then the strategy that developed from that theory would be equally supportable. The observable capabilities of the airplane at the time easily supported access and speed; however, the elements of strategic strike and decisiveness remained unproven. This reality, however, did not keep the officers in the ACTS from developing an airpower strategy based on all four of the airpower theory axioms.

History highlights the accomplishments of airpower during World War II as both extensive and necessary for victory. However, postwar analysis of the European campaigns specifically showed that the ACTS airpower bombing strategy failed to meet its prewar objectives and predictions. The original airpower strategy failed to fully appreciate and recognize the inability of bomber aircraft to effectively defend themselves. Both enemy fighters as well as extensive ground-to-air defenses proved nearly overwhelming. Not only were tens of thousands of aircrew killed during these missions, but the ability of the bombers to actually strike and/or cripple vital industrial centers was nowhere near that predicted. The majority of bombs fell outside the required radius of intended targets, and until U.S. fighter escort became part of the bombing strategy, survival rates were horrific.[6] As noted, the airpower strategy of World War II was perhaps the first major airpower strategy; unfortunately, developers failed to recognize or realize the unintended consequences, second and third order effects, and the adaptive nature of enemy creativity. The prewar airpower thinkers (specifically Mitchell and those at the ACTS) failed to recognize two central requirements in developing effective strategy—translating theoretical axioms into strategy requires extensive consideration of contextual realities; when the axioms of the theory are challenged by new contexts, the resulting strategy will likely need to modify. The prewar airpower strategists assumed the survivability of the self-defended bomber, assumed the accuracy of the bombing, and failed to recognize the complexities associated with connecting the theoretical axioms of access, speed, and strategic strike with the realities of a thinking and capable enemy. In the process, they became wedded to the emerging idea of decisiveness, which compounded an unhealthy perspective and overconfidence. When the theoretical axiom of access was threatened by enemy air defenses, the strategy built upon that axiom had to be modified. When bombers were confronted with faster, more maneuverable German fighters, the axiom of speed became less advantageous. Furthermore, when the realization came that bombing accuracy was significantly less capable than envisioned, the axiom of strategic strike was empirically muddled, or worse—dogmatic. In terms of decisiveness, airpower strategy over Europe simply did not obtain that level of success. Although early airpower theory was generally sound, translating the theory into a feasible strategy became flawed because it failed to consider, understand, or incorporate the full context in which it would be applied.

If the narrative presented to this point were simply the end of World War II, then airpower would have had a difficult time convincing national decision makers that it deserved an independent service separate from the U.S. Army. Based on bombing data from the European campaigns, the airpower axioms of access and speed were supported; the axiom of strategic strike was partially supported; the axiom of decisiveness was not supported. However, in the final operations of the Pacific campaign, airpower accomplished with two flights the most devastating, game-changing events the world has ever witnessed: the dropping of atomic bombs on Japan—ending the war. Those involved in planning the missions clearly linked the theory with the strategy. Airpower theory, combined with the new and devastating atomic capability, provided the access, speed, and ability to strike strategically. The bomber had uncontested access and speed over Japan, carried a payload whose accuracy was of lesser importance (just get anywhere close), and provided for the first time overwhelming strategic-level firepower that all but ensured capitulation of the enemy (decisiveness). From these final events against Japan, an independent Air Force was born. Based on the now empirically proven airpower theory (access, speed, strategic strike, decisiveness), a formal airpower strategy was both adopted and codified in the minds of airmen. From 1947 well into the early 1980s, Strategic Air Command (SAC) dominated the strategic perspective of the newly formed USAF and airpower in general. SAC built a strategy cast in cement—nuclear operations, delivered by aircraft, independent of other services, with near fail-safe routine, rigor, and predictability. However, an airpower strategy is only sound if it appropriately considers changing contextual realities. The limited, often politically restrained wars such as Korea, Vietnam, and Gulf War I hampered and restricted SAC's airpower strategy. While SAC was prohibited from conducting its unlimited nuclear bombardment strategy, it was content with defending the bipolar standoff with the Soviet Union. So the bomber strategy of SAC continued to be a vital mission. The USAF continued developing additional capabilities to fulfill the axioms of airpower theory, and the real-time requirements of limited war demanded a more flexible response—a response the emerging fighter-centric airpower strategy effectively provided. Within the Tactical Air Command (TAC), significant advances occurred in Korea, Vietnam, and eventually Gulf War I—particularly the ability of a fighter-centric strategy to provide limited war capabilities within a highly political context. This contextual change propelled strategy to the forefront. Although the emergence of fighter aircraft as a central and even primary capability fell short of providing decisiveness, the axioms of access, speed, and strategic strike—eventually with precision guided munitions (PGM)—provided a vital complement to the airpower mission and subsequent airpower strategy. In fact, given the changing world dynamic following the fall of the Soviet Union, the fighter-centric perspective became dominant as the USAF not only dismantled SAC, but codified airpower strategy within the new organizational construct of Air Combat Command (ACC).[7]

When ACC activated in 1992, the strategy developed from airpower theory, in relation to the context at the time, became doctrine. Three strategy-enabled requirements emerged from the attributes of the fighter-centric perspective:

- The ability to gain and maintain air superiority
- The ability to accurately strike coveted enemy infrastructure
- The ability to target fielded combatants.

These three capabilities became the hallmark of airpower strategy. Although missing the axiom of decisiveness as presented, they met the enduring axioms of airpower theory (access, speed, strategic strike) and effectively translated those axioms into operational airpower strategy. Perhaps the most significant empirical evidence for this newly codified and organized airpower strategy was provided just prior to the 1992 USAF organizational change—the first Iraq war in 1991. Airpower, under the banner of a fighter-centric strategy, overwhelmed the enemy, shaped the battlefield to U.S. advantage, and dominated both the nature and climax of the war. Given this context and empirical experience, the newly minted fighter-centric airpower strategy formally and firmly held the USAF mantle of power.[8]

The evolution of this strategy can be traced from the initial development of airpower theory, through the years of early USAF independence, filtered through the challenges of limited war in the twentieth century, and culminating in what was thought to be modern war in the 1990s. However, just as the initial bombing strategy in World War II failed to appropriately carry airpower theory to its anticipated heights; and just as the strategic bombing strategy of SAC failed to effectively translate airpower theory in a limited, politically constrained context; so, too, has the current fighter-centric airpower strategy failed to connect airpower theory effectively with the emerging context of asymmetric and unconventional war. In a context where the enemy does not seek or have the capability to challenge the United States for air superiority, the need for advanced air superiority systems is minimized. Furthermore, if targeting coveted enemy infrastructure alienates the noncombatants and pro-U.S. population, strategic strike becomes counterproductive and limited. Finally, if enemy combatants are indistinguishable from the noncombatant population, targeting fielded forces becomes limited to discriminate tactical opportunities. Consequentially, if the three central elements of the airpower strategy fail to offer appropriately how airpower theory can be translated into action within emerging new context, then as has previously occurred, the air-power strategy must be modified. As airpower strategists, we must ask ourselves a vital question: What must our airpower strategy be to connect airpower theory effectively to the emerging and growing spectrum of current and future war?

CURRENT AIRPOWER STRATEGY

The importance of understanding the relationship between airpower theory and the development of airpower strategy cannot be overstated. If the theory remains relevant, it then requires a strategy for translating that theory into actionable reality. However, how that process is accomplished depends on a number of important considerations regarding strategy development in general.

Students of airpower strategy often ask, "What is the difference between a strategy and a plan?" Although the details are much more refined, the most obvious answer is, a strategy not only offers elements of "how" operations will be conducted, but further considers "why" an operation will be conducted. For example, in developing the airpower strategy of bombardment in World War II, strategists outlined the objective of targeting enemy infrastructure, vital centers, and coveted production capabilities. This strategy was underwritten by the idea that an enemy would only be able to compete effectively in warfare if it had the means to continue supporting the war effort. If one could effectively take away the enemy's ability to resupply its war effort, then the logistical realities of resource shortfalls would force capitulation. This dynamic answered "why" targeting of infrastructure, supply chains, and production was part of the bombing strategy. In fact, the recognition of wartime logistical requirements was the driving force behind development of targeting industrial capabilities. Furthermore, knowing that targeting an enemy deep within its traditionally protected vital centers would be confronted by some degree of enemy defenses, the bombing planners prior to World War II developed a strategy for a self-defending aircraft, the B-17. They determined that if the industrial base was in fact a logistical requirement to continue waging war, then the enemy would likely have created some level of protection for those centers. From that consideration, prewar airpower strategists understood that access to those areas (an axiom of airpower theory) was instrumental and therefore their strategy must consider and develop an access capability—self-defended bombers. The strategy was more than a plan in that it addressed realities of why specific elements needed to be considered. Although a plan may offer important insight as to exactly what will be accomplished, a strategy must first be developed that offers important consideration for why an operation will be developed. Airpower theory outlined the military advantage of access; airpower strategy provided the translated need for a self-defendable bomber to provide that access, and then a plan that included specific vital targets could be developed in line with both the theory and the strategy. However, perhaps of greatest importance is the recognition that if the strategy is flawed, then the plan will likely be flawed; if the plan is flawed, the operation will likely not result in the intended effects. This is exactly what occurred in the European bombing campaign in World War II.

Consider again the pre–World War II bombing strategy. The theory appears to have been fairly sound in terms of the advantage airpower can provide in war (access, speed, strategic strike, decisiveness). However, the subsequent strategy failed to consider all of the contextual realities of enemy capabilities. Knowing that access was centrally required to target strategic vital centers, strategists envisioned and procured the self-defended airplane. However, as discovered, the B-17 was unable to adequately defend itself against German fighters and ground defenses. Therefore, because the initial strategy was flawed (i.e., the self-defending bomber could not appropriately self-defend), the subsequent plan of targeting specific locations well inside Germany's vital center did not achieve the anticipated outcome. This was simply a case of appropriate theory married to a flawed strategy, resulting in a less than optimum plan. Again, the important consideration in this discussion is that one must be confident that the theory is in fact appropriately explanatory of a particular phenomenon, and then the subsequent strategy must not only translate that theory into effective operations, but it must do so within the complex context of the environment for which that theory will be applied.

CHANGING CONTEXT, UNCHANGING STRATEGY

> The first, the supreme, the most far reaching act of judgment that a statesman and general officer must make is to try and determine the type of war upon which one is embarking; neither mistaking it for, nor turning it into something alien to its nature.
> —Carl von Clausewitz

As suggested by this insight, failing to appropriately consider all the complexities of the given context will nearly always result in a less than optimum strategy.

SAC developed its codified airpower strategy of predictable, systematic bombing operations in a global context of bipolar strategic competition with the Soviet

Union. Given the initial context of what the United States deemed most important in the 1960s and 1970s, the airpower strategy of SAC was both appropriate and an effective translation of airpower theory. However, as the political and limited nature of war continued to emerge throughout the latter part of the twentieth century, SAC's airpower strategy no longer appropriately addressed the complex context of the global environment. The forcing function of external requirements became a driving factor behind the need to modify the USAF airpower strategy so it could better translate airpower theory into a strategy that reflected current context (limited, politically constrained warfare). Although the airpower strategy that emerged and effectively proved itself in the first Gulf War was appropriate given the context, as the context changed throughout the 1990s, airpower strategy failed to expand or adapt to the emerging exigencies. The fighter-centric airpower strategy was both appropriate and effective given a specific context, but in terms of strategy, it should be viewed as necessary but far from sufficient. It met and even exceeded the context of the first Gulf War, but when the context changed to an asymmetric, unconventional engagement (as it did throughout the 1990s), the strategy needed to adapt. History suggests that as a service the Air Force did not make appropriate changes (adaptation) to its airpower strategy that were required for the emerging new context.

A number of examples can illustrate the changing context throughout the 1990s. Somalia was perhaps the first indication of a context where traditional airpower strategy was not appropriate within the context of the given hostilities. In Somalia there was no requirement to gain and maintain air superiority, little to no coveted infrastructure to target, and combatants blended into the population such that there were no apparent or easily identifiable fielded military forces. In this context, the fighter-centric airpower strategy failed to translate airpower theory appropriately into the complex context of Somalia. Rather than deliberate how it might modify or expand its airpower strategy to address the emerging asymmetric and urban war context, the USAF ignored the reality, categorized it as a type of war it did not prefer or care to fight, and left Somalia following the Mogadishu catastrophe.[9]

Following the events in Somalia, Air Force strategists should have begun developing a strategy appropriate for the emerging reality of asymmetric, unconventional war. Instead, they continued to perceive these types of conflicts as "military operations other than war" (MOOTW). Although formally outlined in Air Force doctrine, the very title alone suggests a secondary or cursory perspective of these types of responsibilities. The remainder of the 1990s continued to offer significant evidence on the limits of the current fighter-centric airpower strategy. It failed to reveal and address appropriately the wider spectrum of operations required by emerging asymmetric realities (context) until the post-9/11 conflicts in Afghanistan and Iraq.

In the months following the 9/11 attacks, the United States was ready and willing to use military force to counter emerging terrorist threats. The obvious attention on Afghanistan and the later decisions regarding Iraq all depended on various military strategies to meet specific U.S. national security objectives. In Afghanistan, the early targeting and bombing of training camps, known enemy locations, and vital logistical centers all fell squarely inside the existing airpower strategy. As long as the context of the conflict fell within the parameters of air superiority, targeting coveted infrastructure, and attrition of fielded forces, existing airpower strategy was appropriate and successful. The same could be said in observing the opening "shock and awe" campaign in Iraq. The context in both countries supported the existing airpower strategy. However, as the next 10 years revealed, once both conflicts transitioned into asymmetric, nontraditional, counterinsurgency operations (a context very similar to Somalia), the existing airpower strategy developed from a fighter-centric perspective failed to appropriately translate airpower theory into advantageous operations. Instead, the USAF began the arduous process of modifying airpower strategy to meet the emerging (real-time) context. What were previously considered secondary operations, less than central, and often underappreciated within the hierarchy of the USAF, quickly became of primary importance. What previously had been considered MOOTW became characteristics of significant war. Daily operations now required tactical airlift, special operations, ISR (intelligence, surveillance, and reconnaissance), close air support, and tightly integrated action with ground forces. Therefore, an ad hoc airpower strategy was developed that understood and coordinated efforts with ground commanders. Survivable intra-theater airlift operations were instituted and tested in real time. The increase in demand for ISR from remotely piloted aircraft (RPA) was "insatiable." However, prior to these emerging demands, the USAF failed to adequately organize, train, and equip for such operations. It lacked a coherent method of translating airpower theory into an effective airpower strategy during the emerging asymmetric context.

Fortunately, over the years of operations in both Afghanistan and Iraq, USAF airpower strategy systematically modified. Evidence suggests Air Force leadership tried to avoid modifying the existing airpower strategy, but the realities and demands of the ongoing conflict became organizational forcing functions that ensured airpower strategy would adapt to an "all-in" posture.[10] The requirement for RPA pilots—once a dreaded and often considered career-ending path—became phenomenally important. Demand for space-based ISR, special operations, and secure command and control gained increased importance. Tight interaction between Air Force operations and ground operations became a paramount requirement—something the Air Force historically (both overtly and covertly) minimized in support of what had been perceived as a constant requirement to prove the importance of its independent status. Fortunately, it was able to adapt its airpower strategy effectively to better meet the required asymmetric context—but not to the level required.

Intra-theater airlift, especially by C-130 aircraft, became the backbone of logistics. The C-130 assumed paramount importance, second only to the helicopter, in nearly every daily mission throughout both Iraq and Afghanistan. Major mobility moves by C-17s, C-5s, and the additional air refueling systems required for long, global logistics (both personnel and equipment) operated at near maximum capacity. The requirement for the AC-130 gunship was overwhelming; the need for direct, near-real-time, ground support capabilities dominated ground commanders' requests. A perpetual lack of requested ISR capability plagued most of both conflicts—especially unmanned platforms. As the years rolled on, the USAF improved in all these areas, adapted operations, and developed to the best of its ability a more qualified airpower strategy.

However, strategists must effectively translate airpower theory into appropriate airpower strategy relative to the existing and emerging contextual complexities—a process that must, in large part, be accomplished prior to hostilities. Although the USAF demonstrated great flexibility adapting over time in Afghanistan and Iraq, the requirement to organize, train, and equip should not be fundamentally a "just-in-time" or ad hoc process.

In hindsight, the understanding of asymmetric and unconventional war that emerged throughout the 1990s should have caused the USAF to develop a tactical intra-theater airlift capability with an increased survivability rate in contested locations—perhaps a smaller, more-efficient airlift platform able to access more potential environments and hardened against small-arms fire. Furthermore, the USAF should have more seriously considered the need for increased air-to-ground systems that could be seamlessly and continually available for close air support, as well as the need for helicopter systems. The lack of substantial USAF helicopters, with their unique and vital airpower capabilities, suggests a possible shortfall in effective planning, or worse, a myopic perspective that only embraces strategic-level airpower technologies or independent systems.[11] In terms of RPAs, no other service is more qualified to procure, organize, train, and equip this vital new capability; if another service (Army, Navy, CIA, etc.) is or becomes more capable, then it is further evidence the USAF failed to proactively usher in these emerging and vital airpower capabilities. Unfortunately, evidence from the early years of both the Iraq and Afghanistan conflicts suggests the service was less than enthusiastic about the increased emphasis and importance being given to RPAs as an arm of traditional airpower strategy. The USAF should also have been better prepared to coordinate within the joint arena, especially in contexts where ground forces have primacy in the fight. It should have recognized, planned, resourced, and trained for these and several other areas when asymmetric and unconventional context began emerging (at least since Vietnam) and well before hostilities erupted.

This discussion is not intended to accuse or denigrate the USAF—just the opposite. As a service we have effectively adapted our airpower strategy in the past to better translate airpower theory into effective, contextually relevant operations. The dynamics that "force" these changes have always been problematic, ambiguous, and difficult. Today, given the expanded contextual realities of asymmetric war, as well as considerations of emerging technologies, a similar requirement exists to modify the fundamental attributes of our fighter-centric airpower strategy.

FUTURE AIRPOWER THEORY

To begin this "predictive analysis," one must first consider how the understanding and implications of enduring airpower theory may have changed over the years. As noted, strategy stems from foundational theory, and theory must be continually filtered through emerging new paradigms and context.

Theory is often an adaptive process where tests, empirical data, and experience help shape and clarify the original theory. As more information is garnered, theory can be updated and refined. There are perhaps three areas of airpower theory where minor clarifications to the original theory will serve to provide better explanatory and predictive power and one consideration where a major change is warranted. Access can no longer be assumed only to mean "over a specific geographical point." Given the advent of space and now cyber operations, access may also mean access to enemy digital networks, access to enemy privacy, or access to enemy secure communications. Although a geophysical phenomenon remains where access is advantageous to military operations, the full spectrum of what is meant by access must now be a wider, more complex perspective. Second, speed, although still vital in terms of the traditional advantage airpower provides, must also be understood to include electrical transmissions with both offensive and defensive capabilities. And third, strategic strike must now include a more robust human element where civilian causalities are no longer socially acceptable, humanitarian operations are directly related to U.S. security interests, and global economies now include multinational infrastructure with a multinational workforce. Finally, the axiom that airpower is decisive should be eliminated from the theory or significantly qualified. Although there may be cases where airpower could be decisive, as was the case in Japan or maybe the 1991 Gulf War, planning for future military engagements would be better served under a banner of synergistic operations across the full range of military capabilities. In an expanded consideration for what access means to airpower theory, the technologies, processes, and physical connections have increased in both number and scope. This requires consideration of both offensive and defensive operations. For example, the ability to cut off enemy communications has long been an important consideration in warfare; however, today the complexities of global cell networks, space-based communication, and even underground hardened communication lines make access to these nodes much more difficult. Furthermore, the requirement to develop equally the same and even more-robust communication lines as a defensive measure against attack requires increased vigilance on what an enemy might be able to access in the United States. Within airpower theory, one must consider a much wider reality and context of what constitutes access as well as the subsequent strategy that develops from that theory.

The axiom that airpower provides speed for military advantage, must now conclude that speed is no longer limited to how fast an airplane can fly. Although the importance of aircraft speed will likely remain relevant into the future, the wider concept of speed will in many ways be measured in terms of electronic, digital, and most importantly, decision-making speed. This suggests that although in the traditional sense, aircraft speed afforded the ability to "get in and get out" (either undetected or at such a speed a belligerent could not appropriately react), speed in this sense may no longer provide an advantage. Given new detection capabilities, advanced radar and targeting systems, and global communications networks that work in nanoseconds, traditional aircraft speed may provide little in terms of advantage. Again, this does not suggest aircraft speed is no longer important; rather, it suggests that widening the possible understanding of what speed means in the future will expand our perspective of speed as an axiom to airpower theory. This wider recognition and definition of speed within the context of airpower theory will have direct consequences on how and why specific airpower strategy is developed in the future.

Third, the traditional dynamic of strategic strike, where a nation consists of internal vital centers wholly owned and operated by citizens of that state, is continuing to decline. Global commerce, multinational companies, and borderless commerce (electronic transfer of wealth) will continue to degrade what has traditionally been central to state sovereignty. Targeting an electrical grid in Country A may take out the operating capacity of an industry in that country owned by one of our allies in Country B. Furthermore, as the future global commons become denser, U.S. economic interests will likely have a footprint in nearly all states across the globe. Traditional strategic strikes may actually result in significant logistical problems at home. Our current bilateral economic dependence on China will only increase in the coming years. It is hard to imagine strategic strikes against China if doing so would risk the potential of significant economic consequences at home. One might consider the future global commons a context in which "mutually assured economic destruction" creates an environment where traditional strategic (kinetic) strikes no longer seem advantageous.

Furthermore, as the world becomes more interconnected; as media and technology provide the vehicle to share massive amounts of live or near-live streaming video; and as social media capabilities continue to connect more people, the future scrutiny of "collateral damage" during strategic strikes will measurably increase. The public backlash over unintended consequences and civilian collateral damage will require more precise strategic strikes than current PGM technology can produce. Moreover, capabilities that produce desired effects without kinetic strike will increase and become the next "insatiable" requirement of commanders. This emerging context will affect the parameters and scope of what we mean by the airpower axiom of strategic strike.

Finally, in terms of the airpower axiom of decisiveness, the USAF must consider the importance of a synergistic perspective. In terms of strategic communication alone, the term *decisive* applied to a single service or capability is by its fundamental understanding an exclusive statement. Although early airpower advocates used the term decisive as a forcing function for a separate Air Force, empirical support through the years has been limited. Furthermore, the twin sister of decisive operations is *independent* operations (clearly connected in Mitchell's early work). This original argument encouraged the term independent for obvious organizational reasons and objectives at the time but could just as well have argued that because U.S. national security "depends" on airpower capabilities, it should be organized under a unique service. Airpower may well retain and even increase its ability to conduct independent operations, but the message this description sends is divisive. Instead, the message regarding both airpower theory and its subsequent airpower strategy should be one whose narrative is best described as dependent. This point is easy to make. In most cases, ground maneuver is dependent on airpower control just as sea maneuver is dependent on airpower control. Likewise, near-immediate humanitarian relief and/or immediate retribution against emerging belligerents are dependent on airpower capabilities (access, speed, strategic strike). Consider that as Mitchell's foundational argument: airpower is so important to the national security of the United States, it required a unique people to lead it (airmen) and a unique organization to control it (USAF). Today, the original argument for independence is not only anachronistic; it is hurting the USAF message. The message today, and likely well into the future, should be about dependence—the security of the United States is dependent on substantial, enduring airpower capabilities. Thus, airpower theory would improve in terms of developing appropriate airpower strategy if the term decisive were eliminated.[12]

Despite this emerging future context, airpower strategists are still responsible for answering the original question: "What must our airpower strategy be to connect airpower theory (access, speed, strategic strike) effectively to the emerging and growing spectrum of current and future war?" Strategists must consider a much wider spectrum of what these elements mean if one is to translate theory effectively into appropriate airpower strategy.

FUTURE AIRPOWER STRATEGY

Airpower strategists should begin by developing a strategy that translates the important axiom of access into an operational reality relevant within the future context. Consider that nearly any significant object on the surface, subsurface, or in the air will be tracked, identified, and potentially targeted. By significant contrast, this prediction suggests one of size, sound, or energy footprint. Only those systems at the micro, near-silent, and ultra-low-energy level will have any

chance of operating undetected (i.e., untargetable). In the technological imperatives of required small size alone, none of these systems will be able to provide the
physiological requirements of manned flight. Moreover, the increase in detection
capabilities, especially ground-to-air weapon systems, is advancing exponentially
in terms of both competency and low-cost production. Today the development
of "stealthy" aircraft is a multi-decade commitment whose cost/benefit ratio has
reached the upper limit. Given this inversely proportional relationship between
detection technology and anti-detection technology, any strategy that relies on
current and traditional physical access using significant systems (traditional aircraft) in the future will likely be disappointing. The USAF must develop systems
(both sensors and weapons) today for tomorrow that are small, undetectable,
modular (so they can be quickly configured for specific missions), and standardized so they can be delivered from a variety of air and space platforms.[13] Airpower
strategy must accommodate and conceptualize not only unmanned systems that
can be much smaller, but also pure drone capabilities. Today's RPA pilots continually emphasize their aircraft are not unmanned but rather manned at a distance.
However, from a strategist's perspective looking at the trends of technology, these
current RPA systems are merely transitional. In the very near future, technology
will provide the opportunity for pure drone aircraft that are small, extremely difficult to track and target, yet highly capable of both ISR and attack (ISRA).
Furthermore, these systems will be "preprogrammed" both to launch and progress autonomously. This autonomous capability will become a requirement due
to the extensive numbers of systems, the vast degree of mission assignments, the
near-global demand, and perhaps most importantly, the need to counter threats
in seconds rather than the traditional time required for human-based decisions.[14]

Airpower theory suggests that access provides a military advantage. Therefore
the USAF must develop systems today for tomorrow that do not rely on manned
control (other than initial programming), are small sized, "on-watch" 24/7, and
can be produced in large numbers for very low cost. Furthermore, an effective
access strategy will require the USAF to continue developing and investing in space
and cyber technologies. In this sense, airpower must be seen not by its original
airplane effect; rather, airpower must in the future be seen as controlling the
domains of air, space, and cyber. Fortunately, the USAF has already made significant organizational strides in this direction. However, in developing relevant
future airpower strategy, it must expand this investment and develop capabilities
to access digital and electrical nodes across the globe. Perhaps most importantly,

the USAF must reorganize how it authorizes, commands, controls, and proportions these capabilities. Under current legal, funding, and "sortie generation" systems, emerging and future cyber capabilities will not be able to function effectively as needed. This will of course require the USAF to divorce itself incrementally from the traditional and primary perspective of manned flight as the central capability for access.

To translate the element of speed into an airpower strategy, one must understand that any speed will likely not be capable of escaping future technologies and their targeting capabilities. For peacetime garrison operations or humanitarian efforts, traditional aircraft speed considerations will remain relevant. However, in contested areas, aircraft will likely not survive. In fact, future operations will no longer call for air superiority as it is conceived today; no country will be capable of gaining and maintaining air superiority due to future advance detection and targeting technologies. Our advantage will come from the speed at which we can deny air operations to a belligerent through our own ground-to-air defenses, the speed at which we can process ISR data into information, and the speed at which our organizational processes allow us to outmaneuver and outthink our enemies. Speed in this sense will be less about technology and more about rapid contextual determination and decision making—rapidly putting the pieces of the puzzle together and thwarting enemy plans. Much of what this strategy suggests is unfolding today, as revealed in antiterrorism procedures. National Security Agency (NSA) data collection is only the beginning of what will be a standard and necessary requirement in the future, where the speed at which one can assimilate data into usable information, synthesize and connect that information to a wider narrative, and act before a belligerent can respond, will determine who has advantage. Given this future strategy, the USAF should invest heavily in secure communication capabilities, highly capable intelligence-gathering competencies, extensive cyber expertise and processes (a significant organize, train, and equip requirement), and personnel with the training and education to work in a fast-paced, proactive environment. These are the strategic characteristics that will effectively translate the theoretical axiom of speed into future airpower strategy.

Finally, future airpower strategy development regarding strategic strike will require significant capabilities in terms of micro, surgical capabilities. Strikes must be capable of engaging single nodes of vulnerability without degrading entire networks. Moreover, strikes must be capable of being "un-done," which means traditional kinetic destruction may no longer be considered the default or single-option capability. Network viruses with available keys that can turn on and off effective directed-energy capabilities that can temporarily degrade systems without destroying the entire infrastructure, and even information overload capabilities that frustrate and degrade a belligerent's ability to make effective decisions—these are just some of the strategic strikes of the future. Consideration for the wider impact of destroying industrial capabilities within a multinational economic context will restrain traditional "shock and awe" strategies.

A common reaction (especially from aviators) to this kind of discussion is: "What you are describing is no longer the Air Force. If you take the airplane out of the Air Force how can it even be called an air force?" In response to this important question, one must first recognize this discussion does not suggest that future airpower strategy will be devoid of aircraft. In fact, as previously noted, significant aircraft capabilities will be required during peacetime garrison operations. Humanitarian lift and airdrop, search and rescue, rapid transportation of personnel and cargo, weather reconnaissance, medical evacuation, fire-fighting operations, tactical domestic surveillance, and other operations will remain both relevant and require extensive aircraft capabilities. Moreover, these operations alone will continue to require air-minded personnel committed to full-time strategic and operational planning for implementing traditional air capabilities. However, in contested areas where an enemy of equal capability challenges our use of aircraft, traditional aircraft operations will no longer be possible. As noted, the technology available to identify, track, and target will have outpaced (and in many ways already has outpaced) the ability of traditional aircraft to hide. The kinetic and combat operations required of future airpower strategy will better translate airpower theory by considering and solving the complexities of context this discussion poses. Finally, in direct response to taking *air* out of *airpower,* one can draw an analogy to taking the *horse* out of *horsepower.* Today, when we talk about horsepower, we are still talking about translating the theory of moving further and/or faster into a strategy that is relevant in today's context. Although the horse in horsepower is no longer present, the theory remains consistent. So, too, is the idea of air in airpower. Although the means of translating the theory will no longer call for traditional combat aircraft, that does not mean future capabilities will not continue to refer to airpower in relation to the theoretical axioms of access, speed, and strategic strike.

CONCLUSION

Predicting the future context of airpower strategies is a risky concern. However, if the ideas presented here begin a conversation about how we might prepare today for an uncertain future, then the risk will have been worth it. The intent of this chapter is to motivate a discussion that can increase the probability of a more prescient, proactive and effective airpower strategy for the future. There will no doubt be those who disagree with these considerations—perfectly acceptable and highly encouraged. For those who perceive a different future or believe airpower should consider a different context: join the debate, offer your ideas, and endure critique. Regardless of the differences this debate generates, future airpower strategy continues to be wed to airpower theory and objective analysis of the expanse and scope of that theory must be realized. As with all organizational change, some will find every reason not to take the future context into account if it means changing what they understand and cherish about today's airpower strategy (mainly manned flight). However, as has been the case with changes in the past, the USAF will work through the needed transitions, shape a new culture that understands and accepts the changes, and think strategically about how the fundamental advantages of access, speed, and strategic strike will remain important theoretical aspects in future conflicts. Given the present and immediate future context posed by potential enemies around the world, current airpower strategy supported by today's air, space, and cyber competencies will remain critical to U.S. national security. Taking into account the ideas offered here, we must understand that our current airpower systems are merely transitional technologies—that may become anachronistic in the coming years. Just as Mitchell argued many years ago, the importance of airpower to the future security and vital interests of the United States is profound. Considering that the Air Force of 2030 will in large part be determined by the decisions we make today, the debate must take place now—at the highest level of strategic decision-making.

NOTES

1. This chapter was originally published as an article in *Strategic Studies Quarterly* (Maxwell AFB: Air University Press, Summer 2014), 74–95.
2. William "Billy" Mitchell, *Winged Defense* (New York: Putnam, 1925).
3. Ibid., 214–15.
4. J. F. Shiner, "The Coming of the GHQ Air Force, 1925–1935," in *Winged Shield, Winged Sword: A History of the United States Air Force*, ed. B. C. Nalty (Washington: Air Force History and Museums Program, 1997), 111–12.

5. Mitchell also offered the idea of airpower being "decisive," but it was the officers at the ACTS who formally considered it in their development of airpower strategy.

6. A. Stephens, "The True Believers: Air Power Between the Wars," in *The War in the Air*, ed. A. Stephens (Fairbain, Australia: Air Power Studies Center, 1994), 61–65; and *The United States Strategic Bombing Survey: Summary Report (European War)* (30 September 1945; reprint, Maxwell AFB, AL: Air University Press, October 1987), www.dtic.mil/cgi-bin/Get TRDoc?AD=ADA421958.

7. Mike Worden, *Rise of the Fighter Generals: The Problem of Air Force Leadership 1945–1982* (Maxwell AFB: Air University Press, 1998). This work outlines and traces the emergence of the fighter perspective and how it eventually dominated the central airpower strategy of the USAF into the 1990s.

8. For a detailed account of the transition from the bomber strategy developed and enforced through SAC to the fighter-centric strategy developed and upheld through ACC, see Jeffrey J. Smith, *Tomorrow's Air Force: Tracing the Past, Shaping the Future* (Bloomington: Indiana University Press, 2014), 58–105.

9. Some might argue that it was not a military decision to "leave" Somalia; rather, the commander in chief ordered us to leave. It might well have been different if the USAF, as just one service example, had offered the president a viable and appropriate alternative strategy that would have proven more advantageous to U.S. national interests. However, given the fighter-centric perspective and dominant airpower strategy of the time, there was limited if any capability for addressing an asymmetric, unconventional context with USAF airpower.

10. USAF chief of staff, Gen Norton Schwartz, 2009, offered in numerous speeches.

11. Carl H. Builder, *The Icarus Syndrome: The Role of Air Power Theory in the Evolution and Fate of the U.S. Air Force* (New Brunswick: Transaction Publishers, 1994). In this work, Builder continually points to events where USAF leaders rejected or slow-rolled certain airpower systems that did not align with their vision of what they deemed important. Within that process, Builder contends that the USAF routinely put the means (systems it preferred to fly) ahead of the ends (maximum military advantage).

12. The airpower theory I propose here is taken from a variety of historical and current observations that all attempt to provide a theory, yet fail to reach the explanatory level that stretches across time and space. Many have developed what they think is an airpower theory but is in reality simply an airpower strategy. Although the USAF has always managed to hit around the edges of an airpower theory, few cases exist where a theoretical framework that describes, explains, anticipates, and even predicts how and why

airpower provides advantage has ever been fully articulated. Future serious discussion on the development of an airpower theory seems exceedingly appropriate at this important time in our development.

13. Much of this discussion was developed through interaction with Lt. Col. John Kepko, USAF, retired, who has spent a lifetime (both in and out of the service) researching, debating, and contemplating future technology-based possibilities. His insight and acumen for recognizing technological trends and synthesizing that recognition into strategic considerations is truly remarkable. This author and many others have garnered a tremendous amount from John's insights and interests in the future of our service.

14. For example, today we are all familiar with antivirus software. These software packages autonomously seek out, quarantine, and even eliminate threats. The future requirement for machine-based digital guardians must exponentially increase to include microsecond decisions to take down entire networks. If a threat to any of our vital cyber systems by an outside digital attack requires a preemptive attack against that network in the few seconds prior to the event, there is no way for humans to make that call in real time—it must be an autonomous action engineered into the cyber system.

CHAPTER EIGHT

Spacepower and the Strategist

M. V. SMITH

In theory there is no difference between theory and practice. In practice, there is.

—Attributed to Yogi Berra

✳

Yogi Berra, the famous Yankee catcher and later manager, probably never read Clausewitz's immortal treatise *On War*.[1] Yet the epigraph above sums up one of the more complex concepts that Clausewitz wrestles with over several pages: Why is there a difference between planning and execution, or between book learning and experience? Why is it that on paper "everything in war is very simple, but the simplest thing is difficult?"[2] The great Prussian master cited "friction" as the cause. He explained it this way: "Countless minor incidents—the kind you can never really foresee—combine to lower the general level of performance, so that one always falls short of the intended goal . . . that more or less corresponds to the factors that distinguish real war from war on paper."[3] More succinctly, the Hall of Famer quoted above elsewhere explained the phenomenon as only he could: "If the world were perfect, it wouldn't be."

Presenting the wisdom of a war theorist and a baseball manager side by side might seem to be comparing apples and oranges, but it is not. Both men were strategists in their own fields, and as Professor Colin Gray points out, "There is an essential unity to all strategic experience in all periods of history because nothing vital to the nature and function of [competition] and strategy changes."[4] While

Berra and Clausewitz had their own specialties and grammars, they shared the same logic as they went about devising their strategies, which Everett Dolman defines as the crafting of "a plan for attaining continuous advantage" over an opponent.[5]

A strategist from any discipline can take some relief in being on the same "strategic playground" regarding spacepower as any other competitive endeavor. As Professor Gray points out, "[Competition] has a grammar, but not a policy logic, of its own. [Competition] in space has its own distinctive [context] that policy must know and respect, but such [competition] has meaning only for the purpose of policy."[6] This means that a person versed in general strategic theory has many skills transferable to the art of crafting and assessing strategies, including for spacepower.

There is a difference between theory and practice, as the previous discussion points out. Theory teaches the rules, whereas experience teaches the exceptions. The exceptions are rooted in the unique context of the environment. It is as simple as the differences among land, sea, air, space, and cyber.[7] This chapter is about the context of spacepower and its employment for strategic effect, which is defined here as doing something in space in the pursuit of the aims of policy. If the policy is properly harmonized with strategy, spacepower will be employed in a manner that seeks continuous advantage in the never-ending competition with other actors. What constitutes an advantage varies. Its pursuit may require space activities for a negative aim of preserving a status quo or for a positive aim of establishing a new order of things.

As interactive servants of policy, strategists, by the way they conceptualize space and spacepower, have great bearing on the crafting of strategies to exploit the space environment. This chapter places spacepower in its supporting role with respect to activities occurring within the terrestrial confines. Spacepower strategy must therefore be embedded in strategies of operations not only in other operating environments but across the panoply of human activities. For example, a commercial telecommunications company must include its space activities in its overall strategic planning as a subset of its enterprise.

It is fair for strategists in the opening years of the twenty-first century to conceptualize space as a place where certain capabilities are based in order to collect and route information. Some may find it useful to think of most of today's space systems as a subset of cyberpower. After all, satellites are merely a set of sensors, receivers, and transmitters connected to computers that route information to terrestrial users via very long wireless connections. While this perspective might be useful to support operations in other operating environments, it fails to take into account all of the activities necessary to assure access to space-derived services while denying the same to an adversary.

The spacepower strategist must therefore work independently to secure space. At the same time, the spacepower strategist must work hand in hand with strategists of other forms of power and commerce to maximize the return on investment in space capabilities. This chapter lays out several considerations that weigh on the minds of spacepower strategists as they go about securing space in ways that allow them to perform their overarching function of providing capabilities to terrestrial users.

WHY IS SPACEPOWER IMPORTANT?

In a nutshell, a relatively small number of satellites in fixed and predictable orbits have become a huge center of gravity. The effect of these satellites cuts across all other sectors and centers of gravity in the modern state. As Clausewitz tells us, the center of gravity is "the hub of all power and movement, on which everything depends."[8] He claims it is "always found where the mass is concentrated most densely."[9] The value of satellites is very high in terms of their pervasiveness and the growing reliance on their services across the fabric of everyday life and critical sectors of the modern state. As such, their target value is disproportionately high for state or nonstate actors who want to strike very heavy and far-reaching blows to modernized state opponents.[10] At present, there is great concern that modern states have become too reliant on space for their security and economic well-being and that they have not taken sufficient precautions to protect and defend their satellites in space.[11]

Spacepower is a vital element of a state's military instrument of power, but spacepower is also a vital element contributing to each instrument of a state's power: diplomacy, information, military, economic, and culture (DIME-C). It is through the use of these instruments that states exercise their ability to influence the world around them in their never-ending pursuit of security, prestige, and wealth. To study spacepower only for its military contribution is to ignore the fact that spacefaring activities are a set of tools that confer far more than merely warfighting capabilities to the state. The tools of spacepower are engines that enable, enhance, and expand the opportunities for success as a state engages its geopolitical surroundings. A word of caution is immediately warranted: the fact that spacepower expands a state's national power makes the spacefaring assets used by a state an attractive center of gravity, one that belligerent adversaries will attempt to counter. They cannot afford to do otherwise.

The strategist must contemplate spacepower in both war and peace. Because space-based assets provide global services, it must be kept in mind that space-based systems provide support to areas at war and other areas at peace simultaneously. Fortunately, the majority of the Earth is peaceful and preoccupied with commerce. However, there are always a few wars of various size and technical sophistication under way across the globe at any one time.

Presented here is a discussion of spacepower in the more theoretical terms of the nexus between policy and strategy, with a focus on the security community. As pointed out above, the spacepower strategist orchestrates systems that engage the entire globe and the space environment itself all at once. At the operational and tactical levels, satellite-based capabilities are apportioned to provide services to practically every form of human endeavor. The onus is on the strategist to learn from others and to gain personal experience with spacepower.

SPACEPOWER IN PEACE

The Primary Value of Spacepower: War Prevention

Spacepower provides different tools with which to manage security concerns. Spacepower provides a matchless opportunity to employ a relatively few satellites to gain global access and global presence. This allows space assets to deliver nearly ubiquitous capabilities from the spaceborne vantage point, which creates some unique opportunities for situational awareness, treaty verification, and interconnectivity for collective security arrangements. Spacepower is ideally suited to assist in war prevention—securing the peace—as a matter of day-to-day statecraft. To restate this in clearer terms, "The primary value of space power is not support to warfighters; rather it is that space capabilities are the primary means of war prevention."[12]

Spacepower provides both direct and indirect methods to achieve war prevention. Direct methods involve the use of force or threats of force. Indirect methods involve cooperative interstate behavior to reduce security concerns without the use or threat of force. Spacepower lends itself more toward indirect methods, such as providing transparency into human activities and expanding broad international partnerships. Direct methods are more hard-power-centric and include capabilities that deliver assurance and dissuasive and deterrent effects, matched with careful diplomacy, in a cost/benefit calculus.

Indirect Methods

TRANSPARENCY. Space-based reconnaissance and surveillance platforms, because of their global and ubiquitous nature, contribute directly to reducing security concerns by providing insight into observable human activities around the globe. Insight into human activity in space is every bit as important as observation of terrestrial activities. When considered together, such insights can alleviate unfounded fears and prevent miscalculations. They also help to detect activities that serve as warnings and indications of activities of genuine concern. This was obvious right from the opening of the space age, during the Cold War, when reconnaissance satellites provided the critical imagery necessary to prove to the Dwight D. Eisenhower administration that there was no missile gap with the Soviet Union and that there was no need to expand defense programs. Spacepower assets alleviated international tensions.[13]

While it is extremely beneficial for any state to have transparency into the actions of another, the other is left at a distinct disadvantage if it has no such reciprocal transparency and hence may experience elevated security concern. Seen thought the realist's lens of international relations, as presented by James Forsyth in chapter 3, self-interest and survival concerns can certainly plant the seeds of war. An alternative view, however, is that given the rising economic interdependency between states in this age of globalization, it is in most states' interests to reduce security concerns among all states and thereby reduce the risk of war. This suggests that the best course of action is to share space-derived surveillance and reconnaissance widely, to reduce everyone's security concerns. States will find this easiest among traditional allies and most difficult with traditional adversaries, but doing so serves to establish the facts with greater certainty, removing much of the ambiguity and enabling a better interplay of diplomacy among all parties. In this way, space-derived transparency does its part in preventing wars. Predictably, transnational actors will find this approach particularly appealing.

Only space-based systems can provide transparency into certain observable human activities everywhere on the globe. This is due largely to the right of overflight in space, as first expressed in National Security Council (memorandum) 5520 and the subsequent Eisenhower space policy—later enshrined in the Outer Space Treaty. Spacepower provides transparency that reduces the "fog" during peacetime (and wartime), increases the certainty of information, and allows contemplation of matters with a better approximation of the facts.[14] This alleviates some of the *chance,* or uncertainty and risk, found in Clausewitz's formulation of the trinity of war. But it is not perfect transparency, and spacepower cannot peer into the minds of people to determine their intentions.

LIMITATIONS OF TRANSPARENCY. Some states will undoubtedly feel an increased security concern if satellite-derived information about their observable affairs is distributed widely. China voiced this concern shortly after the release of Google Earth, but accommodations were made to degrade the quality of images of areas sensitive to the Chinese government.[15] Such concerns must be addressed and dealt with directly, but such accommodations can often be made. Many states will undoubtedly change the way they conduct military and other affairs in ways that are not observable by satellites. India, for example, avoided detection of their efforts to test a nuclear device in 1998. They did so by scheduling activities around the overhead-pass times of U.S. imagery satellites and conducting them during times when sandstorms and intense heat could disrupt surveillance sensors.[16] Such nefarious work-arounds can be eliminated by fielding a large constellation of several dozen reconnaissance and surveillance satellites owned and operated by transnational or state actors and using multispectral technology. If only a limited number of reconnaissance assets are available, stealthy techniques to overfly states of interest at unpredictable and unannounced times could be used. The point is that every inch of the earth can be imaged several times a day using various techniques that can counter concealment efforts.

Perhaps the greatest limitation of transparency is that sharing information about one's own state of affairs gives potential adversaries insight into one's strengths and weaknesses. The adversaries may choose to exploit this information later. This creates an incentive to withhold the most sensitive information or to give misleading or deceptive information. States must not provide transparency naively to those who would prey upon them. Nevertheless, there are many examples of the benefits of transparency as a war-prevention measure. Global transparency efforts are big undertakings and relatively expensive. To be most effective, such efforts require a high degree of international partnering. There will be rogues, so due caution is advisable.

PARTNERING. Another opportunity that spacepower provides for managing security concerns is capitalizing on the opportunity to grow collaborative international-security space arrangements. Multinational partnerships could be formed to provide space situational awareness, space traffic management, and space weather warnings, to name just a few. Such partnerships should not be limited to security-related functions but should cross into civil and commercial endeavors, such as space-based solar power, human missions to the Moon and Mars, space stations, space-based astronomy, etc. In fact, the lack of security classification barriers makes civil and commercial partnerships much easier than military arrangements. The goal is not only to accomplish something meaningful in space but also to use such opportunities as confidence-building measures to build mutual understanding and rapport among the participating states.

Conditions are favorable for increased partnering among states on space projects. Excitement about space remains high among most states, and despite fifty years of spacefaring activities, sending machines and humans to space remains highly complex, requiring a plethora of technologies, as well as exotic materials. As a result, cooperation among states is already required for going to space, if only to acquire the raw resources to fabricate space systems and to achieve the necessary exchange of ideas to advance the art of spacefaring. The goal is to expand the list of partners and the number and types of projects being worked on in cooperation with various states. This has particular ramifications for the strategist, who must weigh the costs and benefits of cooperation versus securitized isolation.

Naturally, it is easier for states to remain inside their comfort zones by building partnerships with their traditional allies, but it is important to broaden the network of space-related cooperative ventures to nontraditional partners, especially developing states that can be brought more fully into the international community through such efforts. Most important of all, however, is the need for cooperation on space activities between potential adversaries. In the past, joint ventures on space initiatives have proven successful as confidence-building measures. This is a modern equivalent of the medieval custom of having the prince or princess live as a guest in the capital of an enemy kingdom as a means of averting war.

The American and Soviet joint venture on the Apollo-Soyuz mission in the mid-1970s is an example. Although the tangible scientific benefits of such efforts are debatable, that instance demonstrated to both participants and to the international community that cooperation on a very challenging task is possible—even between the two Cold War antagonists with widely divergent strategic cultures. This civil spacepower effort became a point of departure for other confidence-building gestures between the two and contributed to the easing of tensions in their homelands and in the rest of the world as well. This reduced security concerns. It must be noted that Apollo-Soyuz was undertaken against the backdrop of detente already under way. The space effort was a continuation of such policies, but it stands out as one of the clearest examples of confidence building between former competitors.

Partnering on spacefaring projects brings together more brilliant minds and resources to solve problems and advance the art. It not only increases the likelihood of success of those programs but over time reduces friction during peacetime between states, decreases the potential for cultural misunderstandings, increases the opportunities for alliances, integrates aspects of each state's economic and industrial bases, and fosters working relationships between governments.[17] This alleviates some of the hatred and enmity found in Clausewitz's trinity of war.

LIMITATIONS OF PARTNERING. Partnering is not always easy, as the members belonging to the International Space Station will attest and as the mostly European states belonging to the Galileo Consortium will point out. In fact, it can be frustrating, if not maddening. It may even result in worse relations between states. Disparate economic strengths, differing distribution of resources, and unequal talent pools give states different values as potential partners. States that are rich in some areas will be highly sought as partners. Poorer states will not. A concerted effort will be needed to draw the developing states into various spacefaring partnerships. All are valuable as prospective partners, as parts of a collaborative international security arrangement.

COMMENTARY ON INDIRECT METHODS OF WAR PREVENTION. The opportunities that spacepower offers spacefaring and nonspacefaring states alike in the forms of global transparency and international partnering as means to prevent wars are not fundamentally different from opportunities resident in other operating environments. What is unique about spacepower, however, is the global vantage point that it provides, as well as how it involves some of the highest technology of any state. The majority of states—especially weaker or developing ones that are not yet spacefaring—will find the indirect methods highly attractive and accrue "soft power" to the leaders of such efforts.[18] These approaches may be sufficient for most states' space-related security needs, while reducing their security concerns inside the terrestrial confines.

Direct Methods

Many states will not feel comfortable resting their security solely on such idealistic constructs as indirect methods. Some states, especially those with more security-minded strategic cultures, will likely acquire or expand space weaponry (overtly or covertly) to alleviate their security concerns, in the form of defensive systems to protect their space assets from attack and offensive systems to deny foes the opportunity to exploit space against them.

In this section the focus is on hard power and space weapons, weapons that create their effects in space against the space segment, regardless of where the weapons themselves are based. This section will not look at spacepower's long history of support to terrestrial forces that are continuously engaged in dissuasion and deterrence strategies or open warfare. The use of space systems to cue and connect nuclear and conventional deterrent forces is well documented elsewhere and will not be addressed here.

Many factors contribute to space-related security concerns faced by states and directly correlate to their likely drives for space weaponry. Each state will perform its own threat-risk calculus and respond accordingly. There are some elements of the threat-risk calculus that must be kept in mind. For example, more advanced spacefaring states have the most at risk in space and therefore greater incentives to field defensive space weaponry. Less advanced states have greater incentives to build offensive space weapons, as asymmetric means of countering the power of space-reliant potential adversaries. Proliferation of space weapons will drive the need for greater space defensive measures. Finally, every state is a user of space services, whether it is spacefaring or not, and therefore all states are space actors and must consider their space threat-risk calculi.

Acquiring space weapons is not a sufficient precursor to war, and as the peaceful conclusion of the Cold War illustrated, massive nuclear arsenals mated to launch-ready delivery systems are not automatic triggers for war. War has political roots. In fact, the possession of hard-power capabilities managed in a responsible and constrained manner enables the war-preventive strategies of *dissuasion* and *deterrence,* as were used to avert hostilities in the Cold War. An important point must be made here: states must openly acknowledge their possession of space weapons if those weapons are to be useful tools in hard-power dissuasion and deterrence. There is no war-prevention benefit in keeping space weapons secret, other than avoiding a space arms race—which may be desirable but may also fail to serve the cause of preserving peace. A potential adversary must clearly perceive a credible space weapons capability if dissuasion and deterrence strategies are to work.

ASSURANCES. The concept of "assurances" is borrowed directly from nuclear-related literature. It involves guarantees between stronger and weaker states made for the purpose of preventing proliferation of war and weapons of mass destruction. There are negative and positive security assurances. These concepts can be related to space weapons and warfare. Negative assurances would be guarantees by space-weapons states not to use or threaten the use of such weapons against states that have formally renounced them. Positive assurances would be the agreement between a space-weapons state and a nonspace-weapons state that assistance would be given to the nonspace-weapons state if attacked or threatened by a state that uses space weapons against it. This could include defending the satellites of the nonspace-weapons state, sharing space-derived data with it, and striking its adversary's counterspace systems.

Presently there are no known assurances between space-weapons states and nonspace-weapons states in the international community. This is a wide-open area, awaiting diplomatic engagement. Presumably the threat posed by space weapons has not yet raised the level of security concerns among the international community to the point of stimulating assurance-making among states.

LIMITATIONS OF ASSURANCES. As we have seen in the nuclear community, some states will give public assurances not to proliferate while working covertly to acquire weapons. There is always the risk of being hoodwinked, which highlights the need for greater transparency and other soft power–related means of securing the aims of policy. Many states possess devices that can interfere with satellites, and many have done so. Nevertheless, the term "space weapon" remains hotly debated. Many well-meaning people contend that space is a sanctuary and refuse to concede that space weapons exist, are proliferating, and have been used in warfare against satellite services several times in recent years. Iranian jamming of European satellite signals to prevent foreign news from entering Iran typifies the current state of space warfare.[19] It is not heroic, nor does it meet the Clausewitzian concept of violence, in the sense of bloodshed.[20] But it does meet the Clausewitzian definition of war in the sense of a form of engagement used for a political purpose against the will of another state or states.[21] Ironically, and perhaps paradoxically, wishful thinking and denial of the fact that space warfare is already upon us are not helping to bolster the war-preventive abilities of spacepower.[22]

DISSUASION. Dissuasion, like soft-power methods, rests on the ability to shape the preferences of others so they behave in a certain desired manner. But unlike soft power, where you induce others to choose courses of action you would like them to pursue simply because they find them attractive, dissuasion is really about persuading an actor who may pose a threat before that actor acquires the capability actually to pose a danger.[23] Dissuasion is a discussion or negotiation of sorts, where one party talks the other out of developing a system or systems that the former would consider threatening. It typically includes rewards and incentives for good behavior but usually also threats of escalating punishment for noncompliance. Such punishments may span from economic sanctions to preemptive military strikes. The goal is to cut a deal to preserve the peace by removing potential security dilemmas. Like deterrence, which will be discussed below, practitioners of dissuasion must be credible and capable. The dissuaded must rationally decide to comply because they deem the costs of noncompliance to outweigh the benefits of acquiring the new capability.

In its most familiar form, dissuasion is a method attempted by powerful, long-established nuclear states to persuade nonnuclear states not to proliferate. They approach states who pose threats before they do proliferate and directly attempt to dissuade them from going any further with their programs. Often economic incentives, such as the lifting of sanctions, trade deals, and foreign aid, are offered. Threats of the use of force are seldom emphasized in the media by the negotiating states, but sometimes "red lines" are established that clearly identify unacceptable behaviors that could elicit military responses. The goal is for the state to decide on its own that joining in the nuclear competition is not in its interest.

As applied to spacepower, a state that demonstrates a robust defensive and offensive capability may tacitly dissuade others from attempting to compete against that state not only in space but also in arenas that require space support.[24] Conversely, a state whose overall power, especially military power, appears directly tied to its space-based assets—a center of gravity—but has no visible means for defending them or denying other states from exploiting space for military gain, almost baits potential adversaries into fielding space weaponry.

LIMITATIONS OF DISSUASION. The evidence shows mixed results for dissuasion. This is most evident regarding nuclear proliferation. Since the mid-1990s Pakistan and North Korea have acquired nuclear weapons, and Iran appears to be well on its way, in spite of often very intense dissuasive efforts by the international community. Libya may be a success story. After lengthy discussions with international diplomats, Libya's leaders made a cost-benefit analysis that resulted in terminating their nuclear program by 2010. However, once Libya had met all United Nations' demands for eliminating its nuclear weapons program it found itself embroiled in a foreign-supported civil war that overthrew its government. In other cases, some states may have been dissuaded from proliferating nuclear weapons, but the evidence is not clear.

There is an important note to add regarding spacepower. A state that has overwhelming spacepower may successfully dissuade another actor from competing militarily in space or in other space-supported venues. However, if the former lacks the ability to negate space systems nonlethally (with respect to people) and in ways that could assist in achieving its aims, its options might be limited to pursuing asymmetric and potentially more violent means. In other words, space weapons poised against uninhabited satellites constitute nonlethal force "in being." Using such weapons in lieu of lethal means is in keeping with the spirit and intent of the law of armed conflict, which seeks to minimize human suffering in war. Here again, the good intentions of the arms-control community, which seeks to ban space weapons and all attacks on space systems or their signals, may otherwise actually lead to increased casualties and human suffering in war. Irony and paradox are visited once more.

DETERRENCE. When soft power and dissuasion fail, spacepower has a central role in deterrence strategies to prevent war. Deterrence is the prevention of war based on coercion whereby one actor threatens to impose unacceptable damage on an adversary if that adversary uses already existing capabilities against the former's interests.[25] Threats must be credible and deemed sufficient of inflicting unacceptable damage. This describes the standoff between the United States and the Soviet Union during the Cold War.

During the arms race of the Cold War, U.S. and Soviet space systems became thoroughly integrated into their respective states' nuclear-attack warning systems, command and control, assessment, targeting, planning, and most every aspect of finding, targeting, and potentially destroying each other's assets. The end of the

Cold War and the reduction of security concerns that followed allowed the focus of space systems to evolve rapidly from strictly nuclear-force support to support for all warfighting activities, including conventional and covert operations. It remains clear, however, that spacepower assets, as deeply integrated as they are in all aspects of the military operations of advanced spacefaring states, will continue to be an interconnecting glue making terrestrial deterrence possible.

It may be possible to deter an advanced spacefaring adversary who is heavily reliant on space systems but who has taken few or no precautions to defend them. In this case, possession of a credible set of offensive space weapons may cow the adversary into avoiding confrontation. Sensing this prospect, however, the adversary may initiate a crash program to acquire space weapons of its own.

LIMITATIONS OF DETERRENCE. Unfortunately, deterrence is based on the abstraction that there is no limit to the violence that can be threatened in retaliation. As Clausewitz noted, "Each side, therefore, compels its opponent to follow suit; a reciprocal action is started which must lead, in theory, to extremes."[26] This tendency can easily lead to arms racing.

COMMENTARY ON DIRECT METHODS OF WAR PREVENTION. Dissuasion and deterrence come with risks. They presuppose that both sides of a potential confrontation are equally rational, have an equal understanding of the stakes, and are using the same or similar rational calculi to establish policy in an interactive fashion.[27] Given differences in strategic cultures, these presumptions can never be the case in reality.[28] As a result, there are margins of error associated with every calculation. A state that builds offensive space weapons overtly for the purpose of enabling dissuasive and deterrent strategies for war prevention may be misunderstood as having hostile intentions that trigger security dilemmas for other states. The same is true for a state that builds what it considers to be a defensive system but has an apparent dual application as an offensive system. China's test of a direct ascent antisatellite (ASAT) weapon in January of 2007 may be a case in point.[29] A state may do its best to tailor its forces to support dissuasive and deterrent strategies and focus them at whatever they suspect the enemy holds dear, only to discover that the enemy reacts quite differently than expected. There are no guarantees.[30] A way to reduce the margins of error and the risk associated with direct hard-power war-prevention strategies is to include them within the policy-driven context of both indirect strategies suggested above—within the framework of global transparency and within broad international partnerships.

The use of declaratory policies may be a useful way to blend indirect and direct means of war prevention strategies involving spacepower. This could take the form of announcing the possession of space weapons but explaining to the international community exactly under what circumstances they would be used and how. This could stimulate a constructive international debate while at the same time drawing clear lines in the sand between potential belligerents.

As shown above, a strategist can employ spacepower in a structural manner to ameliorate and mitigate mistrust, misdeeds, misperceptions, and miscalculations on the world stage. This creates a more peaceful, predictable, and secure environment for commerce and other human activities. However, war remains a part of the human condition, and while most of the world is at peace, there are always, as we have noted, wars under way. Sometimes the spacepower strategist will be an observer to others' wars. Sometimes the spacepower strategist's own nation will be engaged in war, and space warfare may be a part of it.

SPACEPOWER IN WAR

When War Prevention Fails

The primary mission of security spacepower at all times is war prevention. To that end, constabulary and martial means must assure freedom of access to space and freedom of action in space for all lawful and nonhostile spacefaring activities. Martial space forces are those that work to provide space security when it is contested. When war is waged in space, the goal is to limit the effects only to belligerents while allowing the rest of international commerce and other activities in space to continue unimpeded. Space control with respect to hostile space forces will likely be required in order to achieve this.[31]

We are well within the age of space warfare, wherein satellite services are engaged and negated for political purposes. In the words of Colin Gray:

> It is a rule in strategy, one derived empirically from the evidence of two and a half millennia, that anything of great strategic importance to one belligerent, for that reason has to be worth attacking by others. And the greater the importance, the greater has to be the incentive to damage, disable, capture, or destroy it. In the bluntest of statements: space warfare is a certainty in the future because the use of space in war has become vital. . . . Regardless of public sentimental or environmentally shaped attitudes toward space as the pristine final frontier, space warfare is coming.[32]

What Does Spacepower Bring to Warfare?

Spacepower provides an exponential advance in cutting the fog and friction of war on a global scale. Today's most prolific spacepower, the United States, uses its wide variety of space systems as the key components of a global reconnaissance-strike complex.[33] This complex allows commanders to integrate rapid and synchronized attacks from air, land, sea, and cyber forces anywhere on the globe to maneuver and to provide "fires" (that is, strikes of various kinds) across the depth of an enemy's homeland with a rapidity, precision, and tempo that can overwhelm an adversary. Space assets form a ubiquitous global infrastructure—a communications and information backbone—into which friendly forces stationed or deployed anywhere in the world can plug to receive services that increase situational awareness, improve precision engagement, and expedite command and control.[34] The mechanism is the same as German blitzkrieg at the outset of World War II—reduce friendly fog and friction while expediting rapid and synchronized maneuvers and fires to increase the fog and friction experienced by the enemy.[35] With today's spacepower it could be called *astrokrieg*.

The Chinese have described the contributions of spacepower as the *informatization* of warfare and believe it will be the single greatest contributor to warfare in the coming century.[36] There is little doubt that the ability to collect and route information during wartime is critical. This is consistent with John Boyd's "OODA-loop" theory, wherein space-derived information is used by commanders to observe situations, orient their understanding of them, decide what to do about them, and act on their decisions.[37]

Offense and Defense

It is often said that defense is the stronger form of warfare.[38] This is not true in space—today. Defending satellites and their data links is a difficult proposition at best. Satellites are delicate, fragile devices that can easily fall prey to any number of space weapons that currently exist, such as lasers, radio-frequency jamming, and brute-force directed-energy weapons, as well as surface-to-space missiles with kinetic-kill vehicles—many of which are relatively small and highly mobile or transportable systems. While satellites in low earth orbit are the most vulnerable to lasers and lofted kinetic-kill vehicles, satellites all the way out in the geostationary belt and in highly elliptical orbits share a universal vulnerability to radio-frequency jamming and electromagnetic brute-force attacks.

Satellites need not be physically destroyed to be rendered ineffective. Satellites are tasked (as applicable) and provide their services to ground stations and users via the electromagnetic spectrum. Hence there is a rule: no spectrum means no spacepower. The rapid proliferation of counterspace jammers and electronic intrusion devices around the world in recent years is a testament to the general recognition of this rule.

It must be noted at this point that negating satellites via temporary and reversible means, such as brute-force jamming or laser dazzling, requires that such weapons engage their targets continuously. This makes such systems detectable and targetable by weapons resident in the operating environment, wherever they are located. For example, a jammer in Cuba that is negating an American satellite can be geolocated and countered by diplomatic moves or by air or land attacks. It is apparent that a country with a policy of achieving space superiority or space control against a prolific user of space systems via temporary and reversible means necessarily must have a large number of such counterspace weapons, a number commensurate with the number of space systems in use by the adversary. In addition, it must have a robust intelligence community that can identify, characterize, and prioritize such targets. It must also have sufficient defenses to protect such weapons, because their very use makes them vulnerable to attack.

Conversely, a state may configure its counterspace forces to conduct a cyber-style attack against a satellite's internal programming or strike with permanent effects to degrade or destroy adversary satellites. This configuration approach may satisfy the requirement for continuous engagement, thereby improving the survivability of one's counterspace weapons and obviating the need for defending them with other forces. In addition, it means that one weapon can be used successively to negate multiple satellites permanently. It seems, then, that permanent negation becomes both a cost- and resource-saving option. However, resorting to only one form of attack seriously curtails strategic options, which can be highly problematic. For example, during wartime, modern militaries employ commercial and third-party satellites to provide war-essential services. Using permanent methods of negation against commercial and third-party satellites could dramatically expand the conflict and the list of belligerents faced by the attacker. In contrast, using discrete, limited-duration temporary and reversible methods of negation against such targets will not likely expand the conflict, as evidenced by the fact that hostilities have not been caused by the numerous episodes of satellite jamming that have already occurred.

Efforts to defend space systems have been paltry at best. An adversary with robust counterspace weapons may be able to negate all friendly space systems in a matter of hours; therefore, it is imperative for spacepowers to acquire the ability to find, fix, track, target, and destroy an adversary's space weapons very quickly. Such hostile systems may reside on land, at sea, in the air, or in space. It will require close coordination with terrestrial forces to engage space weapons wherever they reside at the behest of the space commander.

The many examples of satellite jamming, lasing, and signal piracy indicate that we are well into the age of space warfare. Like war in all other realms, it is a contest of political wills using specific means to achieve the ends of policy. We know what space warfare looks like. It has appeared in several different forms—most being nonlethal, temporary, and reversible. As indicated in preceding paragraphs, we know enough about space warfare to anticipate how it will manifest itself in other, more destructive forms.

Ironically, the law of armed conflict may drive actors toward space warfare. It is quickly noted that engaging targets in space creates effects on Earth in ways that do not kill people (at least not directly). The law of armed conflict requires belligerents to behave in ways that minimize human suffering. Therefore, it is incumbent on belligerents to consider negating satellites in ways that obviate the need to resort to lethal force inside terrestrial confines. In other words, jamming a communications signal on board a satellite would be far more consistent with the law of armed conflict than bombing transmission or reception towers in populated areas. A case in point occurred during Operation Allied Force.[39] The Serbians were using a satellite to distribute command-and-control communications to their army in Kosovo, which was engaged in dehousing the ethnic Albanians living in the area. NATO used lethal force against transmission stations in Belgrade; if instead it had discreetly jammed the Serbian signals, it would not have had to do so, and civilian deaths and other collateral damage would have been avoided.

There is a drawback to temporary levels of negation: it is exceptionally difficult to determine if the application of a nondestructive weapon is achieving the desired effect. Permanent levels of negation may produce more easily observable confirmation of results. This is somewhat analogous to the problems in assessing tank kills in operation Desert Storm. Some commanders considered a tank killed if its unit had been attacked and the tank was no longer moving. Others did not. But all agreed that a tank with its turret blown off had been killed.

It must be kept in mind that a small number of very powerful directed-energy space weapons used in quick succession can permanently negate dozens of satellites. On the other hand, it would take several dozen space weapons that, like jammers, only cause temporary effects to sustain negation effects on the constellations of the larger spacefaring states. Since noise jammers are only effective when broadcasting and broadcasting jammers are relatively easy to find and target, there are incentives to develop space weapons that cause permanent effects—but do not create additional space debris.

Temporary and reversible methods of attack have proven the most popular. Space debris created by destructive engagements in space creates long-term hazards for all spacefaring parties—including the attacker. To preserve one's own freedom of action in space, the creation of space debris must be mitigated, especially during wartime, when access to space-derived services is most critical.

Space Control

Space control is not only provided for military purposes. Space control allows civil, commercial, and other space activities to continue uninterruptedly around the globe. It provides the benign environment that is a necessary precondition for most spacefaring activities. The importance of ensuring uninterrupted space commerce cannot be understated. All states are increasingly reliant on space systems for matters critical to their economic well-being.

Space control efforts must minimize disruptions to the flow of the global economy. During war every effort should be made to limit the effects to the belligerents only. This minimizes the risk of war expansion caused by the drawing in of other states seeking to protect their own interests by force. Space control also requires preventing the creation of space debris, because, as noted, it becomes a hazard to spacefaring activities and denies freedom of action in space to all actors in the vicinity of debris fields. Such are the negative aims of space control.

Achieving the negative aims of space control requires the passive or active defense of space systems under attack. This may require attacks to suppress or destroy the adversary's offensive space weapons, which may be based in the air, on land, at sea, in space, or within the cyber medium. It may be necessary to drive a foe all the way to the point of offensive culmination (that is, its maximum effort, all reserves committed, after which its assault wanes) of its counterspace forces to arrive at the security required to assure free passage of commerce and other activities. The policy, strategy, and situation will dictate the degree of offensive space control that is used. Factors to consider will be the time and place where space superiority must be gained, how rapidly it is needed, what parts of the adversary space systems are vulnerable, how to mitigate collateral damage, how quickly space control can be achieved (if it is even possible), how long space control must be sustained, and the desired level of negation (e.g., destruction, degradation, denial, disruption, deception, deterrence, or dissuasion) to achieve the ends of policy. Space control does not need to be permanent to be effective. In fact, attempting to impose total space control over an adversary, dominating all decisive points, including the equatorial choke point would be counterproductive, as preparations to do so would drain the budget and be highly wasteful.[40]

Space superiority and space control efforts also have a positive aim. The positive aim is to sustain the requisite degree of freedom of action to enable friendly space forces to engage the missions of *direct space support* to friendly forces, *space denial* of adversary space services (if required), *space logistics* to sustain friendly operations in orbit, and someday perhaps *space strike* (striking adversary targets in the terrestrial environment from space). Each of these missions will have priorities dictated by the policies and strategies they support.

Space situational awareness is a vital component of spacefaring. Freedom of access to space and freedom of action in space require timely and reliable information about what is actually happening in orbit. It includes what could be called "space traffic management" and debris avoidance, in addition to characterization of threats, anomaly detection and attribution, and attack assessment. The ability to characterize accurately what is happening in space becomes more critical as the world becomes more space reliant, as the number and frequency of spacefaring activities increase, and as space weapons proliferate.

Competition for space superiority and space control is not limited to warfare. Such competition also occurs during peacetime negotiations of treaties, international law, and codes of conduct. Many of these instruments seek to curtail the freedom of access to space or freedom of action in space in certain ways. This is why some countries are very cautious about entering into such negotiations. The long-term implications of various forms of agreements are difficult to anticipate. There is little doubt, however, that additional treaties, laws, and codes of conduct are warranted to codify the appropriate and inappropriate behaviors of spacefaring actors. This will soon be critical as it becomes necessary to accommodate a rapidly increasing number of satellites in orbit, space tourism, space hotels, and lunar as well as asteroid resource development.

DIRECT SPACE SUPPORT. Direct space support to terrestrial forces includes all of the space force enhancements and information services to which modern militaries have become accustomed. The negative aim of direct space support includes providing all of the space services associated with what is coming to be called the *surveillance-strike complex*. The surveillance-strike complex includes all those sensors, communications links, and other space capabilities that allow terrestrial forces to operate day to day and to defend friendly interests. It includes such things as warnings, tip-offs, indications, cross-sensor cues, and assessments of attack by air, land, sea, cyber, or space forces. It includes all space systems used in any way to integrate passive and active defensive measures. One example involves the satellites associated with the Defense Support Program and the Space-Based Infrared System, which form parts of the missile-warning network of the United States. That network uses satellites to detect and characterize missile launches, routes the data into the fire-control systems of missile defense batteries, and connects the batteries with commanders via communications satellites.

The positive aim of direct space support to terrestrial forces mentioned above includes providing all the space services associated with the *reconnaissance-strike complex* (as distinct from the "surveillance-strike complex" mentioned above). The reconnaissance-strike complex includes all space sensors, communications links, and other space capabilities that allow terrestrial forces to attack the enemy. It includes the entire space-enabled ability to find, fix, track, target, engage, and negate enemy targets and then to assess the results. An example is a reconnaissance satellite finding an enemy tank, routing this data to a strike aircraft via communications satellite, and guiding aircraft munitions to the target via the Global Positioning System, while observing battle-damage indications from other satellites in space.

The surveillance- and reconnaissance-strike complexes of most actors have many space-related elements in common. The Global Positioning System, for example, provides data that is typically critical to both complexes. Of particular note is the blending of commercial assets, such as communications satellites, into the strike complexes of states and nonstate actors. Commercial space systems used by the enemy to advance its war effort, including satellites in orbit, become valid military targets. Their likelihood of being attacked is directly related to the intensity of the war aims of the belligerents and their ability to strike relevant commercial systems.

SPACE DENIAL. Denial of adversary space forces is as important as space control. Its essence is the use of space weapons to negate services provided by adversary space systems. Its negative aim is to defend friendly interests by negating the enemy's space systems associated with its reconnaissance-strike complex, thereby increasing the fog and friction inherent to the enemy's offensive efforts and to hasten their offensive culmination.

There are two positive aims for which space denial can be used. The first includes space denial attacks against an adversary's space systems associated with its surveillance-strike complex to facilitate subsequent attacks against enemy forces and to hasten their defensive culmination. The second positive aim of space denial has received little attention. It involves negating adversary space systems simply to raise its costs in the war effort, in an attempt to coerce it into accepting terms. This can be done as part of an overall punishment strategy or risk strategy of imposing costs on the enemy with the promise of imposing even greater costs in the future.[41] An interesting twist to this strategy might be limiting strikes to satellites in orbit. Nobody dies, but tangible costs are imposed. It might be possible to coerce a state that is heavily reliant on space services into accepting modest terms by negating only its satellites in orbit. Such prospects heighten the need for effective space defenses for highly reliant states. States that do not find themselves heavily reliant on space have far less need for space defenses and may become concerned when others merely discuss defensive systems, since the line between offense and defense is so easily blurred.

It is important to remember that an adversary's satellites are global assets. It may be politically untenable for a number of reasons to damage an adversary's satellite permanently. For example, while an imagery satellite may threaten to disclose friendly troop movements in one region, that same satellite might perform treaty verification on the opposite side of the globe or other missions for which there are friendly interests in preserving. In many scenarios, space denial might best be limited to very localized and temporary effects.

Space-denial efforts will be complicated if an adversary is using third-party launch facilities, satellites, or ground-control systems provided by commercial vendors, international consortia, or allies. Diplomatic efforts will likely be required to eliminate third-party support to adversaries, but if the political factors demand, friendly forces must be ready to expand the conflict by striking suppliers of space support to adversaries. If diplomatic efforts fail and policy does not allow expansion of the conflict to strike third-party targets, the adversary has a sanctuary that will undoubtedly be exploited.

SPACE LOGISTICS. The next mission to consider is space logistics. Space logistics are those activities undertaken to sustain satellites and their capabilities in orbit. It includes launching satellites to orbit, checking out on orbit, maintaining, refueling, and repairing, inter alia. With regard to wartime space logistics it is imperative for spacefaring states to repair or replace lost satellite capabilities in orbit for which they have insufficient terrestrial redundancy. The goal is to restore capabilities rapidly before their loss affects political, economic, or combat operations. Activating on-orbit spares, leasing commercial satellite services, launching new satellites to replace those lost through attrition, or gaining access to an ally's satellite services may do this.[42] It is also essential to repair or replace lost satellite ground-control systems. Methods for doing this may include transferring ground-control responsibility to another location (fixed or mobile), leasing commercial support, or obtaining ground support from an allied state.

A word of caution is warranted regarding the launch of new satellites to replace those lost to enemy attack. Unless there is complete certainty that the adversary is culminated offensively and that all adversary space weapons have been accounted for and successfully negated, launching a satellite of the same design into the same orbit will be like throwing skeet in front of a shooter. In practice there is no way to be absolutely certain that the threat is completely removed.

SPACE STRIKE. Space strike, meaning striking terrestrial targets from weapons based in space, is the last mission area to be discussed. It is possible that state or nonstate actors will put in orbit weapons that can strike terrestrial targets in the air, land, sea, or cyber operating environments. Space strike could have a negative aim of striking an adversary's advancing forces or offensive systems as a matter of defending friendly interests and hastening the offensive culmination of an adversary. Space strike could also have two positive aims. The first could be striking adversary forces or their defensive systems to expedite their defensive culmination. The next could be attacking their centers of gravity directly as part of the war-winning effort.

There are many good reasons for not putting space-strike weapons in orbit around the Earth. Among them is the enormous expense and their vulnerability once there. But a paradoxical logic of warfare increases the likelihood of someone's actually doing it. It works like this: there are many good reasons not to put terrestrial strike weapons in space; putting such weapons in space makes no sense; no one is expecting such weapons in space; therefore one achieves the element of surprise by putting such weapons in space!

THE COMBINED-ARMS APPROACH. During times of peace, spacepower assets monitor the globe, helping to identify and characterize potential threats. When a threat emerges, political and military leaders may opt to send terrestrially based surveillance and reconnaissance sensors into the area of interest to get a closer look. Should hostilities break out, space forces must secure whatever degree of space control is required and contribute whatever they can to help friendly forces in-theater in terms of space support to the surveillance- and reconnaissance-strike complexes. But space forces must still watch the rest of the world, in every other theater, looking for tip-offs, warnings, and indications of other threats.

No claim is made that spacepower by itself can be decisive in general conventional warfare, but in certain circumstances it may help set the conditions for continued success by friendly forces. Conversely, the defeat of one's spacepower capabilities may turn the tide of the war against friendly forces and contribute to overall defeat. There may be certain forms of limited warfare wherein the information gleaned from space or strikes into or from space, kinetic or otherwise, may achieve the political and military aims of an operation. On such occasions it would be proper to say that spacepower has been decisive.

CONCLUSION

Modern strategists find themselves having to integrate a far broader set of tools in many different operating environments than did their predecessors. Nevertheless, the nature of strategy and competition remain the same. As in ancient times, the outcomes of events on land matter most, because it is on land that people live, work, and conduct politics from which policies are devised. The advent of spacepower has changed nothing in this classic dynamic, other than opening a new operating medium where tools of high strategic value are placed. This warrants the defense of these tools and their use to drive the desired outcomes of policy.

It must be remembered that the primary value of spacepower is war prevention, not support to warfighters. It prevents war by providing transparency into certain observable human activities around the globe and in space itself. This removes many uncertainties and may alleviate security concerns or allow them to be addressed by politicians with a better approximation of the facts. Spacepower enables and enhances all of the instruments of power: diplomacy, information, military, economic, and culture. This makes space assets a center of gravity for developed states that use space-derived services prolifically. Spacepower also provides opportunities for cooperative ventures on spacefaring activities across all sectors. These ventures can become the framework of better international relationships and confidence building between potential adversaries. Powerful spacefaring states may be able to use martial spacepower in ways that prevent wars by providing assurances, as well as employing dissuasive and deterrent strategies. The use of declaratory policies by states can take much of the uncertainty out of the system and create a basis for much-needed international dialog.

Sometimes war cannot be avoided. We are currently living, and forever will be, in the age of space warfare. War has already spilled into space, not because space warfare is an end in itself—it is not—but because assuring friendly access to space services while denying the same to adversaries is of growing importance in the prosecution of war. When war breaks out, the first priority of space forces is gaining relative space superiority and, in some remote cases, total space control over adversaries—while not interfering with other lawful and nonhostile users. The second priority of space forces in war is support to terrestrial warfighters. The overarching concern throughout space warfare is keeping the international lines of commerce and communications open and minimizing the impact to others. Space debris must be avoided in all but the most extreme circumstances, and when created, it should be promptly cleaned up, although methods for doing so remain on drawing boards.

Because spacepower offers nonlethal means of negating satellites that are critical to some adversaries' reconnaissance- and surveillance-strike complexes, there is a moral requirement expressed in the law of armed conflict to consider striking key satellites in lieu of using lethal force on Earth to achieve desired effects. This means air, land, sea, and cyber target lists should be studied closely by space forces and that in cases where the desired effect can be achieved; counterspace strikes should be used instead of lethal force in the terrestrial environment.

The international arms control community would do well to "give up the ghost" of space as a sanctuary.[43] Banning interference with satellites during warfare will escalate the use of lethal force against humans and property in the terrestrial confines. In their zeal to ban space weaponry, arms controllers have not taken into account that such bans—if followed—would be a death sentence for countless humans. The irony of this point invokes an ancient saying: "The road to hell is paved with good intentions."

Space is heavily militarized, with powerful spacefaring states attempting to enable their surveillance- and reconnaissance-strike complexes in ways that accelerate the scale, timing, and tempo of combat operations far beyond the ability of nonspacefaring actors to cope. It enables *astrokrieg,* which has all the shock-and-awe components of blitzkrieg but on the scale of global reach. Weak actors are likely to employ space weapons in attempts to counter the advantage that spacepower confers on powerful states. The most dangerous situation, however, occurs if two powerful spacefaring states go to war with each other. If the motives are powerful, it is likely that the belligerents will be forced to counter each other's space systems in the very early stages. At present there are inadequate defenses for space systems, but defense is possible, even required, if only to secure space systems from criminal activity, up to and including advanced methods of attack. Space-denial strategies will evolve wherein a belligerent attacks an adversary's space systems to inflict costs or to inflict strategic paralysis on the enemy before offering terms. Finally, space is very much a part of the military mix of all actors—state and nonstate. It must be recognized that military spacepower is not a replacement for terrestrial forces but an additional set of tools that deliver unique capabilities.[44] "[T]here is nothing special about space, strategically speaking."[45] It is just another venue for normal human activity, which must include the constabulary and the martial means of enforcing the rule of law and securing the peace.

Spacepower is of growing importance to the strategist and therefore requires continuous study. It provides a unique set of tools that must be considered in the formulation of strategies for war and peace—two conditions that coexist in the minds of space professionals in commanding their global spacepower assets. War prevention is the primary role of spacepower, but sometimes war is unavoidable. At such times, it is best to keep in mind another Berra quote, "The other teams could make trouble for us if they win."[46] Keep the strategic advantage.

NOTES

1. The author apologizes to fellow members of the Red Sox Nation for beginning this chapter with a quote, if perhaps apocryphal, from an archrival team member (recently departed).
2. Carl von Clausewitz, *On War,* ed. and trans. Michael Howard and Peter Paret (Princeton, N.J.: Princeton University Press, 1984), 119.
3. Ibid., 119.
4. Colin S. Gray, *Modern Strategy* (Oxford: Oxford University Press, 1999), 1. The word "competition" has been substituted for "war," which appears in the original text. The author intends to show in this chapter that space-power provides benefits beyond the scope of war.
5. Everett C. Dolman, *Pure Strategy: Power and Principle in the Space and Information Age* (New York: Frank Cass, 2005), 6.

6. Gray, *Modern Strategy*, 256–57. "Competition" is substituted for "war," and "context" for "characteristics."
7. The operating media are presented here in the order in which human strategic experience expanded into them.
8. Clausewitz, *On War*, 595.
9. Ibid., 485.
10. This point is made by Colin Gray as a "rule of strategy, . . . that anything of great strategic importance to one belligerent, for that reason has to be worth attacking by others." He states, "[S]pace warfare is a certainty in the future because the use of space in war has become vital." Colin S. Gray, *Another Bloody Century* (London: Phoenix, 2006), 307.
11. This point is raised in several sources, for example, *Report of the Commission to Assess United States National Security Space Management and Organization* (Washington, D.C., 11 January 2001), i.
12. The claim that the proper primary mission for spacepower is to prevent war was first made to the author of this chapter by Dr. S. Pete Worden, Brig. Gen., USAF (Ret.), in the fall of 2005. He expands this to claim that spacepower is the primary means that states can use to prevent wars. S. Pete Worden, "Future Strategy and Professional Development: A Roadmap" (paper submitted to the National Defense University Space Power Theory Team, 2006), 1.
13. The security concern faced by the Eisenhower administration with regard to a Soviet missile attack was so great that the president and congressional funders accepted twelve successive failures of Corona systems before the thirteenth actually delivered usable imagery. Described in William E. Burrows, *This New Ocean* (New York: Modern Library, 1999), 217, 232–33.
14. Clausewitz, *On War*, 140. In describing what he calls the "uncertainty of all information," Clausewitz describes the quality of information in war as affected by a kind of fog, which he claims "tends to make things seem grotesque and larger than they really are."
15. Google Earth is an Internet-based imagery database set in an easy-to-use imagery-manipulation program that is expanding to show relatively high-quality images of the entire Earth. "Google Earth" is a licensed trade mark of Google Incorporated of Mountain View California.
16. Tara Shankar Sahay, "Pakistan Feels Let Down by US Spy Satellites," Rediff on the Net, 13 May 1998, http://www.rediff.com/news/1998/may/13spy.htm; Krishnan Gurswamy, "India Tricks US Satellites," Associated Press, 19 May 1998, http://abcnews.go.com/sections/world/DailyNews/India980519_nukes.html.
17. Clausewitz, *On War*, 119–21.
18. "Soft power" is defined in Joseph S. Nye Jr., *Soft Power: The Means to Success in World Politics* (New York: PublicAffairs, 2004), 5.

19. Christoph Seidler, "How Iran Silences Unwanted News," ABC News/International, 1 April 2010, http://abcnews.go.com/International/iran-jamming-satellite-signals-carrying-foreign-media/story?id=10258000 (accessed 12 Oct 2010).

20. The author thanks Professor Harold Winton and Dr. James Kiras of the School of Advanced Air and Space Studies for sharing their thoughts on this matter. Professor Winton asserts his belief that violence in the sense of bloodshed is what Clausewitz had in mind in defining "war," although Professor Winton also accepts that "war" in the sense by the author is an acceptably "elastic term." Dr. Kiras points out that while Clausewitz's logic is sound, his conception of war and warfare is dated and electronic warfare is warfare nonetheless. Both interviewed by the author at Maxwell Air Force Base, 2 September 2010.

21. Clausewitz, On War, 75.

22. As Edward Luttwak points out, the realm of strategy is often punctuated by irony and paradox. See Edward N. Luttwak, Strategy: The Logic of War and Peace (Cambridge, Mass.: Belknap Press, 2003), xii.

23. Glen M. Segall, "Thoughts on Dissuasion," Journal of Military and Strategic Studies 10, no. 4 (Summer 2008): 1, http://www.jmss.org/jmss/index.php/jmss/article/viewFile/73/83.

24. This is part of the central thesis found in Everett C. Dolman, Astropolitik: Classical Geopolitics in the Space Age (London: Frank Cass, 2002).

25. Thomas C. Schelling, Arms and Influence (New Haven, Conn.: Yale University Press, 1966), 3.

26. Clausewitz, On War, 77.

27. Michael Krepon, PhD, interview by author, Washington D.C., 10 May 2007.

28. "Strategic culture" comprises a state's or nonstate actor's shared beliefs and modes of behavior, derived from common experiences and narratives and that shape ends and means for achieving national security objectives. See "Glossary of Key Terms," National Strategy Information Center, n.d., http://www.strategycenter.org/programs/adapting-americas-security-paradigm-and-security-agenda/glossary-of-key-terms/.

29. Earlier ASAT tests by the United States and the Soviet Union from the early 1960s through the 1980s may also be examples of this phenomenon. It is by no means limited to the Chinese. See description of U.S. and Soviet ASAT tests in Clayton S. Chung, Defending Space: US Anti-Satellite Warfare and Space Weaponry (New York: Osprey, 2006), 32–37.

30. Jeffrey Lewis, PhD, interview by author, Washington, D.C., 27 May 2007.

31. "Space control" is not an absolute term, nor does it imply destruction, damage, or debris creation. It merely refers to stopping the hostile or unlawful use of a capability provided by a satellite. There is no need to "wipe the sky"

of the adversary's satellites and no need to engage an entire satellite. The use of various cyber techniques to negate a small subset of very discrete satellite signals in temporary, nondestructive, and reversible ways is preferred. To date, such activity has not been defined as "warfare" in the classic sense under international law. The term also refers to preserving one's freedom of action to operate in the space environment.

32. Gray, *Another Bloody Century,* 307.

33. The "global strike complex" includes those satellites whose sensors and data links are integrated into the architecture used to find, fix, track, target, strike, and assess targets for attack.

34. See M. V. Smith, *Ten Propositions Regarding Spacepower* (Maxwell Air Force Base, Ala.: Air University Press, 2002), 70.

35. Michael Lee Lanning, *The Military 100: A Ranking of the Most Influential Military Leaders of All Time* (New York: Barnes and Noble, 1996), 276–79.

36. Department of Defense, *Annual Report to Congress: Military Power of the People's Republic of China, 2006* (Washington, D.C., 2006), 13–14, 17.

37. John Boyd's OODA loop, as described in Robert Corum, *Boyd: The Fighter Pilot Who Changed the Art of War* (New York: Back Bay Books, 2002), 327–44.

38. Clausewitz, *On War,* 84. See also *Warfighting: The Marine Corps Book of Strategy* (New York: Currency-Doubleday, 1994), 30.

39. The author served at the Combined Air Operations Center in the Strategy, Guidance, Apportionment, and Targeting Cell during the war and was involved in many discussions contemplating the benefits of the use of counterspace methods instead of lethal force. Lt. Gen. Michael Hamel, USAF (Ret.), was also involved in these discussions.

40. This point was brought out by Mahan with regard to command of the sea: total control is not necessary. This point is developed in relation to spacefaring activities in Dolman, *Astropolitik,* 34. The equator is a choke point for all satellites in earth orbit, as every satellite must cross the equator twice in each orbital rotation.

41. A good description of these strategies is found in Robert A. Pape, *Bombing to Win: Air Power and Coercion in War* (Ithaca, N.Y.: Cornell University Press, 1996), 20.

42. "On orbit" is an industry term that means more than merely "in" orbit. It implies that the satellite is within the desired orbital parameters.

43. Space as a sanctuary is asserted by many, but one of the most vociferous advocates of the concept is Washington, D.C.–based Michael Krepon of the Stimson Center. See Michael Krepon and Samuel Black, *Space Security or Anti-Satellite Weapons?* (Washington, D.C.: Stimson Center, 2010), 4.

44. See Smith, *Ten Propositions Regarding Spacepower,* 104–6.

45. John B. Sheldon, Marshall Institute Fellow (comments as panel discussant at "National Security Space: Policy and Program Developments," Marshall Institute, Washington, D.C., 6 October 2010).

46. The author apologizes once again to fellow members of the Red Sox Nation for drawing this work to a close with a quote (this one apparently authentic!) from an archrival team member. The author must point out that during a 1986 interview with a Long Island journalist, Berra admitted, "I really didn't say everything I said." Nevertheless, his brilliance as a strategist in the game of baseball is beyond question.

CHAPTER NINE

Four Dimensions to the Digital Debate

*How Should We Think Strategically
about Cyberspace and Cyberpower?*

RICHARD J. BAILEY JR.

The problem is to find a form of association which will defend and
protect with the whole common force the person and goods of each
associate, and in which each, while uniting himself with all, may still
obey himself alone, and remain as free as before.

—Jean Jacques Rousseau, *The Social Contract* (1762)

❋

The history of our human experience adapting to new technologies is lit-
tered with stories of friction and turbulence. It is not surprising that we
use the word "revolution" to describe scientific as well as governmental
upheavals.[1] Our current struggle adjusting to the information revolution provides
a case in point. Scanning the current research on cyberspace and cyberpower
reveals a myriad of diverse opinions regarding this relatively new scientific frontier.
As a result, crafting a coherent strategy for its use has been problematic. Often
both scholars and government authorities focus on the unique physical (or analogous) characteristics of cyberspace as a launching point for expressing concern
about the U.S. unpreparedness for war using these technologies. While helpful
and important, these views tend to overlook a much more foundational aspect
of cyberspace, one that perhaps presents an even greater challenge—social (and
ultimately political) tensions that our experience with cyberspace brings to the
surface. The three most visceral of these tensions are *liberty versus order, cooperation versus isolation,* and *transparency versus privacy.* While cyberspace technology
itself is a powerful resource in terms of its influence on economic, diplomatic,

and military power, it is this stoking of societal tensions that makes this domain fundamentally different and therefore presents obstacles to our strategic understanding.

This chapter offers an analysis of three of the most common debates in the prevalent literature on cyberspace and cyberpower:

- Challenges in defining cyberspace
- Arguments about whether our current military and governmental structures are organized in ways that will foster productive operations in this environment
- The question of whether this technology has the potential to change warfare in a fundamental way.

Taken collectively, this literature seems to focus on defining cyberspace as a domain (a view with implications for military applications), on reviewing present military and governmental structures (and exposing shortcomings in terms of how to address challenges unique to the application of cyberpower), and in articulating what effect this technology has on the nature and character of warfare.

In addition to the three common debates above, this study introduces a fourth concept, a point largely missing from the literature on cyberspace and cyberpower. Specifically, it highlights the need for a much more robust dialogue among cyberspace stakeholders concerning the three societal tensions described above. Just as the authors of the *Federalist Papers* struggled with these main tensions in arguing for a strong central government in the then-experimental fledgling American republic, so too does our still relatively brief experience with cyberspace and cyberpower expose challenges. This research does not present an argument for a specific target on the spectrum of these three tensions but simply calls for (1) a deeper understanding of these forces in the current debate and (2) a recognition that until these tensions are addressed, we will not understand cyberpower in a strategic way.

Ultimately, strategy depends on two fundamental endeavors—attempting to understand one's environment more fully and adapting to the effects of uncertainty that often appear in complex undertakings. In this chapter, the four dimensions of the digital frontier (the three debates commonly found in current cyberspace literature and the additional social dynamic) serve as starting points for understanding the environment of cyberspace and cyberpower. Without a basic comprehension and appreciation for these concepts, one's strategic journey cannot begin.

CYBERSPACE AND CYBERPOWER:
THE THREE PUBLIC DEBATES

> Warfare is the greatest affair of state, the basis of life and death, the
> Way (Tao) to survival or extinction. It must be thoroughly pondered
> and analyzed.
>
> —Sun Tzu, *The Art of War*

Most studies of cyberspace and cyberpower are still relatively new and therefore difficult to categorize or generalize. But they seem to attempt to answer one (or more) of three central questions: (1) How should we define cyberspace and cyberpower? (2) Are our existing military and governmental structures sufficient for both optimizing its possible strengths and defending against malicious attacks? (3) To what extent does this technology change warfare?

Defining Cyberspace and Cyberpower

William Gibson coined the term "cyberspace" in a short story called "Burning Chrome" in 1982, but his use of it in 1984's *Neuromancer* made it popular enough to join the common vernacular. Gibson's science-fiction novel is a dark and (at times) horrifying glance into the future but stands as one of the most prescient works about the integration of technology and society. Since then, a wide variety of cyberspace definitions have been published, each with its own justifications. Perhaps the biggest reason for this divergence in opinions and perspectives is that "cyberspace" is, in essence, a metaphor. To illustrate, the U.S. Air Force broadened its mission statement in 2005 to call on its airmen "to fly, fight, and win . . . in air, space, and cyberspace."[2] When we consider cyberspace as an *area* of military operations alongside air and space, it is easy to imagine it as analogous to a geospatial entity. But the actual boundaries of cyberspace are much more nuanced. In reality, "cyberspace" doesn't refer to a physical *space* at all (unless one considers the physical architecture that provides the infrastructure for its utilization). Rather, cyberspace is a metaphor helping us to visualize a domain in which information travels via networked computer systems. Ultimately, this makes defining cyberspace a unique challenge and complicates strategic understanding.

One of the most complete definitions of cyberspace is posited by Daniel Kuehl, who describes it as "a domain characterized by the use of electronics and the electromagnetic spectrum to store, modify, and exchange information via networked information systems and physical infrastructures."[3] Martin Libicki refers to three distinct layers of cyberspace: the *physical* (routers, wires, switches, etc.), the *syntactic* (the information systems themselves, along with the protocols for formatting and distributing information), and the *semantic* (the nexus between the information being transferred and the human reception and understanding of that information).[4] The synthetic aspects of these layers make cyberspace a unique operating environment. As opposed to other domains of military power (land, sea, air, and space), human-made objects must be present in order for it to exist.[5] While humankind creates objects in order to traverse and optimize the use of the physical domains, only in cyberspace is our intervention required to *create* the domain. But a pause for reflection is required here. Even if we recognize cyberspace as a unique domain by virtue of its human-made architecture, what are its associated strategic implications? Put bluntly, they are either nonexistent or irrelevant. In the extreme, the only possible connection would exist in a scenario where either the global Internet architecture was destroyed (which is difficult to imagine, considering the redundancies inherent in cyberspace's infrastructure now) or through a cataclysmic event (perhaps an electromagnetic pulse so powerful that it disables all electrical power on the planet). Ultimately, that cyberspace is a synthetic domain has little or no effect on crafting strategy. Rather, it is how we *think* about cyberspace that matters.

Cyberspace has no physical boundaries, and thus there exists no simple method of partitioning either responsibility or control. That characteristic has forced military strategists to look beyond traditional assumptions about the application of military force in a physical setting. Consider for example the factor of distance. In a physical confrontation, the distance to an enemy target is of paramount importance in a land or sea engagement and relatively important in an air engagement, but it is almost negligible in cyberspace. A skilled computer hacker with advance knowledge of an enemy's computer vulnerabilities may be able to wreak havoc not only on that enemy's computer networks but on his or her *physical* assets as well. No matter where the target is located, the hacker can engage it from practically anywhere on the planet in literally fractions of a second. Just as unsettling, dependence on computer systems and networked information has prompted many scholars and government agencies to sound alarms regarding the potential for disaster. In an age when many critical infrastructures (electrical power, pipelines, water supplies, etc.) are tied to (and dependent on) computer systems for day-to-day maintenance and operation, the full suite of cyberpower applications now unfortunately implies much more sinister possibilities.[6]

The other notable difference in defining cyberspace as a domain is that it is founded upon the flow of information. In the 1940s, Norbert Weiner, a professor of mathematics at the Massachusetts Institute of Technology, began to call for the increased use of statistical analysis to explain societal phenomena. He also began to interpret the interaction of systems (biological, mechanical, and even societal) as forms of communication, with feedback mechanisms and, more importantly, predictive qualities.[7] Weiner and his colleagues became the foundational pioneers of a transdisciplinary field of study he termed "cybernetics." For many military strategists during the middle part of the twentieth century, cybernetics offered hope that through a thorough analysis of regulatory systems, one might be able to learn enough about the enemy (and about war itself) to mitigate uncertainty in conflict. For decades, strategists began to challenge the warning of the renowned Prussian military strategist Carl von Clausewitz that "war is the realm of chance."[8] Theorists started to refer to a "Revolution in Military Affairs" (RMA) positing that information, if processed carefully and dutifully, could fundamentally change the very essence of warfare. RMA literature embraced Chinese strategist Sun Tzu's philosophy that "one who knows the enemy and knows himself will not be endangered in a hundred engagements."[9] From a military standpoint, it is why a rapidly increasing capacity to transmit, receive, and interpret data led to a new way of strategic thinking regarding warfare. Cybernetics (and the operations-research emphasis that followed) looked at ways to optimize the use of data collection and information processing to solve the complexities inherent in warfare. But according to some theorists, cyberneticists' overconfidence in the ability of communications and statistical analysis to counter uncertainty in warfare led to the "spectacular inefficiency and failure" of strategy in the Vietnam War.[10] Even after that experience, however, military strategists still looked for ways to use information and its applications to create lasting advantages in warfare. Thus, as cyberspace began to grow at a dizzying pace, with its seemingly limitless possibilities in terms of data transfer and flow, new ideas for employing that power started to emerge.

Are Current Structures Adequate?

One of the main themes present in literature on cyberspace and cyberpower is the inability of current structures to optimize their use or to defend users against malicious attacks. These structural deficiencies are found both in military organizations and in domestic and international civilian enterprises.

As stated in the section above, many definitions of cyberspace, particularly within the context of military power, use the term "domain" to describe it as an area in which operations are planned and executed in order to achieve a desired effect. One could make the argument that the U.S. military is organized more or less in terms of these domains. For example, even though the U.S. Army owns and operates air and sea assets, its primary focus is land-based warfare. In the years following World War I, advocates for airpower lobbied for a separate air service. Their main argument was that land-based strategies (and strategists) would be incapable of fully realizing what airpower could bring to a war effort. This debate was not without its drama, and airpower's most staunch advocates, like Brig. Gen. William "Billy" Mitchell, endured personal sacrifices to publicize their cause. Mitchell was actually court-martialed in 1925 for championing a separate air force and challenging the status quo.[11] Today, the U.S. military is still trying to determine the best way to organize to optimize the use of national cyberpower. While proposals for a separate cyber service have been whispered, no unified campaign has taken place. In fact, after more than ten years of structural and bureaucratic experiments, each service now utilizes cyber forces and cyber operators, and the interoperability of such forces is still far from seamless. U.S. Cyber Command (or CYBERCOM, for short) is now a subunified command under U.S. Strategic Command (with the director of the National Security Agency dual-hatted as the CYBERCOM commander), but it has far smaller forces than the service's organic cyber personnel strengths, which may call into question the DoD's desire for a holistic approach to cyber operations. Efforts have been made to increase the number of CYBERCOM personnel from nine hundred to five thousand;[12] however, given how Russia and China are both organizing professional cyber-warrior forces and potentially sanctioning thousands more in less formal groups, U.S. efforts might be insufficient.[13]

Organizing for cyberspace is also challenging civilian institutions. Consider, for example, a corporate entity based in Denver whose payroll accounts are hacked. The corporation's security office informs local police (this is unlikely, actually, but for the purpose of the discussion let us suppose the authorities are notified), who arrive on scene to investigate. The scope of the crime necessitates federal intervention, so the Federal Bureau of Investigations (FBI) gets involved. It discovers that the perpetrators diverted funds to an offshore account (which has since been drained) and that several foreign Internet protocol (IP) addresses were apparently used to complete the transfer.

These IP addresses simply pinpoint the location of senders and receivers of Internet transmissions. While not perfect investigative tools (deceptive techniques have already been used), the IP addresses provide clues to investigators in terms of potential suspects. The problem is that the FBI's jurisdiction does not automatically extend to other countries. Its own website notes that on "foreign soil, FBI special agents generally do not have authority to make arrests except in certain cases where, with the consent of the host country, Congress has granted the FBI extraterritorial jurisdiction."[14] Thus, unless a foreign country authorizes agents access (and the U.S. Congress allows such intervention), the trail stops cold. This example highlights a few structural shortcomings. First, as in any noncyber-related crime, national sovereignty complicates an investigation. International law-enforcement entities such as Interpol have attempted to overcome such obstacles, but the traditional Westphalian construct still grants nations the right to deny external access. Similar to the military example of kinetic effects described in the previous section, the factor of distance is no longer an issue in cyber crime. A clean getaway is now a matter of only a keystroke (a well-planned and crafted keystroke, but a keystroke nonetheless). Ultimately, no international agency exists to respond to crimes in cyberspace.[15] Second, what would the U.S. response have been if the target had been the U.S. Government Reserve Bank and the goal for the attack had been to cripple the American financial system? Just as puzzling, what organization would investigate and respond to the attack? This new twist illustrates not only the blurred distinction between war, terrorism, and crime in cyberspace (a distinction that is difficult enough in the physical world) but also how overdue is a whole-of-government approach (tying together the Department of Defense, Department of Energy, Federal Communications Commission, Department of Homeland Defense, etc.) to defend against potential cyber threats.[16]

Internationally, the challenge that calls for a unified approach to cyberspace (and cyber security) is even more complex. Take for example a letter sent by the Chinese and Russian governments to the United Nations (UN) in September 2011 that called for an "International Code of Conduct for Information Security."[17] While some states agreed that the UN should take a more central role in regulating Internet usage (or at least promoting standards of Internet security), the United States opposed such measures. It feared that the proposal would provide legitimacy to states that currently suppress access to online information to protect their authoritarian regimes.[18] While the UN is considering possible action, no coherent policy plan has taken shape. Thus, the only current body that has any viable regulatory control over cyberspace is the International Corporation for Assigned Names and Numbers (ICANN), a private, nonprofit organization formed by private Internet stakeholders that coordinates unique addresses to computers so that individuals or entities can find one another online.[19] ICANN does an admirable job of organizing an almost incomprehensible expansion of global Internet users, but its mandate falls well short of establishing (and more importantly, enforcing) cyber-security standards.

In summary, much of the current literature on cyberspace and cyberpower points to domestic and international organizations that are currently ill equipped to address many of the concerns about war, crime, and terrorism in the information age. This has impacts both in the private sector and in the military, for which providing national security becomes a much more complex challenge.

How Does This Technology Change Warfare?

Theorists today debate the scope of the effect that cyberpower has (and will have) on warfare. It is not unlike what occurred in the years during and just after World War I, which had a dramatic effect on the thinking of budding airpower theorists. Consider historian John H. Morrow Jr.'s account of the thinking of airpower advocates just after the war: "Air warfare was the apotheosis of warfare in modern, technological, and industrial society. It literally and figuratively enabled its combatants to rise above the anonymity of mass society and modern warfare to wage a clean and individual struggle. It allowed the preservation of notions of sport and individual combat in a war in which land and naval conflict amply demonstrated that modern warfare had rendered such ideals obsolete and ludicrous."[20]

To some, as awkward as it seems, military airpower provided an element of glamour and elegance to a ground war that the entire world saw as horrific and barbaric. But more importantly, it sparked a dialogue about what airpower could do from a strategic standpoint. Giulio Douhet's classic work *The Command of the Air* captures this perfectly: "To have command of the air means to be in a position to wield offensive power so great it defies human imagination."[21] If airpower could strike directly at the heart of an enemy, it might convince that nation to end hostilities earlier, or in an even more desirable outcome, reject the notion of war altogether. Armies had always been assembled to push toward an objective or fortify a defense of the treasured populace. But against airpower those armies could no longer shield the city. Aircraft could, by design, circumvent those defenses and deliver an assault to the decision-making body itself. This gave airpower advocates an added motivation, particularly given an interwar period characterized by abhorrence of war and an insistence on doing whatever it took to prevent the atrocities of World War I from reoccurring. Think tanks such as the Air Corps Tactical School in Montgomery, Alabama, assembled some of the preeminent airpower advocates to establish tactics, techniques, and procedures to employ airpower in combat, laying the foundation for airpower doctrine. In fact, many of those founding principles are still pertinent to air forces. America's relatively scant experience with cyberpower has yet to yield either outspoken advocates or unified strategies. The U.S. Air Force is considering the creation of a formal Cyber Air Corps Tactical School, modeled after its airpower namesake, but has yet to provide proper funding or full-time personnel.

Some cyberpower advocates have claimed that the new technology changes how states should organize, train, and equip forces for future conflicts, just as airpower advocates did in the years between the two world wars. Much of the RMA literature offered the possibility that cyberpower would make war almost obsolete, particularly if potential enemies could be deterred directly at the source of decision-making authority (just as airpower advocates saw targeting hubs of industry and war-making infrastructures). This led some to predict a sea change in military thinking. Consider Martin Libicki's prophecy from 1995: "Future changes in information technology will . . . certainly rewrite the assumptions—both political and military—on which national security rests."[22]

But in many ways, while airpower advocates were justified in pushing for a new way of thinking about war and certainly for a new way of utilizing airpower to alter the battlespace, airpower did not (as some had predicted) become a panacea for warring nations. In the century since airpower was first used in combat, warfare has continued (for the most part) to rely on a nation's ability to employ land and naval power in conjunction with air forces.

Ultimately, the debate over whether cyberpower will revolutionize combat must come down to a distillation of the key elements inherent in war. One of the most pertinent elements of the cyberspace discussion is conflict's *human* element. Some cyberpower advocates have applied Douhet's philosophy of airpower to cyberspace, claiming that cyberpower might render the other, more traditional military forms of power almost obsolete. If the political object is the "original motive" for war, as Clausewitz suggests, how does the human aspect of the application of cyberpower affect this dynamic?[23] Early airpower advocates rested their arguments on the ability of air forces to penetrate enemy defenses without interference, thereby directly influencing (through overwhelming destruction) the enemy's will to fight. Could the same be true for cyberwar? If cyberpower has the potential to take down power grids, degrade water supplies, and shut down transportation control mechanisms (among many other things), can it directly influence a state's ability to wage war or a populace's willingness to support it?

In addition, one must ask whether humankind's early embrace of cyberpower as a military weapon is indicative of a next step in an evolution of warfare, one that looks for ways to minimize its barbarism and close-up conflict. In line with Morrow's quote about the elegance of airpower, cyberpower to some may provide an even less costly way to coerce, compel, or even cripple an enemy to achieve one's political objectives. The current national debate regarding the use of unmanned aerial drones provides another example.[24] In essence, this evolution may indicate a tendency to *remove* the human element from the war equation. It still must be stated, however, that even if one imagines potential future cyber-centric conflicts without human beings as directly involved in combat as in previous, physical battles, the effects will still be visceral and devastating. Human dependence on networked systems for the daily conveniences of their lives has given rise to a dramatic vulnerability (particularly in ties to critical infrastructures and financial networks), one that cyberpower literature strongly addresses. The human element will also be present in both the decision to employ cyberpower and on the losing side to yield. As David Lonsdale puts it, "Regardless of what character a war assumes, it is always a human activity, in that humans do the fighting and also that war is a contest between opposing human wills. The involvement of humans is essential to the existence of the climate of war."[25] If war is waged to achieve political objectives and humans define those objectives, war will remain a human endeavor, even if the tactics become more and more automated.

AN ADDITIONAL FRAMING OF THE CYBERSPACE DILEMMA: A TAPESTRY OF SOCIAL TENSIONS

To be provident is impossible, for without social regulation there can be no obligation to respect the interests, rights, and property of others.
—Kenneth Waltz, *Man, the State, and War*

America has always been torn between the ideal and the real, between noble goals and inevitable compromises.
—Jon Meacham, *Thomas Jefferson: The Art of Power*

The preceding analyses focused on three debates prevalent throughout the nascent literature on cyberspace and cyberpower: the difficulty in defining cyberspace, the argument over the inability of current structures to respond to the new technology, and a disagreement over its effect on warfare. While helpful and important, these debates seem to have overshadowed a fourth, and perhaps the most important, debate regarding cyberspace. This fourth debate may actually be the biggest obstacle to understanding cyberpower strategically, yet it is rarely discussed. It concerns the social impact of the technology, and it affects our most basic human principles. If one assumes that power is inherently socially constructed, a strategy for using power must be defined as "the creation and manipulation of social relations that allows for the exercise of national resources toward a common goal."[26] The social (and ultimately political) tensions that the human experience with cyberspace brings to the surface have yet to be addressed in a meaningful way, either by theorists or policy makers. The three most visceral of these tensions are: *liberty versus order, cooperation versus isolation,* and *transparency versus privacy.* Cyberspace technology is a powerful and (arguably) game-changing resource in terms of economic, diplomatic, and military power, but this stoking of societal tensions makes this domain fundamentally different from the others and therefore presents obstacles to our strategic understanding.

Liberty versus Order

In 1958, President Dwight Eisenhower secured funding for a new research wing for the Pentagon, and the Advanced Research Project Agency (ARPA) was born. Originally, the agency's mission was to advance the understanding of nuclear and ballistic-missile technology, but it was a side project of an engineer, J. C. R. Licklider, that made ARPA famous.[27] His vision of sharing computer power in an open forum led to partnering with university research centers and planted the seeds for the modern Internet. But these early developers were much more hopeful about what sharing information could bring than fearful of any harm that could come from a misuse of the technology. In fact, most cyberspace historians posit that the early pioneers were so enamored with the idea of a rapidly evolving marketplace of ideas (the liberty of thought and the freedom to share those thoughts) that they paid very little attention to the propensity for nefarious activity.

Today, individuals have the ability to share their views instantaneously with audiences larger than ever before, but this ability brings both positive and negative side effects. On the one hand, it is evident that cyberspace provides a mechanism for rapid social mobilization. A policy memorandum from the Program on New Approaches to Research and Security (PONARS) Eurasia in May 2011 states: "No region, state, or form of government can remain immune to the impact of new information and communication technologies on social and political movements."[28] On the other hand, the memo grants that the technology can have different effects, depending on political and social contexts.

The dark side of Internet freedom, as Evgeny Morozov interprets it, is the by-product of *cyber-utopianism* (the belief in the "emancipatory nature of online communication") and *Internet-centrism* (the practice of reframing social problems to fit within an Internet-driven solution set).[29] When embraced together, these concepts lead to a naiveté about the process of social and political reform and, in extreme cases, overconfidence in the ability of this technology to spur a global democratic revolution independently. Authoritarian regimes, however, are not likely to cede power automatically; they have learned to use the technology to strengthen their control over their subjects through modified propaganda techniques, targeted censorship, and highly advanced surveillance of proposed threats.[30] In essence, cyberspace has established itself as a new battleground where different views are competing for legitimacy and influence in the age-old struggle over the role and scope of government.

As stated in the previous section, several nations (China and Russia being the most vocal) are pressuring the United Nations to take a stronger role in Internet governance. But because freedom of expression is a fundamental characteristic of Western democracies, many nations will eschew strong central control over cyberspace, even at the risk of a higher level of vulnerability.

In the United States specifically, the struggle between liberty and order can be found in the dialogues concerning how to respond to threats in cyberspace. For example, since the early days of the American republic, fears of overreach by the federal government have been manifested in structural safeguards. Long-held practices like *posse comitatus* (which dictates that the government cannot use military forces for law enforcement purposes) continue to be put to the test, particularly as the already-blurred lines between crime, terrorism, and war become even more muddled in cyberspace.[31] While the number of reported malicious acts in cyberspace continues to rise (by some estimates at an exponential rate), the U.S. government has still not settled on what entities are best equipped and designed to respond to them. Without a doubt, the Department of Defense, Department of Homeland Security, and the National Security Agency have vested stakes in the process. But the Federal Communications Commission, the Department of Commerce, the Department of Energy, and civilian corporations who own and operate the nation's banking and critical infrastructure systems should also be on the list of stakeholders and therefore need to contribute to a response mechanism.

But no matter what the shape of the response force or which agency or agencies take the lead, most preventative measures will call for some type of screening or monitoring in cyberspace. Such measures will keep the entities charged with response and security measures better informed of potential malicious activities. But suspicions will arise that simple monitoring may empower the government to dictate online content and ultimately overreach in terms of regulating what ideas and views are to be shared online.

Cooperation versus Isolation

Former secretary of state Henry Kissinger opined that George Washington's warning about permanent international alliances (from his farewell address) reflected America's view at the time that it "could best serve the cause of democracy by practicing its virtues at home" rather than influencing others abroad.[32] If true, the nation's view regarding international engagement has certainly matured over the last two centuries; the United States has signed over 150 international treaties since the ratification of the Constitution. Perhaps these obligations support the argument of Robert Axelrod, who states that "mutual cooperation can emerge in a world of egoists without central control by starting with a cluster of individuals who rely on reciprocity."[33] At the heart of the debate lies a fairly straightforward question: Does U.S. cooperation help to advance the nation's interests, or would isolationism help it to focus energies and resources better to foster greater domestic prosperity and security? National leaders have been tasked with answering this question since the birth of the republic, and at critical times the result has meant the difference between war and peace.

Thus far, the U.S. experience with cooperation in cyberspace has been characterized by cautious engagement. As stated in an earlier section, the United States voiced opposition to the Russian-Chinese proposal of a UN code of conduct. While such an agreement would in some ways serve as a symbol of international cooperation, its underpinnings would be antithetical to this nation's commitment to freedom of expression. However, in May 2011, the White House released its *International Strategy for Cyberspace,* a road map for future cooperation: "The benefits of networked technology should not be reserved to a few privileged nations, or a privileged few within them. But connectivity is no end in itself; it must be supported by a cyberspace that is open to innovation, interoperable the world over, secure enough to earn people's trust, and reliable enough to support their work."[34] The document does an admirable job of expressing its goals for networked cooperation but falls short in terms of identifying agency mechanisms for accomplishing those goals.

The line between cooperation and isolation in cyberspace is complicated also by the hesitancy of advanced cyberpowers to share technological advantages with either near peers or less advanced states. This hesitancy probably stems from the nature of cyber weapons themselves. Consider a cyber attack by state A to disrupt an electrical power grid in state B. First, state A studies the supervisory control and data acquisition (SCADA) system that monitors and regulates State B's grid. For convenience, that SCADA system is connected to the Internet; that way, engineers can adjust settings from remote locations. This is not an uncommon practice today for most critical infrastructure systems. State A designs a computer virus that will dupe the SCADA system into throwing generators off cycle, thereby collapsing the power grid completely. The virus, however, exploits a particular network vulnerability in state B's architecture. Once the virus is discovered, state B would be able not only to patch its network vulnerability but to study and replicate the virus to use on its adversaries.

The preceding example illustrates why cyber weapons are sometimes referred to as "one-trick ponies," which can be used only once, because victims will quickly develop defenses against them and be able to employ them as well. Logically, then, these types of weapons are likely to influence decision makers in two fundamental ways. First, there is a hesitation to use them; decision makers would be unlikely to use a particular cyber weapon, for example, if they feared they might need to employ it in a larger, more important conflict later (that is, were unwilling to show their cards too early). Second, and critical to the cooperation-isolation discussion, is that states are deterred from sharing information on such weapons with others by the fact that the more widespread the knowledge regarding specific tactics in cyberspace, the less likely those tactics will be of any use in conflict. This may explain why many states classify their cyber programs at the highest levels. As the discussion below will highlight, however, keeping secrets in an age of ever-increasing information flow is becoming a much more daunting task.

Transparency versus Privacy

Closely related to the two tensions discussed above is a debate over how much transparency is needed to craft a coherent strategy; it continues to generate strong opinions. Consider the following critique from Thomas Rid's 2013 article in *New Republic:* "[It] is telling that an administration that vowed to be unprecedentedly open and transparent with the public, while being tough on national security leaks, has chosen to ignore these principles in its approach to cyber security. The Obama White House treats cyber security as a mission that the public can be informed about through furtive leaks and unidentified officials, cloak-and-dagger style."[35] As mentioned in the previous section, it is expected that increased international cooperation will probably require more transparency in the form of information and technology sharing.

But will cooperation even among U.S. entities require more transparency? One problem that security experts are observing, for example, is that corporations are not generally sharing information on attacks against their infrastructures, nor are they admitting it when proprietary information is hacked. They keep quiet for two reasons. First, corporations don't want to shine a light on vulnerabilities of their computer networks. Such publicity might invite repeat attacks. Second, and perhaps just as important, exposing security vulnerabilities might lower stockholder confidence and do financial harm to the company. Thus, corporations are beginning to accept greater intrusions, a situation exacerbated by the increasing complexities of daily threats: "Defenders can no longer routinely assume that threats will be identifiable, singular, and sequential; they must also be able to respond to aggregated threats that can be labyrinth in structure and discontinuous in occurrence."[36]

Transparency is not necessarily a matter of choice, however. One need only contrast the strong language then-secretary of state Hillary Clinton used to promote Internet freedom in January of 2010 and the seemingly incongruous actions the government took in the aftermath of Pvt. 1st Class Bradley Manning's infamous Wikileaks file-sharing scandal just weeks later. These actions included denial of Wikileaks website's U.S. domain name and allegations of government monitoring of Twitter accounts.[37] In fact, some argue that as it is getting harder to guarantee computer network security, so too is it harder to keep anything secret. Joel Brenner states: "As we have seen over and over again, these technologies are creating previously unimaginable transparency—voluntary and involuntary, good, bad, and indifferent—in all walks of life: personal, commercial, governmental, and military."[38] This forced transparency may not be as bitter a pill to swallow for younger generations, who have virtually grown up online and have grown accustomed to having their private lives available for public consumption.[39] But for older generations, the modicum of privacy they were raised to expect is no longer guaranteed. That can be a disconcerting revelation.

How does this loss of privacy affect the debate over cyberspace? First, as related to the tensions previously described, individuals might be asked to forfeit some control over their own private Internet usage and allow governing authorities the ability to monitor systems for security risks. Corporations might be forced to admit breaches to their own systems in order to assist in securing other networks. Nations might soon be mandated by international law to share in best security practices with other nations and to open their borders to assist in international cybercrime investigations.

As for the military, the loss of privacy may have massive ramifications. Consider an extreme example in which no network was impervious to intrusion. The intelligence community would need to shift its efforts substantially away from collection, focusing instead much more on deception. Thus, strategy would involve creating duplicate files with purposefully erroneous information to throw off intruders. Military planning would also be hugely affected. If planners had no guarantees that their operational plans could be kept private, would that change the way they planned? Would it force military planners to adopt and utilize new tactics? The possibilities for and probabilities of change are staggering.

Each of the three social tensions highlighted above is rarely described in the literature on cyberspace and cyberpower, yet all are critical to gaining strategic insight for using the technology. Ultimately, the United States will have to address these issues honestly and frankly. Without that dialogue, we will never fully understand cyberpower strategically.

CONCLUSION

> It will be forgotten, on the one hand, that jealousy is the usual concomitant of violent love, and that the noble enthusiasm of liberty is too apt to be infected with a spirit of narrow and illiberal distrust. On the other hand, it will be equally forgotten, that the vigour of government is essential to the security of liberty; that, in the contemplation of a sound and well informed judgment, their interests

can never be separated; and that a dangerous ambition more often lurks behind the specious mask of zeal for the rights of the people, than under the forbidding appearances of zeal for the firmness and efficiency of government.

—Publius (Alexander Hamilton), *Federalist No. 1*

A review of the top CNN news stories of 2013 reveals that Hamilton's concerns are still alive and well in the United States. Edward Snowden's release of National Security Agency documents ranked near the top of the list of the biggest news events of the year, behind only the election of Pope Francis, the Boston Marathon bombings, and the death of Nelson Mandela.[40] It reinforces the point that the United States is still struggling with how to balance the social dynamics of the virtual world.

There are several different perspectives to the debate on cyberspace and cyberpower. The three most prevalent discussions in the literature concern challenges in defining cyberspace; arguments about whether our current military and governmental structures are organized to be able to operate in this new environment; and whether or not this technology has the potential to change warfare fundamentally. A fourth dimension to the debate, however, rarely discussed, concerns three societal tensions (liberty versus order, cooperation versus isolation, and transparency versus privacy) critical to the development of a viable cyberpower strategy. Until this social dimension is explored through both cultural and legal frameworks, cyber-integrated coherent national (and international) strategies will remain difficult to construct.

Everett Carl Dolman defines *strategy* as "a plan for attaining continual advantage."[41] In the context of crafting a strategy for a nation, it is useful to broaden that definition slightly: *Strategy is a continuous, artistic endeavor to optimize competitive advantage through an understanding of one's environment and an adaptation to uncertainty.* As stated at the start of this chapter, two fundamentals of any strategic venture are trying to make sense of context and adapting to the unknown or unforeseen. The last two decades of our exploration with cyberspace and cyberpower have resulted in introductory attempts to identify the environment of cyberspace. Strategic cyber goals generally center on maximizing the freedom of information (and the benefits that can result from an unobstructed marketplace of ideas) while guaranteeing a modicum of security, a balance that can be extremely difficult to attain. The manifestations of cyberpower (national policies, international laws and treaties, and generally accepted practices) and the intricacies of employment tools (infrastructure, network, supply chain design, and hardware and software standards) are seldom clearly articulated. Thus, further explorations of the common debates in cyberspace are required, in addition to serious discussions about the societal tensions inherent in our relatively new human experience with cyberspace and cyberpower.

The purpose of this analysis is not to advocate specific policy positions but rather to offer ways to think about how to create a strategy for cyberspace and cyberpower. Questions that will have to be considered and addressed in relation to the three social tensions might resemble the following:

- How much personal liberty are we willing to sacrifice to secure the cyberspace domain? In other words, would we allow the government to monitor our Internet use if there were assurances that the detection software only looked for *malware* (malicious software) but ignored the *content* of our activity? Policy makers and technical experts will need to discuss methods of Internet scanning to determine the limits of the possible.

- Similarly, are individuals (and larger entities) willing to give up some level of basic privacy in order to make cyberspace more transparent (and therefore more stable)? For example, should the government *mandate* that corporations report all cyber intrusions? Although that would potentially cause turbulence with shareholders (who would feel less confident in the security of their investments), it would create a level of awareness that would force more comprehensive security reforms.

- Do we need to cooperate more with other nations in this global regime, or should we focus more on isolating and protecting national networks? In other words, should the United States start to look for diplomatic ways to adjust the language of the proposed International Code of Conduct for Internet Security to make it more palatable? Should it permanently open its cyber borders to international criminal investigations?

The preceding questions are presented solely to show the gravity of the implications of future policy debates. But as mentioned earlier, these determinations (and many others) could form a necessary foundation for a sound (and comprehensive) strategic understanding of cyberpower.

The quote from *The Federalist* at the beginning of this section alludes to the societal debates that the original architects of the U.S. democracy faced. While it is certainly audacious to claim that the task that lies ahead can compare to the monumental struggles that shaped the radical American democratic experiment, there are definitely echoes of the past that will again need to be confronted. Ultimately, we must frame the debate by considering that power, in essence, is a socially constructed phenomenon:

> Hiding within our common-sense use of power is a rather more banal but crucial observation: that power is only produced through the interactions of social beings, and has no existence outside of social action. Power does not exist without the relationships through which it is manifest. The operations of power may release the potency of an actor's capabilities, but without social interaction these capabilities may as well not exist. Power is not inherent, but must be somehow produced, and it is only made apparent by the effects it has on others. All power can therefore be characterized as "the production, in and through social relations, of effects on actors that shape their capacity to control their fate."[42]

The recognition that power is a social commodity leads to the conclusion that societal tensions must be confronted, as a basis for understanding strategy more fully. Until these tensions are explored in cyberspace, the full potential of our strategic understanding in this domain will, unfortunately, remain elusive.

NOTES

1. Thomas S. Kuhn, *The Structure of Scientific Revolutions* (Chicago: University of Chicago Press, 1996), 93–94.
2. The U.S. Air Force's mission statement is published on its public website ("Our Mission," U.S. Air Force, http://www.airforce.com/learn-about/our-mission) along with the organization's values, core competencies, and history.
3. Daniel T. Kuehl, "From Cyberspace to Cyber Power: Defining the Problem," in *Cyber Power and National Security,* ed. Franklin D. Kramer, Stuart H. Starr, and Larry K. Wentz (Dulles, Va.: Potomac Books, 2009), 26.
4. Martin C. Libicki, *Conquest in Cyberspace: National Security and Information Warfare* (New York: Cambridge University Press, 2007), 8–9.
5. John B. Sheldon, "Toward a Theory of Cyber Power: Strategic Purpose in Peace and War," in *Cyberspace and National Security: Threats, Opportunities,*

and Power in a Virtual World, ed. Derek S. Reveron (Washington, D.C.: Georgetown University Press, 2012), 212.

6. For an excellent example of a nightmare scenario involving the use of cyber-power to inflict chaos on American society, see Richard A. Clarke and Robert K. Knake, *Cyber War: The Next Threat to National Security and What to Do about It* (New York: HarperCollins, 2010), 64–65.

7. Adam Brate, *Technomanifestos: Visions from the Information Revolutionaries* (New York: Texere, 2002), 18.

8. Carl von Clausewitz, *On War,* ed. and trans. Michael Howard and Peter Paret (Princeton, N.J.: Princeton University Press, 1976), 101.

9. Sun Tzu, *The Art of War,* trans. Ralph D. Sawyer (Boulder, Colo.: Westview, 1994), 179.

10. Antoine Bousquet, *The Scientific Way of Warfare: Order and Chaos on the Battlefields of Modernity* (New York: Columbia University Press, 2009), 160.

11. Conrad C. Crane, *Bombs, Cities and Civilians* (Lawrence: University Press of Kansas, 1993), 16.

12. Amber Corrin, "Pentagon Staffing Up to Address Cyber Concerns," FCW: The Business of Federal Technology, 28 January 2013, http://fcw.com/articles/2013/01/28/cybercommand-hiring.aspx.

13. For an analysis of Russia and China's approach to cyberpower, see Nikolas K. Gvosdev, "The Bear Goes Digital: Russia and Its Cyber Capabilities" (173–190), and Nigel Inkster, "China in Cyberspace" (191–206), in Reveron, *Cyberspace and National Security;* and Timothy L. Thomas, "Nation-State Cyber Strategies: Examples from Russia and China," in Kramer, Starr, and Wentz, *Cyber Power and National Security,* 465–90.

14. The Federal Bureau of Investigation's formal website publishes information about the organization, including its jurisdiction (and the limits on that jurisdiction): "Frequently Asked Questions," The FBI: Federal Bureau of Investigation, http://www.fbi.gov/about-us/faqs. The FBI website also has a page devoted to its cybercrime division, with in-depth accounts of cases where the agency did get international cooperation to topple cyber-driven theft operations. See "Cyber Crime," FBI, http://www.fbi.gov/about-us/investigate/cyber.

15. For an in-depth review of the problems of cybercrime and organizational challenges, as well as a legal framework for the blurred distinction between war, crime, and terrorism in cyberspace, see Susan W. Brenner, *Cyberthreats: The Emerging Fault Lines of the Nation State* (Oxford: Oxford University Press, 2009).

16. Joel Brenner provides a compelling case for an overhaul of government cyberpower capabilities by examining the 1986 Goldwater-Nichols Act, which helped the Department of Defense integrate its service forces for more joint operations. He recommends that model for a whole-of-government

approach to responding to cyber threats. See Joel Brenner, *America the Vulnerable: Inside the New Threat Matrix of Digital Espionage, Crime, and Warfare* (New York: Penguin Books, 2011), 218–19.

17. Timothy Farnsworth, "China and Russia Submit Cyber Proposal," *Arms Control Today,* November 2011, http://www.armscontrol.org/act/2011_11/China_and_Russia_Submit_Cyber_Proposal.

18. For an analysis of the authoritarian use (or misuse) of cyberspace to bolster power, see Evgeny Morozov, *The Net Delusion: The Dark Side of Internet Freedom* (New York: PublicAffairs, 2011).

19. For detailed information, visit ICANN, http://www.icann.org.

20. John H. Morrow Jr., *The Great War in the Air: Military Aviation from 1909 to 1921* (Washington, D.C.: Smithsonian Institution Press, 1993), 366.

21. Giulio Douhet, *The Command of the Air,* ed. Joseph Patrick Harahan and Richard H. Kohn (Tuscaloosa: University of Alabama Press, 2009), 23. The original Italian title translates more directly to *"The Dominion of the Air."*

22. Martin C. Libicki, *The Mesh and the Net: Speculations on Armed Conflict in a Time of Free Silicon* (Washington, D.C.: National Defense University, 1995), 24.

23. Clausewitz, *On War,* 81.

24. Here I am referring to unmanned aerial vehicles (UAVs) or remotely piloted aircraft (RPAs). My colleagues who operate these systems detest the term "drones," and understandably so, because of the human energy and talent involved in their use. Unfortunately, however, "drone" has become the term of choice in the public sphere. It is with my apologies to the RPA community that it is used here.

25. David J. Lonsdale, *The Nature of War in the Information Age: Clausewitzian Future* (London: Frank Cass, 2004), 36.

26. For an analysis of the social aspect of power and its application to cyberspace, see David J. Betz and Tim Stevens, *Cyberspace and the State: Toward a Strategy for Cyber-Power* (London: International Institute for Strategic Studies, 2011), 42–48.

27. See more about the contributions of J. C. R. Licklider, as well as an analysis of his "Man-Computer Symbiosis," in Brate, *Technomanifestos,* 86–113.

28. Ekaterina Stepanova, *The Role of Information Communication Technologies in the "Arab Spring": Implications beyond the Region,* PONARS Eurasia Policy Memo 159 (Washington, D.C., May 2011), 3.

29. Morozov, *Net Delusion,* xiii–xvii.

30. Ibid., 82.

31. S. Brenner, *Cyberthreats,* 177–79.

32. Henry Kissinger, *Diplomacy* (New York: Simon and Schuster, 1994), 32–33.

33. Robert Axelrod, *The Evolution of Cooperation* (New York: Basic Books, 1984), 69.

34. Barack H. Obama, *International Strategy for Cyberspace: Prosperity, Security, and Openness in a Networked World* (Washington, D.C.: Office of the President of the United States, May 2011), 25.

35. Thomas Rid, "Cyber Fail: The Obama Administration's Lousy Record on Cyber Security," *New Republic,* 4 February 2013, http://www.newrepublic.com/article/112314/obama-administrations-lousy-record-cyber-security.

36. S. Brenner, *Cyberthreats,* 54.

37. Dan Sabbagh, "Hillary Clinton's Speech: Shades of Hypocrisy on Internet Freedom," *Guardian,* 15 February 2011, http://www.guardian.co.uk/world/2011/feb/15/hillary-clinton-internet-freedom. For an in-depth discussion of PFC Manning's trial and assumption of full responsibility for the leak, see Spencer Ackerman, "Bradley Manning Takes 'Full Responsibility' for Giving WikiLeaks Huge Government Data Trove," *Wired,* 28 February 2013, http://www.wired.com/threatlevel/2013/02/bradley-manning/.

38. J. Brenner, *America the Vulnerable,* 184.

39. For a discussion of how different experiences with the Internet have created a generation gap in terms of expected rights to privacy, see Emily Nussbaum, "Kids, the Internet, and the End of Privacy: The Greatest Generation Gap since Rock and Roll," *New York Magazine,* 12 February 2007, http://nymag.com/news/features/27341/.

40. For a full list of the top ten news stories of 2013, see "What Stories Got You Talking in 2014?," CNN, n.d., http://www.cnn.com/interactive/2013/12/specials/yir-top-stories-vote/.

41. Everett Carl Dolman, *Pure Strategy: Power and Principle in the Space and Information Age* (New York: Frank Cass, 2005), 6.

42. Betz and Stevens, *Cyberspace and the State,* 42.

CHAPTER TEN

Staying Regular?

The Importance of Irregular Warfare to the Modern Strategist

MARK O. YEISLEY

A s the other contributors to this collection thus far have pointed out, strategy is a multifaceted ideal that is informed by a wide variety of academic and military disciplines. Since humans emerged on the African plains they have faced threats and adversaries that have challenged and often outclassed them in terms of power and position. Gaining the advantage has demanded the development of strategy to prevail over these adversaries, and the pursuit of useful and correct strategy has been carried out for thousands of generations. From Hannibal's envelopment of the Roman legions at Cannae to the defeat of Napoleon's forces at Waterloo, generals of nations either have developed and implemented strategy effectively to defeat the armies of enemy states that challenged them in battle or have themselves faced defeat.

Twentieth-century conflict was in many ways no different: two devastatingly costly wars spanned nearly the entire globe, a nuclear stalemate developed between the superpower winners of World War II, and the United States emerged as the global hegemon following the collapse of the Soviet Union. The two world wars, though fought for differing strategic and operational imperatives, were waged using military strategies that would have been familiar to such classical strategic thinkers as Carl von Clausewitz, Basil Liddell Hart, or Alfred Thayer Mahan.[1] Militaries faced each other in formal battles decided by maneuver, deception, and operational brilliance; although friction and the "fog" of war played their respective parts, victory was usually attained by the side that outthought and outfought the other.

U.S. grand strategy during the Cold War focused on the twin concepts of containment and deterrence; strategic- and operational-level plans were laid out in the greatest detail to allow the United States to act proactively to contain Soviet expansion and prevent a nuclear Armageddon. Since the end of the Cold War, however, the United States has struggled to define a strategic role for itself. From Mogadishu to the ongoing crises in the Middle East and Afghanistan, the United States has assumed a more reactive role, responding to multiple contingencies that tax its military might in irregular warfare rather than in conventional state-on-state engagements. Despite its victories in the aforementioned conflicts, the United States is now in what some scholars characterize as an "era of strategic failure," struggling to understand and meet the demands of irregular war. This chapter looks at the characteristics of irregular warfare, how classical and modern strategists have viewed this phenomenon, and how airpower can contribute to victory in these types of campaigns in the future.

Since 2001 the United States has conducted ongoing counterinsurgency and counterterrorism operations in Afghanistan, Iraq, Pakistan, Yemen, the Arabian Peninsula, and across the Horn of Africa. As of this writing the United States is engaged in airstrikes against the Islamic State of Iraq and Syria (ISIS) and is debating whether airpower will be enough in the coming years to quell this movement. During the same period there have been only two cases of conventional conflict where the United States has faced a state-level adversary.[2] Thus while conventional conflict has become increasingly uncommon, incidences of irregular warfare have remained anything but.

The United States was indeed a force to be reckoned with in the conventional state-on-state conflicts of the twentieth century, but it has had far less success when it comes to unconventional warfare. It failed to keep South Vietnam from falling into communist hands and has paid a heavy toll in blood and treasure in its ongoing struggle against al Qaeda, ISIS, and other nonstate actors. While the airpower arm of U.S. military power has served brilliantly in these conflicts, it has not always succeeded in deterring its adversaries from continuing to pursue their goals.

Some claim the United States has struggled to integrate its instruments of power correctly to meet the challenges of modern unconventional adversaries. Others argue that the underlying strategies employed to address these adversaries are designed more for conventional enemies and provide little traction against terror groups such as ISIS. This leads one to wonder: Is the problem a failure to match desired ends with the means available? Or is it a lack of an effective use of the instruments of power? Or the ways we seek to achieve our ends? The answers to these questions are beyond the scope of this short chapter, which offers instead a frank discussion of how both classical and modern strategic thinking can be applied to modern unconventional conflict. In addition, a critical review of airpower theory will show that strategies for the application of airpower against these threats already exist and can be used effectively in current and future conflicts of this type. An examination of the characteristics, causes, and effects of irregular warfare will help set the stage for the remainder of this discussion.

CHARACTERISTICS OF IRREGULAR WARFARE

A robust understanding of some of the characteristics of irregular warfare is essential to the modern strategist, for three reasons. First, winners in these conflicts are more difficult to predict a priori than they are in conventional ones, making strategic calculations for engaging in them uncertain and risky. Second, these conflicts often last longer than their conventional counterparts, as challenger groups do not desire a return to the status quo ante and states usually do not wish to risk the appearance of weakness by appeasing challengers' demands. Third, they are costly in both blood and treasure due to their extended durations and zero-sum nature.

Who Wins and Who Loses? Not Always an Easy Question

When diplomacy fails, states may attempt to resolve contentious issues between them via the use of military force. During these "conventional" conflicts state military forces are pitted against each other on fields of battle; the disputes are formally decided when both sides recognize which of them has the superior force and the weaker side yields. Since each side's military force is usually discernible, determinations of relative strength are made via intelligence collection and analysis. Since states should not risk squandering military might in conflicts where they may not prevail, they will usually make rational decisions not to engage in unequal power struggles. This by extension often limits both conflict duration and casualty potential, as wartime decision matrices are more or less clearly defined.

Decisions for participation in irregular conflicts are more difficult; while state military and police power is usually well known, deducing the strength of challenger forces is demanding (if not impossible) prior to the outbreak of hostilities. A state's forces overwhelm those of the challenger in most cases; the latter are thus unlikely to reveal their numerical and material strengths until it becomes necessary.[3] Since information asymmetries often exist until forces have engaged in conflict, determinations of relative superiority remain unclear during the initial stages as well. While the primary goal of the state is to retain its hold on sovereign power, it is difficult (if not impossible) to deduce the true goals of the challenger force; these are also often malleable as the conflict progresses over time.[4] Since information on relative power and group goals is difficult to discern, there is less incentive for challenger groups to admit that they are likely to be defeated; leaders of challenger groups are often able to convince civilian populations to continue supporting them even when defeat appears inevitable.

The (Often) Extended Nature of Irregular Warfare

Since states usually possess the preponderance of military and police forces in asymmetric conflicts, challengers must make strategic choices about when to fight and what methods to employ. In the early stages of irregular conflict, challengers are often too weak to engage directly with forces of the state; instead, these groups often apply indirect methods, such as terrorism or guerrilla warfare's "hit and run" tactics.[5] Military and political decisions for conflict initiation and sustainment become muddled as each side struggles with targeting, force employment, and execution. States must be careful in militarized responses to challenger actions, as undue violence can be used by the challenger to win support.

Challengers must take care to maintain or increase the support of the population, as they depend on the people in most cases for sanctuary, support, and resupply. A return to the preconflict status quo is never palatable for challengers; in addition to the return to conditions extant at conflict initiation, challengers (and their loved ones) may face sanctions for failed attempts. Sanctions often mean imprisonment or death; challengers thus have little to lose by continuing to pursue their goals using violence. States are inclined to pursue and prosecute responsible leaders on the challenger side, to punish those attempting to weaken state control, and to deter future challengers to its authority. Both individual and group cost-benefit calculations on both sides of the conflict therefore favor continuing the fight, causing irregular warfare to be characterized by its often extended duration.

The High Costs of Irregular Warfare

Challengers in irregular conflicts are drawn from the population, often from groups with little or no voice in the political process or from the otherwise disenfranchised. When representing a population as the active political or military arm of a popular movement they are often able to hide among the people when not actively engaged. This brings the conflict into direct contact with civilians, who may or may not be participating, whether through direct action on the part of the state or via retaliatory or other measures inflicted by challenger groups. States can direct violence at the population to repress future rebellion or to punish perceived criminal behavior on behalf of the rebel group.[6] Challengers can conduct reprisal attacks on those they suspect of being disloyal to the cause or to make examples so as to minimize any tendency to cooperate with the state.[7] This widens the circle of violence, leading to higher casualties and larger population displacements.

During the Cold War, the nuclear stalemate made direct superpower conflict unthinkable; many instances of irregular warfare were the result of proxy conflicts conducted by the USSR (i.e., the Soviet Union) and United States within or among their client states.[8] Each contributed resources to its client forces; this support generally came in the form of funding, weapons/technology transfers, and technical or advisory support. In the years prior to and following the collapse of the USSR, money was no longer available to spend on proxy conflicts, and Soviet support ended; without a communist threat the United States also lost interest in funding such conflicts.[9] Without superpower support, proxy conflicts often ended, as sides in conflict sought strategic alternatives to violence. Yet irregular warfare continues to tax both the United States and the international community. The conflict in Afghanistan against Taliban and al Qaeda forces is estimated to have cost the United States over $100 billion annually. Despite the massive outlay of blood and treasure by the United States, Taliban fighters number only between 20,000 and 40,000, and their own spending on the conflict is estimated at as little as $100–200 million annually.[10] The United States thus annually spends on average one thousand times what the Taliban does, making the cost of this irregular war high indeed.

CAUSES OF IRREGULAR WARFARE

The U.S. Army/Marine Corps field manual on counterinsurgency defines irregular warfare as a broad category of conflict that includes both insurgency and counterinsurgency, but this definition applies only to movements designed to overthrow established governments via the use of force and other actions taken to oppose authorities.[11] More broadly, irregular warfare implies the use of violence among state and nonstate actors for legitimacy and influence over particular populations. While challengers prefer to employ force indirectly and in an asymmetric fashion, force can also be applied using the whole gamut of military and other capabilities. Thus irregular warfare comprises all conflicts that pit against one another combatant groups of differential technological and military skill levels; these conflicts range from coups to terror campaigns to full-scale civil war. Scholars have found such conflicts often take place when central governments are inept or corrupt and are weak enough to make violent change attractive, to offer rebels with often limited economic and military means opportunities to challenge state sovereignty successfully.[12]

Theories of irregular warfare cover a wide variety of causal factors, but the primary motivator of conflict is usually a lack of political means by which individual or group grievances can be addressed, whether at the local, regional, or national level. Without any means of redress, groups have no choice but either to abandon further efforts to obtain it and thus accept the status quo or to express their grievances through some form of conflict. These expressions take many forms, most of which are nonviolent in nature; the passing of handbills, town meetings, orations from bully pulpits, marches, sit-ins, and strikes are common examples of primarily nonviolent conflict expression. Violent expressions include riots, armed uprisings, insurgencies, and civil war.

While the spectrum of irregular warfare is broad, scholars have identified specific "issue spaces" that often lead to violent conflict of this type. Scholars continue to debate which issues most often lead to grievances and conflict, and no list of issues of sufficient salience has yet been compiled. Early research identified relative deprivation, wherein levels of perceived actual welfare do not meet expected values, as a key motivator of conflict.[13] Utility theory predicts that if those desiring rebellion perceive the benefits to be derived outweigh the costs, they will choose strategies of conflict. Other scholars treat rebellion as a form of organized crime, in which rebels desiring access to rents derived from resource endowments will confiscate those resources and then defend themselves against government forces. Since the latter are generally well armed, rebel leaders will make such attempts only if they believe they can survive government attack and make a profit.[14]

Further financial motivations can be found in the works of Collier and Sambanis, who argue that while weak economic development is a major grievance, a descent into civil war is a function of the opportunity to organize and then finance a rebellion.[15] Economic inequality as well is a powerful predictor of political unrest and rebellion; with a "Gini coefficient" measured at 0.45 (the Gini coefficient is a measure of state inequality among the population, with a value of zero equating to perfect equality and one with total inequality) in 2000, China was in historically dangerous territory. Gini coefficient values above 0.4 are considered dangerous in terms of the likelihood of rebellion; China's values (as of 2008) were estimated to be as high as 0.5 or 0.6.[16]

Ethnic violence, broadly defined, meets at least one of the following three criteria: it is motivated by some animosity toward an ethnic group, the victims are chosen because of specific ethnic criteria, or attack is carried out on behalf of an ethnic group. Ethnicity prior to the end of the Cold War was an understudied conflict component; ideology was the primary focus of strategy makers and elites during this period. One was either a communist or not, and ethnicity was considered largely epiphenomenal. Intergroup ethnic violence remains rare in the post–Cold War era, however; most instances of lethal ethnic violence since World War II have been either the results of state repression of specific ethnic groups or between a state and members of a group claiming to represent an ethnic grouping.[17]

Early work on conflict among ethnic groups began the modern debate, citing the importance of societal structure to determine whether ethnic conflict between groups would erupt. In hierarchical societies where social status is relatively fixed among groups there is little chance of upward social mobility; subordinates in these societies are generally dispersed, making mobilization difficult and conflict unlikely. In unranked societies, subordinates think in terms of both ethnicity and class, often demanding regional autonomy if regionally concentrated, which can lead to conflict if these demands remain unmet.[18] Others see identity as fluid and able to change as the situation requires; this helps explain how ethnic identities dormant in the former Yugoslavia were aroused by President Slobodan Milosevic, leading to extreme acts of violence.[19] When ethnic cleavages are particularly durable, violent ethnic conflict can result when a given minority group perceives that its ability to improve its position vis-à-vis its neighbors will only decline over time.[20]

Nationalism can be defined as any collective action whereby actors seek congruence between the boundaries of an ethnic group and those of the state. Using Spain, France, and England as case studies, Marx shows how religious intolerance was used by leaders of these states, when newly created, to target minority religious groups for expulsion. This served not only to rid the ruling elites of problematic factions that might eventually challenge royal rule but also to create a binding mechanism for the populations of the new nations.[21] When central governments appear weak, elites and citizens alike may perceive opportunities to improve their social condition; if an ethnic group senses bias directed against it under these conditions and is spatially concentrated, self-determination movements become more likely.[22]

Religious motivators for conflict at the subnational level are many and vary among the multitude of religious groupings extant today. Religious factors on their own seemingly have little explanatory power in occurrences of ethnic conflict; however, when one combines religion and desires for separatism, religion becomes a major causal factor indeed. Muslims have been found more likely to rebel against the state than to protest; however, this is unsurprising, as most Muslims live in authoritarian states, where avenues of protest seldom exist.[23] Thus regime types and the threat of repression likely carry more explanatory weight in these cases. When religious and territorial issues intersect, violence is more likely to obtain; because both issues have fixed and known boundaries, little room for compromise exists and violence becomes more likely.[24]

Polity types and their responses to requests for political change can also lead to group mobilization and the escalation of movements into rebellion. Autocracies are particularly ripe for rebellion, as often they offer no pathways for political access; groups that seek political change must either agitate peacefully or use violent forms of protest. Financially and bureaucratically weak states can make insurgency strategically more feasible for groups desirous of change; weak internal security forces, including corrupt or inefficient police, weak counterinsurgency forces, and poorly trained and equipped militaries offer conditions more favorable to insurgencies.[25]

EFFECTS OF IRREGULAR WARFARE

Irregular warfare tends to have destabilizing effects, domestically, regionally and not infrequently internationally. As violence rises within the state, domestic order breaks down, institutions are threatened, and personal security declines; if the protective capabilities of local and regional police or other security forces are inadequate, individual security becomes more problematic or fails altogether. This often results in large population movements to neighboring states, where individuals seek shelter from the violence at home. As of this writing, nearly four million Syrian refugees have been registered in Turkey, Egypt, Iraq, Jordan, and Lebanon as a result of the Syrian civil war and the ongoing threat of ISIS.[26] However, if state borders are porous, conflict can also transcend them, allowing challenger groups to seek refuge and resupply in neighboring nations. If sovereignty cannot be sustained by neighboring states, they too can descend into anarchic conditions, affecting trade, business and security. Often such conflicts become proxy wars for more powerful states that seek to gain advantage over others without engaging in direct conflict; without careful control these conflicts can escalate to international wars with far-reaching implications.

It is clear that irregular warfare is a growing concern as groups like al-Shabaab, al Qaeda in the Arabian Peninsula, and ISIS continue to employ widespread violence and terror to achieve their goals. It is not clear whether effective strategies exist for dealing with groups like these, which employ unconventional methods of conducting military campaigns. The following sections will examine both classical and modern theoretical perspectives on warfare and strategy to determine what may be both applicable and useful for current and future irregular conflicts.

CLASSICAL STRATEGIC THEORISTS AND IRREGULAR WARFARE

As many of the authors in this volume have already discussed, deep thinking on military strategy has been under way for thousands of years. Modern strategists would be remiss if they did not study the works of Sun Tzu, Clausewitz, and Jomini, as they have much to offer those wishing to understand and master the art of military strategy making. Yet many would argue that these works, while valuable in comprehending the complexities of "traditional" conflict between warring armies, have little to offer those interested in irregular warfare. This argument is easy to counter: many of these classical theorists speak directly to the complexities of irregular warfare. One must only be willing to examine their writings closely to find pertinent material, and it is to this purpose that this section is dedicated.

Sun Tzu

Sun Tzu's writings are, like those of so many military theorists, products of the time and context in which he lived. Dating *The Art of War,* his classic treatise on warfare in ancient China, is difficult, but many place its origins in the fourth century BCE.[27] During this "Warring States" period, large armies commanded by generals met on fields of battle—yet numbers meant little to Sun Tzu. Instead, he valued a deep understanding of the battlefield and the enemy, the use of deception, and the indirect approach. He greatly valued moral strength, intelligence, adaptability, and flexibility in responding to the enemy as keys to success in battle.[28]

Protracted warfare was abhorrent to Sun Tzu; no country had ever benefited from such a conflict, and thus it was to be avoided.[29] Attacking the enemy's strategy, rather than his troops, was most important, for "[t]o subdue the enemy without fighting is the acme of skill."[30] Sun Tzu's thoughts on strategy are thus directly applicable to irregular warfare today, as understanding the motivations and goals of groups like ISIS and al Qaeda and attacking their strategy, rather than meeting them kinetically on the battlefield, may defuse and defeat these movements with less expenditure of blood and treasure.

Thucydides

Thucydides, a one-time Athenian general who was exiled for failing to save the city of Amphipolis from the Spartans, also lived in the times about which he wrote. Although his narrative concerns the war between the states of Athens, with its powerful navy, and Sparta, with its heavily armed land forces, it has many lessons for irregular warfare strategy. As Colin Gray so astutely observes, there is little difference between the motivations of those who fought the Peloponnesian Wars and the leaders of ISIS and al Qaeda. The concerns of both are "about political power: who gets it, and as a rather secondary matter, what to do with it."[31]

Thucydides believed that conflict between Athens and Sparta would be "inevitable and terrible," given the lack of adherence to traditional rules of warfare and the absence of any political common ground on which to attempt to establish a real and lasting peace.[32] This corresponds rather well to the current conflict between ISIS (which seeks political power and legitimacy) and Western forces, between whom there appears to exist little in the form of common ground for negotiation. It therefore seems likely that Thucydides, considered the father of realist theory, would expect the West to utilize its extensive military might as its primary means of addressing the current Middle East crises and to adopt an annihilation strategy against groups such as ISIS and al Qaeda. But while such a strategy could ultimately result in a victory for the West in terms of destroying the threat, it would likely mean a further lessening of U.S. soft power and perhaps mean a difficult and protracted conflict indeed.

Clausewitz

Now approaching its two-hundredth anniversary, Carl von Clausewitz's *On War* has been studied, interpreted, and misinterpreted, by generations of military officers and scholars of both military strategy and history. In it Clausewitz describes war as a continuation of policy by other means, means by which states, as the creators and arbiters of national policy, force other states to do their will.[33] This Westphalian viewpoint, some scholars argue, minimizes the value of these theories in the modern era, as they do not account for nonstate actors (which by Clausewitzian standards would be incapable of conducting policy at this level). Others argue that his theories do not account for the changing nature of war in the modern era.[34]

Yet dismissing Clausewitz outright shortchanges the reader, who with a little digging would uncover additional thoughts by this theorist specifically on irregular warfare. Clausewitz does indeed write of such conflicts in *On War*— his magnum opus devotes a relatively short, yet illustrative chapter entitled "The People in Arms" in Book Six to it. Although Clausewitz admits that at the time of the writing this type of warfare was rare and understudied, he does provide a theoretical framework for its conduct. Distance from military and police forces of the state and suitable topography were musts for success.

Rebels must also concentrate their efforts against the state only at the periphery, where their actions would foment uneasiness and fear and "deepen the psychological effect of the insurrection as a whole."[35] The goal was thus not the defeat of the enemy (state) forces but exhaustion of the state by the insurgent's actions, akin to what al Qaeda has been doing for over a decade as of this writing. By understanding these theoretical concepts, forces countering these insurgent strategies can properly focus their own strengths and marginalize the efforts of the terrorist groups they seek to defeat.

It becomes apparent, then, that these classical strategic thinkers do indeed have much to offer those who are interested in developing strategies for irregular war. Understanding the enemy's motivations and goals and attacking his strategy instead of his troops may indeed pay bigger benefits than kinetic action alone. The use of overwhelming military power, the hallmark of major powers in the international system, can be beneficial when insurgent goals and strategies are unclear, but the benefits might be outweighed by the damage to soft power and prestige. By understanding insurgent group tactics, the United States can minimize losses along the periphery and avoid exhaustion from prolonged combat. We now turn to more modern strategic thinkers and theorists to see what seekers of strategies for irregular war can understand and employ.

MODERN STRATEGIC THEORISTS ON IRREGULAR WARFARE

Although "modern" is somewhat ambiguous, it is used here less as a temporal divider than as a means of denoting the beginning of the current era of irregular warfare and terrorism. For the purposes of this chapter, I define modern works as those written in the twentieth and twenty-first centuries, as they incorporate the latest in tactics and strategy in their theories. For this reason I begin this section by examining the works of Col. C. E. Callwell and move on through the current day.

Callwell, a British officer who served in many campaigns, draws heavily on the works of Clausewitz and to some degree those of Sun Tzu to explain how best to defeat insurgent forces in irregular conflicts. His *Small Wars: Their Principles and Practice* is now a classic. The first step is to set clear goals for the campaign, then to do a rational assessment of one's own capabilities, as well as those of the enemy, before deriving strategies for achieving the goals. The operational and strategic goals were the same: to "achieve the collapse of enemy resistance as quickly as possible."[36] In this way one's forces would not be drawn into a protracted conflict and atritted by enemy forces. Speed is thus of the essence, to avoid the lengthy conflict so abhorred by both Sun Tzu and by the British public at the time.

From the beginning of the twentieth century until 1934, the U.S. Marine Corps (consisting of just over 11,000 men until the United States entered World War I) engaged primarily in small wars with the goal of pacifying indigenous peoples. The 1940 *Small Wars Manual* was an attempt to provide every Marine with a single volume dedicated to understanding and fighting these conflicts. The use of military action differed greatly from that in conventional warfare, where maximum force was expected. In small wars the population mattered to the political outcome, so violence would be kept to a minimum. Time spent reducing popular opposition was far more valuable than speed for its own sake; getting the population to side with U.S. forces would allow well-equipped guerrillas to be more easily identified and prosecuted.[37] Despite the extensive review of counterinsurgency practices contained in the *Small Wars Manual,* however, the manual would be all but disregarded as America entered Vietnam just over two decades later.

The *Small Wars Manual*'s focus on the population was prescient, as shown by the writings of several post–World War II theorists on the conduct of insurgencies. Mao Tse-tung recognized the importance of popular unity to the revolution that eventually united China under communism; he cited the need to both inform and educate the public on the need for revolution.[38] Robert Taber, in his classic tome on guerrilla warfare, explained the criticality of revolutionary leaders who could explain and rationalize the often confusing character of revolutionary conflict as it was under way. Since the populace often saw only isolated acts of violence, it was important for leadership to incorporate these acts into a coherent revolutionary "whole" that could be used to rally the populace to the cause.[39] "Che" Guevara concurred with the need for public support for the guerrilla, to be obtained by indoctrination and good moral conduct. The guerrilla would ensure cooperation by "helping the peasant technically, economically, morally and culturally as a sort of guardian angel."[40]

Given this dependence on the population, any strategy for defeating insurgents in an irregular conflict must naturally revolve around protecting the population from their influence and violence. The French theorist of modern (what he terms "subversive" or "revolutionary") warfare Roger Trinquier believed in employing the population in a comprehensive self-defense organization that would secure cities and surrounding territories.[41] David Galula, another French theorist on irregular warfare, expanded on the idea of population involvement. After separating the insurgents from the population and properly training local security forces, the counterinsurgent forces should focus on actionable intelligence obtained from the protected population.[42] The tasks involved are not easy, but they are vital.

Supporting and protecting the civilian population thus needs to be a central part of the overall strategy. As Kilcullen avers, "Effective counterinsurgency provides human security to the population, where they live, 24 hours a day. This, not destroying the enemy, is the central task." The work thus comes down to basics: securing villages, valleys, roads, and population centers. But still, Kilcullen warns, it is essential to reassure the population that you are not there to occupy their dwelling places.[43]

In an increasingly globalized world, however, the "populations" to which these authors refer have been expanded greatly—mass communication, migratory flows, and the connectedness of the global society today mean that the focus on population is no longer confined to the state where conflict has arisen. Populations today "stretch around the world in an archipelago of individuals, cells and communities; they have no territory, and exist instead in isolated but interconnected groups that are horizontally related rather than vertically ordered, and their shared sense of outrage is regenerated by the exertions of the media and the visibility of the campaign. In these wispy, informal patterns, without territory and without formal command structures they are not easily touched by the kinetic blows of a formal military campaign."[44] Clearly the effort to sway the population in conflicts the United States faces today with al Qaeda and ISIS requires a higher level of effort and a much more inclusive scope.

For much of the twentieth century, insurgent groups were more often driven by ideology than by ethnic factors. This changed with the fall of the Soviet Union, as noted, and ethnicity rather than ideology has become one of the primary motivators for conflict. A major component of ethnicity is religion, and it is to this banner that groups like ISIS, al Qaeda, and others call the faithful to take up arms and fight. Given the rigid and monotheistic nature of some religions, is it possible to dissuade these groups from continuing their campaigns of violence? Can modern strategic theorists offer anything to address this thorny problem?

Atran believes nearly all major ideological movements (political or religious) require an "imagined kinship"—the subordination of the family to the larger community of figurative brothers and sisters. Globally, people believe that devotion to sacred or cultural values that incorporate moral beliefs is (or ought to be) absolute and inviolable.[45] One problem, however, is that while people revere their own sacred values, they often ignore or downplay the other side's. Understanding sacred values is about understanding human nature—what it is to be human. This is, of course, part of what Sun Tzu spoke of when discussing the importance of knowing one's enemy, and it should be a critical part of strategy making.

Given the focus each of these strategists has placed on understanding, educating, and protecting the populations involved in irregular warfare today, is there still a logical place for the employment of military force? Thucydides was convinced that a "might makes right" mind-set clearly indicated that military force was an irresistible means of conducting war (and therefore policy) against an intransigent adversary. Yet after over a decade of kinetic war the United States finds itself little nearer its goals in Afghanistan and now perhaps faces a much larger threat in ISIS.

Gen. Sir Rupert Smith wrote, "In international affairs we tend to place the highest priority on what we do rather than on what will achieve our ultimate object."[46] The United States has done well in the use of its formidable airpower both to deter and defeat states that have threatened its national security. Not since World War II have U.S. surface-based military assets faced a threat from above, thanks to air superiority. U.S. airmen have done an incredible job in facing nonstate and transnational actors in the last several decades as well, both in kinetic attack and in every other airpower mission that exists. What do modern airpower theorists have to say about the utility of airpower in irregular conflicts? The next section ponders this question and sets the stage for this chapter's concluding remarks.

AIRPOWER AND IRREGULAR WARFARE

Airpower has been used in irregular conflicts from the earliest days of manned flight. In March 1916, for example, eight Curtiss JN-3 "Jennys" were dispatched with their crews from the 1st Aero Squadron to assist Brig. Gen. "Blackjack" Pershing in his pursuit of the Mexican rebel Francisco "Pancho" Villa.[47] Although

General Pershing never caught Villa, the Mexican Punitive Expedition showed the utility of airpower in irregular war. However, the Army thereafter focused instead on how airpower could shape the European battlefields of World War I and tested almost every airpower mission (with the exception of in-flight refueling) in the skies over the trenches.

Airpower theorists after World War I (such as Giulio Douhet, Hugh Trenchard, John Slessor, and Arthur Tedder) continued to focus almost exclusively on airpower's future contributions to conventional war. It was not until the Vietnam War that theorists again began to consider seriously airpower's effect in irregular campaigns. John Boyd and John Warden both argued that destruction or degradation of the enemy leadership's ability to control military forces was the primary role of modern airpower. While Warden focused on the actual destruction of leadership, Boyd focused on the process whereby friendly forces would be able to think (and act) faster than their adversary, thereby denying the latter control of their forces.[48] Although designed primarily for conventional conflicts, the ideas presented in these theories have great applicability to irregular conflicts as well. Killing Osama bin Laden, for example, was a critical milestone in the ongoing conflict with al Qaeda, as has been the destruction of many senior leaders of this group. However, the United States has not had the same level of success getting ahead of the information curve, as groups such as ISIS and al Qaeda continue to be able to use the Internet to teach, inform, and recruit members.

The actual use of airpower over Vietnam was not as successful as its supporters had hoped it would be, at least in terms of addressing irregular conflict on the ground. Clodfelter argues that U.S. civilian and military leaders entered the Vietnam War blinded by "a modern vision of air power that focuses on the lethality of its weaponry rather than on that weapon's effectiveness as a political instrument."[49] They had conflated lethality with political results; this resulted in the misapplication of airpower and made it ineffective in deterring the North Vietnamese. Strategic bombing in North Vietnam and elsewhere in the theater had little effect on the North prior to Operations Linebacker and Linebacker II, and the North Vietnamese Army and Vietcong by April 1975 were able to bring their total war for reunification to a successful conclusion.

Lambeth argues that the use of airpower during the early days of Operation Enduring Freedom (OEF) was a stark contrast to the Vietnam experience. Coalition aircraft struck thirty-one targets the first day, then turned to support both the Northern Alliance/special-operations forces (SOF) effort against the Taliban and attacks against cave complexes. In just two months the Taliban had been routed, and the focus switched to the mountains of Tora Bora and the killing of Osama bin Laden. Despite late notification from the Army, air assets supported Operation Anaconda and provided close air support in an incredibly small and crowded airspace. OEF also saw the integration of fused intelligence, surveillance, and reconnaissance (ISR) information from SOF teams, Air Force forward air controllers, and feeds from the Predator and Global Hawk remotely piloted vehicles, which led to better target identification and destruction.[50]

U.S. airpower continues to contribute to irregular warfare today; as of this writing it is providing intelligence, airlift, and kinetic support to the ground conflicts in Iraq, Afghanistan, Syria, Yemen, and many other locations. Scholars seem to agree on the need for a comprehensive strategy when dealing with actors engaged in irregular conflict. While in a conventional conflict forces can seek a decisive military victory leading to unconditional surrender, seldom is this possible in irregular wars. In many cases a political compromise between the state and the insurgents is the best that can be achieved and is as much a victory as the defeat of an enemy's military forces.[51]

Robert Pape has cited four major coercive strategies regarding strategic bombing: punishment (raising the cost of continued resistance), denial (making enemy strategy futile), risk (raising possibility of suffering), and decapitation (removing leadership). While each has value, Pape insisted, only denial has a chance of being successful, although he does admit that it can be very difficult and take a long time.[52] Regarding the current use of airpower in the struggle against terror groups like ISIS and al Qaeda, the United States seems to be employing a combination of punishment and denial strategies. Although the results of this strategy are still being debated, it seems that airpower is having an effect on the ability of these groups to communicate with, command, and control their forces.

Corum and Johnson have noted that airpower provides a level of flexibility and initiative that cannot be gained in other ways; while these factors used to work in favor of the insurgent, multiuse platforms and remotely piloted vehicles for ISR seem to have returned their advantages to the state.[53] Aircraft such as the F-15, F-16, and B-52 continue to conduct interdiction missions against ground targets, and the A-10 continues to create fear in the hearts of insurgents throughout the Middle East. The number of remotely piloted vehicles in use against these groups is on the increase; they continue to provide twenty-four-hour surveillance, intelligence, and other valuable information to U.S. commanders. Given the increasing number of such platforms in each of the services today, it is likely that their utility in future prosecution of irregular wars will only grow.

THE FUTURE(S) OF IRREGULAR WARFARE

Scholars are divided as to what forms the future causes of warfare will take; however, there are many serious challenges currently facing the United States and humanity as a whole. Geopolitical analyst and author Robert D. Kaplan noted back in 1994 that global stressors such as overpopulation, disease, resource exhaustion, and the erosion of state borders resulting from migrations of peoples would only worsen over time.[54] The contentious political geography of much of the Third World and the plight of the indigenous peoples of the nonindustrialized southern zones suggest his arguments are not as far-fetched as they might have seemed at the time. Hundreds died and thousands got sick in 2012 from a severe cholera outbreak in the shantytowns of Sierra Leone and Guinea, as well as in Mali and Niger.[55] The so-called Lord's Resistance Army, operating out of Uganda, continues to promote a radical form of Christianity involving the rape, torture, and murder of Ugandans and others and fills its ranks primarily with kidnapped and brainwashed children.[56] The resulting instability affects both Uganda and the surrounding region.

India continues to face a severe water shortage from weak monsoon rains, and poor water management in Pakistan has dropped water availability per capita by more than two-thirds.[57] Forced migration will also continue to be a global problem in the near future; the Arab Spring movements have generated nearly a million refugees, and nearly four million have left Syria during its ongoing civil war.[58] One hundred thousand refugees made the crossing from Somalia into Yemen in 2012, and refugee flows from Africa into southern Europe are increasing annually.[59] Elites and scholars have long considered these humanitarian concerns proximate causes of conflict, especially at the subnational level. Overpopulation and disease can lead to migratory behavior as individuals and groups seek greater security and opportunity; this often leads to internal power imbalances and hostilities within states. Loss of resources, whether of water, due to drought or pollution, or of arable land, owing to periods of poor climatic conditions or external threats, can lead to conflict between haves and have-nots within a state or between groups sharing a common border.

Seth Jones, associate director of the International Security and Defense Policy Center at the RAND Corporation, believes the United States will continue to face irregular warfare challenges from nonstate actors, including terrorist groups, international drug cartels, and violent global activists. In addition, he believes, the United States will be under threat from states, to include those that deliberately create irregular warfare challenges and weak states whose insufficient governance does so inadvertently. These challenges will be amplified by inadequate interagency cooperation, lack of military doctrinal and material support for these operations, overtaxed military forces, and the increasingly technological savvy of the challengers the United States will face.[60]

The conduct of irregular warfare affects the domestic political order and can adversely affect the regional and international system. Realists and liberal thinkers view future perturbations in the international system as likely to induce conflict between states that can lead to war.[61] As nuclear powers become more prevalent, wars and their consequences will grow increasingly dangerous; it is thus imperative that strategic thinkers concern themselves with irregular conflicts at the domestic level that have the potential to create international disputes. Strategists must then carefully consider these global stressors when devising strategies for detecting, preventing, and, if necessary, intervening to end irregular conflict.

Perhaps the most difficult decision facing the modern strategist when considering future irregular warfare is whether or not to intervene in the struggle; issues of sovereignty are at stake, and states (particularly the United States) doing so over the last several decades have often been drawn into lengthy and costly conflicts.[62] Generally only strong states will choose to intervene in the affairs of others, since they have the requisite force to do so and can rally sufficient domestic and international support for such actions. Although humanitarian interventions have been common in the modern era, states will also intervene if domestic struggles threaten to undermine the larger international order.

A final question, then, is not whether states, particularly strong ones, *can* intervene—but the proper question might be whether they *should*. While force is a necessary precondition for such a decision and may be essential to separate warring parties in a particular conflict, it has been shown that it is not a sufficient condition for sustained peace. Force has to be coupled with political and social intervention programs to ease the underlying grievances that existed prior to the violence; if not, violence will likely return when the intervention comes to an end.[63] Thus interventions of this type will likely be long-term and extraordinarily costly, even to strong states; political decisions to intervene in such conflicts will by necessity be multilateral, if taken at all. Weighing the costs of intervention against the ramifications of regional instability will perhaps be the greatest challenge for future strategists as they inform political decision makers about the efficacy of engaging in future conflict of this type.

CONCLUSIONS

Since the end of the Cold War the United States has struggled to find its place in a world where containment and nuclear deterrence are no longer the end-all of national strategy. The United States cannot afford to remain reactive in a world where challengers to regional and global security are increasingly well mobilized and equipped to oppose its interests without reliance on purely conventional forces. Given that U.S. military hegemony will likely remain intact for decades, challengers will choose asymmetric means to disrupt U.S. strategic interests, based on rational cost-benefit calculations. The continuation of nationalist movements such as the Arab Spring will lead to more regional instability abroad, to the detriment of U.S. interests outside its borders. The erosion of autocratic regimes in Latin America and continued struggles against drug cartels in this hemisphere could bring irregular conflict to our borders in the near term.

Given the ubiquity of these threats, the United States needs to prepare better to face the reality of future irregular warfare, as it will do so sooner rather than later. While military hardware is essential to defeat our adversaries, armed conflict remains costly in blood and treasure. Moreover, as one scholar has noted, "Military effectiveness does not equal strategic effectiveness . . . [a]t the strategic level, additional factors such as social, political, cultural and economic elements shape military responses."[64] It is thus more cost-efficient to monitor and prepare for these conflicts *before* they erupt; to accomplish this we must labor to understand the characteristics of irregular warfare and teach them to our future military strategists.

Asymmetric information flow between states and challenger groups makes strategic calculations of relative power and intent difficult to predict; therefore, decisions to engage in irregular warfare will often be based on incorrect assumptions. Irregular wars are often long in duration and quite costly in terms of blood and treasure, and they can be ultimately destabilizing, both domestically and regionally. Modern strategists must be able to assess accurately the likelihood of such conflicts before the disputes turn violent; to do so they must understand the primary causes and become familiar with strategies for dealing with conflicts that become violent. They will then (ideally) be able to use this knowledge to inform senior decision makers as to whether and when to engage in these issue areas while simultaneously minimizing the costs of doing so. Reliance on a reactive posture will only ensure future losses of U.S. blood and treasure; a detailed knowledge of irregular warfare and how to address it will give the modern strategist the means to minimize these losses as well.

The modern strategist must have the tools necessary to predict, assess, and respond to irregular warfare before it spirals into uncontrolled violence. Professional military education currently exposes midlevel officers to irregular warfare all too briefly; a concerted effort must therefore be made to make the teaching of irregular warfare a part of a continuum of education that stretches the full length of an officer's career. Modern strategists, both civilian and military, need to understand better why these conflicts start, to predict better when they will become violent, and to address in the best way insurgent grievances to avoid continued bloodshed. As of this writing, the United States still struggles with all of these issues, and the evolution of strategy in meeting the challenges of irregular warfare has been limited. Educating modern strategists to understand these concepts may prepare them to meet the challenges of irregular warfare far more effectively and efficiently than they have in the past. They and the nation deserve nothing less.

NOTES

1. Clausewitz, Carl von, *On War,* trans. and ed. Michael Howard and Peter Paret (Princeton, N.J.: Princeton University Press, 1976); Basil Henry Liddell Hart, *Strategy,* 2nd ed. (New York: Penguin Books, 1991); and Alfred Thayer Mahan, *Mahan on Naval Strategy: Selections from the Writings of Rear Admiral Alfred Thayer Mahan,* ed. John B. Hattendorf (Annapolis, Md.: Naval Institute Press, 1991). Each of these theorists has made crucial contributions to the concept and formulation of modern strategy.

2. The first was the assault on the regime of Saddam Hussein. Although initially fought as a conventional conflict, the campaign remained such for less than sixty days; violence thereafter was asymmetric for another eight years, claiming the lives of 4,500 U.S. servicemen and leaving 22,000 wounded. The second was Operation Enduring Freedom, which began with special operations forces working in concert with Northern Alliance troops to defeat the Taliban in October 2001. This phase was largely over by December of that year, but the U.S.-led coalition has continued to conduct asymmetric operations in that country for over a decade.

3. James Fearon, "Rationalist Explanations for War," *International Organization* 49, no. 3 (Summer 1995), makes a similar argument for why states tend to go to war even when the costs and risks of fighting argue against it. Leaders on both sides may have cause to withhold or misrepresent information about military capabilities and resolve; in addition, one side could

have incentives to renege on any negotiated agreement. These information asymmetries are more likely in irregular-warfare situations, when challenger capabilities and resolve are difficult to discern, especially early in the conflict.

4. Bard O'Neill in *Insurgency and Terrorism: From Revolution to Apocalypse* (Washington, D.C.: Potomac Books, 2005), argues that challenger group leaders often change their goals as campaigns unfold or as it becomes clear that less ambitious goals have better chances of success. In addition, factional leaders within a movement often have different, even mutually exclusive goals.

5. Ibid., 35–36.

6. See Jeremy Weinstein's discussion of state repression during the Mozambique civil war, in *Inside Rebellion: The Politics of Insurgent Violence* (New York: Cambridge University Press, 2007), 270–74.

7. Stathis N. Kalyvas, *The Logic of Violence in Civil War* (New York: Cambridge University Press, 2006).

8. See Mark O. Yeisley, "Bipolarity, Proxy Wars and the Rise of China," *Strategic Studies Quarterly* 5, no. 4 (Winter 2011).

9. Stathis N. Kalyvas and Laia Balcells, "International System and Technologies of Rebellion: How the End of the Cold War Shaped Internal Conflict," *American Political Science Review* 104, no. 3 (August 2010).

10. Seth G. Jones, *"The Future of Irregular Warfare" (CT-374, The RAND Corporation) Testimony Presented before the House Committee on Emerging Threats and Capabilities on March 27, 2012,* Washington, D.C.

11. *U.S. Army/Marine Corps Counterinsurgency Field Manual 3-24* (Chicago: University of Chicago Press, 2007).

12. James D. Fearon and David D. Laitin, "Ethnicity, Insurgency and Civil War," *American Political Science Review* 97, no. 1 (February 2003), apply this logic primarily to insurgencies and civil wars in the post–Cold War era.

13. Ted Robert Gurr, *Why Men Rebel* (Princeton, N.J.: Princeton University Press, 1970).

14. Paul Collier, "Rebellion as a Quasi-Criminal Activity," *Journal of Conflict Resolution* 44, no. 6 (2000).

15. Paul Collier and Nicholas Sambanis, eds., *Understanding Civil War: Evidence and Analysis* (Washington, D.C.: International Bank for Reconstruction and Development, World Bank, 2005).

16. Steven R. David, *Catastrophic Consequences: Civil Wars and American Interests* (Baltimore, Md.: Johns Hopkins Press, 2008).

17. James D. Fearon, "Ethnic Mobilization and Ethnic Violence," in *Oxford Handbook of Political Economy*, ed. Barry R. Weingast and Donald Wittman (Oxford: Oxford University Press, 2006).

18. Donald L. Horowitz, *Ethnic Groups in Conflict* (Los Angeles: University of California Press, 1985).

19. See for example Henry Hale, "Explaining Ethnicity," *Comparative Political Studies* 37, no. 4 (May 2004), and his explanations of identity "thickening" in response to elite persuasion.

20. Fearon, "Ethnic Mobilization and Ethnic Violence."

21. Joel S. Fetzer and J. Christopher Soper, *Muslims and the State in Britain, France, and Germany* (Boston: Cambridge University Press, 2004).

22. Michael Hechter, *Containing Nationalism* (Oxford: Oxford University Press, 2000).

23. Jonathan Fox, *Religion, Civilization and Civil War: 1945 through the Millennium* (Lanham, Md.: Lexington Books, 2004).

24. Ibid.

25. Fearon and Laitin, "Ethnicity, Insurgency and Civil War."

26. "Syrian Regional Refugee Response," UNHCR: The UN Refugee Agency, 25 June 2015, http://data.unhcr.org/syrianrefugees/regional.php.

27. Cf. Samuel B. Griffith, *The Illustrated Art of War* (Oxford: Oxford University Press, 2005), showing that Sun Tzu most likely lived between 400 and 320 BCE.

28. Sun Tzu, *The Art of War*, trans. Ralph D. Sawyer (Boulder, Colo.: Westview, 1994), chap. 1.

29. Ibid., chap. 2.

30. Ibid., chap. 3.

31. Colin S. Gray, "Irregular Warfare: One Nature, Many Characters," *Strategic Studies Quarterly* (Winter 2007).

32. Robert B. Strassler, *The Landmark Thucydides: A Comprehensive Guide to the Peloponnesian War* (New York: Free Press, 1996), xix.

33. Clausewitz, *On War,* chap. 1.

34. For example, see John Keegan, *A History of Warfare* (New York: Alfred A. Knopf, 1993).

35. Clausewitz, *On War,* 482.

36. C. E. Callwell, *Small Wars: Their Principles and Practice* (Lincoln: University of Nebraska Press, 1996), xii.

37. Ronald Schaffer, "The 1940 Small Wars Manual and the 'Lessons of History,'" in *Small Wars Manual: United States Marine Corps 1940* (Manhattan, Kans.: Sunflower University Press, 2004).

38. Mao Tse-tung, *On Protracted War* (Honolulu: University Press of the Pacific, 2001), 111.

39. Robert Taber, *War of the Flea: The Classic Study of Guerrilla Warfare* (Washington, D.C.: Brassey's, 2002), 152.

40. Ernesto "Che" Guevara, *Guerrilla Warfare* (Lanham, Md.: Scholarly Resources, 1997), 73.

41. Roger Trinquier, *Modern Warfare: A French View of Counterinsurgency.* Westport, Conn.: Praeger Security International, 2006, 28.

42. David Galula, *Counterinsurgency Warfare: Theory and Practice* (Westport, Conn.: Praeger Security International, 2006), viii.

43. David Kilcullen, *The Accidental Guerrilla: Fighting Small Wars in the Midst of a Big One* (Oxford: Oxford University Press, 2009), 266.

44. John Mackinlay, *The Insurgent Archipelago* (New York: Columbia University Press, 2009), 6.

45. Scott Atran, *Talking to the Enemy: Faith, Brotherhood and the (Un)Making of Terrorists* (New York: HarperCollins, 2010), 375.

46. Rupert Smith, *The Utility of Force: The Art of War in the Modern World* (New York: Vintage Books, 2008), 379.

47. James S. Corum and Wray R. Johnson, *Airpower in Small Wars: Fighting Insurgents and Terrorists* (Lawrence: University Press of Kansas, 2003), 11.

48. For more on these two theories, cf. John Andreas Olsen, *John Warden and the Renaissance of American Air Power* (Dulles, Va.: Potomac Books, 2007), and John Richard Boyd, "Destruction and Creation," Goal Systems International, 3 September 1976, http://www.goalsys.com/books/documents/destruction_and_creation.pdf.

49. Mark Clodfelter, *The Limits of Air Power: The American Bombing of North Vietnam* (New York: Free Press, 1989), 203.

50. Benjamin S. Lambeth, *Air Power against Terror: America's Conduct of Operation Enduring Freedom* (Santa Monica, Calif.: RAND, 2005), 337–42.

51. Corum and Johnson, *Airpower in Small Wars,* 426.

52. Robert A. Pape, *Bombing to Win: Air Power and Coercion in War* (Ithaca, N.Y.: Cornell University Press, 1996).

53. Corum and Johnson, *Airpower in Small Wars,* 434–35.

54. Robert D. Kaplan, "The Coming Anarchy: How Scarcity, Crime, Overpopulation, Tribalism, and Disease Are Rapidly Destroying the Social Fabric of Our Planet," *Atlantic Monthly* 273, no. 2 (1994).

55. Adam Nossiter, "Cholera Epidemic Envelopes Coastal Slums in West Africa," *New York Times,* 22 August 2012.

56. "Terrorist Organization Profiles," National Consortium for the Study of Terrorism and Responses to Terrorism, http://www.start.umd.edu/start/data_collections/tops/terrorist_organization_profile.asp?id=3513.

57. Michael Kugelman and Robert M. Hathaway, eds., introduction to *Running on Empty: Pakistan's Water Crisis* (Washington, D.C.: Woodrow Wilson International Center for Scholars, Asia Program, 2009), 5.

58. "Stories from Syrian Refugees," UNHCR, http://data.unhcr.org/syrianrefugees/syria.php, accessed 26 September 2013.

59. "Record number of African Refugees and Migrants Cross the Gulf of Aden in 2012," Briefing Notes, UN High Council on Refugees, 15 January 2013.

60. Jones, *Future of Irregular Warfare*.

61. Kenneth Waltz, *Theory of International Politics* (Boston: McGraw-Hill, 1979), introduces "structural realism," wherein states in an anarchic international system must respond to shifts in the international balance of power or face the consequences of inaction in the presence of such shifts.

62. The ongoing conflicts in Iraq and Afghanistan have claimed thousands of U.S. lives and cost the United States hundreds of billions of dollars as of this writing.

63. Martha Finnemore, *The Purpose of Intervention: Changing Beliefs about the Use of Force* (Ithaca, NY: Cornell University Press, 2003).

64. James D. Kiras, *Special Operations and Strategy: From WWII to the War on Terrorism* (New York: Routledge, 2006).

CHAPTER ELEVEN

Two Sides of a Coin

The Strategist and the Planner

STEPHEN E. WRIGHT

Strategy without a plan is akin to hallucination, and a plan without
strategy relies on serendipity for any possibility of success.

In a perfect world, a given planning process would serve both the strategist
and the planner, and preparing either person to conduct either activity would
be a straightforward process. For military strategists and planners, the Joint
Operation Planning Process (JOPP) should cover, in theory, the activities of both
strategy and planning, from planning initiation to execution and to the new end
state that results. In fact, Joint Publication (JP) 5-0, *Joint Operation Planning*,
places operational design activities within the JOPP under "planning initiation,"
as the first step of course-of-action development and approval and subsequent
plan or order development.[1] In that perfect world, clear guidance including goals
and objectives, desired end state(s), and interagency clarity of purpose comes from
the president and the National Security Council. The real world is somewhat
different.

Every time I have participated in a war game or political-military crisis-action
exercise, we have always received plenty of guidance from the echelons above us
and a plethora of detail regarding scenario, commander's intent, and force availability. Every time I went into contingency or crisis-action planning, we always
started from scratch. Always! In 1994, I received a call on a Saturday night around
midnight from our numbered air force vice commander telling me to prepare to
deploy for up to six months and that I was leaving on a plane the next day. Sunday

afternoon I was in a strategy cell at Headquarters Central Air Force at Shaw Air Force Base, South Carolina. This response became one of many crisis-action efforts that airmen of my generation euphemistically call, collectively, "Operation Deny Holiday."[2] The U.S. Air Forces Central Command (CENTAF) commander, then Lt. Gen. John Jumper, tasked us to develop the first three days of a plan while the rest of CENTAF deployed into theater. Despite our lack of "adult leadership," we were making great progress until a lone CENTAF lieutenant colonel looked in on us as we were working through the strategy portion of the plan and exclaimed rudely and loudly, "Strategy?!? We don't need a [expletive] strategy! We need an ATO [air tasking order]!" Aside from having to start from scratch, strategy and planning do not always elicit insightful help.

In addition, many crises seem to catch us by surprise. Perhaps we should not be shocked, for all too often the "next" crisis occurs in a place we are not watching, as opposed to those commanding our minute attention. For example, the Arab Spring crisis of 2010 came as a surprise to many outside observers. This crisis spread across North Africa and beyond and eventually, in 2011, drew the North Atlantic Treaty Organization (NATO) and coalition partners into an armed response in Libya. The United States had diverted its attention from Libya after its President Muammar Gaddafi gave up his quest for weapons of mass destruction in 2003. The nation had realigned its intelligence capabilities to the "current fights," focusing on Iraq and Afghanistan, forgetting about Libya. When the Libyan crisis emerged in February 2011, the United States, its allies, and partners had no operational orders of battle that had been updated since 2003 or current intelligence on Libya.

So, if strategy and planning do not occur in a perfect world of clear guidance and on-demand intelligence preparation of the operational environment, how does one prepare the strategist and planner to meet the challenges of the real world? In this chapter, we will focus on linking concepts to practice. That is right, we are going to "make some sausage," or at least see how to make strategy in a practical sense.

The organization of this chapter is a simple one, but the discussion very diverse. First, I work to help us understand ourselves and then to understand the differences between strategists and planners, recognizing that in the real world the same individuals might be both. Next, I bring together the strategist and the planner, using a figure to illustrate their development and their key elements, followed by a short conclusion. The starting point for our discussion is the same one Sun Tzu wrote of long ago as the "way to victory," and that is to "know yourself."[3]

KNOW THYSELF

In one of my favorite *Calvin and Hobbes* comic strips, by Bill Watterson, Calvin is daydreaming during geography class about an alternative, prehistoric universe. The teacher finally gets Calvin's attention and demands that he tell the class what state he lives in. Calvin replies, "Denial." Now, while knowing that one is living in a "state of denial" is preferable to not knowing, the strategist and planner have to see the world clearly, and that starts with a truthful understanding of herself.

So, who are the strategists and planners in the U.S. Air Force (USAF) and, more broadly, the Department of Defense (DoD)? Well, "we" are mostly male, with educational backgrounds in STEM—science, technology, engineering, and mathematics. The Air Force and the Department of Defense recruit almost exclusively from STEM graduates for the officer corps.[4] If you took a survey of officers in a typical unit, you would find that most earned bachelor of science degrees as undergraduates. U.S. Air Force Academy graduates, even those with social science degrees (political science, for example), spend nearly two-thirds of their undergraduate degree program in core STEM coursework. Moreover, most of us STEM types are linear thinkers.

Now, before someone cries "Foul!" at being called a linear thinker, let me note that the Air Force, like the military writ large, needs many linear thinkers—we have lots of linear tasks to do. In fact, most of what the military does is linear tasking, for which linear thinking is perfectly suited. I do not mean to use the term pejoratively; rather, it simply acknowledges that we are the people who like to get things done in an orderly manner, moving from step one to step "last" in an efficient and effective manner. In addition, most of us have type A personalities—you know, the people characterized as competitive, highly work-oriented, who work with a sense of urgency, and who display a higher level of aggressiveness than other personality types.[5] Truly, we are the "git 'er done" people of the world. We are the people who roll the rocks up the hills however big the rock or steep the hill—we get it done. As long as the challenges we face are ones we can resolve in a linear fashion with lots of hard work, we will be "as sound as a pound."[6]

The problem is that the challenges we face in the security business are almost all "wicked problems." As Rittel and Webber argued, "Planning problems are inherently wicked."[7] The problems they describe are societal ones—and conflict and war assuredly are societal phenomena. The Chairman, Joint Chiefs of Staff *Capstone Concept for Joint Operations: Joint Force 2020*, looking to the future observes, "threats and crises grow more complex[;] . . . [they are] driven by—and in turn drive—transnational dynamics."[8] Our colleagues at the Army's School of Advanced Military Studies have provided a key insight into the breadth of potential meanings for "wicked problems" observing, "What one author calls a wicked problem, another refers to as an ill-structured problem, a problem situation, a complex adaptive problem, a complex adaptive system, or even a mess."[9] No matter the terminology, war and warfare are highly complex activities.

While I ascribe to the idea that warfare whenever it occurs is a complex, wicked problem, I do see the potential for more issues to be and become wicked problems, due to the increased social and societal interaction enabled by the Internet and the ease of international travel. These interactions are at the core of many social and societal problems. As we contemplate budget sequestration, force structure reductions, and new threats from new technologies, we begin to realize just how "wicked" and complex the future challenges our forces meet might be. These are not the kinds of problems resolved with linear thinking.

The conundrum we face is that we are linear thinkers attempting to resolve nonlinear, abstract, wicked problems. Some might ask, "Don't we have abstract thinkers in the military?" I answer, "Not many, and those we have, hide." Most of us who have been military officers recall the new lieutenant in the (say) squadron who, when some new task required rolling yet another rock up another hill asked, "Why this rock; why this hill?" The typical response was to send the lieutenant to the corner. If she persisted with "why" questions, we marginalized her or, worse, showed her the door. The concern for us is this one—that lieutenant was the abstract thinker. Unfortunately, the demand for linear thinking from junior officers morphs into a demand for abstract thinking ability, especially from strategists and very senior officers, whose daily activity revolves around the wicked problems of the day. The "deaths" of our abstract thinkers result from a thousand cuts, not single strokes. For example, the title of the Air Force officer evaluation form is the "Officer Performance Report" (OPR). The Air Force structured the OPR to report on what the officer has done; not one block on the form asks about how well the officer thinks.

Who are we? By accession, activity, and evaluation we are STEM-oriented linear thinkers with strong personality tendencies toward accomplishment rather than reflection. The few exceptions to this picture are those linear thinkers also capable of, or at least comfortable with, abstract thinking; however, all of them I have ever met in the military had very strong type A personalities. In other words, these exceptions to the rule might think abstractly, but at the end of the day they knew they had to produce something. They had to "git 'er done." So, as prospective leaders, since we may not be abstract thinkers ourselves, we must work hard to create or cultivate those people with abilities to deal with wicked, nonlinear problems, using the best abstract thinking skills and coupling them to the best accomplishment efforts in order to develop well-structured options for ill-structured problems. Perhaps even more important, we may need to protect our abstract thinkers while they transit the "linear" portions of their careers. These distinctions between linear and nonlinear (abstract) thinking are stark when we look at the strategist versus the planner.

THE STRATEGIST: COMPARED TO THE PLANNER

Building from the previous discussion, let us examine the differences between strategists and planners. At its core, the difference between the two, at least in my mind, results from the different activities and outcomes required from each. The strategist must think about context and problem definition and then use the outcomes of these efforts to frame the problem, producing the guidance that shapes what planners do. Planners, on the other hand, take framing guidance and look for solutions. Once a solution is accepted, the planners produce the detailed plans that make it possible for others to execute the option selected by leadership. In short, strategy gives focus to determining what needs to be accomplished; planning is what planners do when they know what it is that needs to be achieved. Two vignettes help illustrate these differences.

This first illustrates the difference between the drive to produce a solution and the need to understand context and the problem. So, imagine driving home after a long, challenging day at the office. We might think to ourselves, "Man, all I want is a cold beverage, dinner, some TV, and early to bed."[10] Then we open the front door. On the other side, our spouse awaits after an equally long day at home with three kids, all under the age of six. Our spouse lays into us with all the things gone awry during the day, detailing one problem after another. Now in "crisis response mode," we respond with the fateful words, "If you had only done this or that differently, then you would not have had this or that problem." Eureka, we think, in one fell swoop we have found the solution to our spouse's day.

Sometime later, preparing after a cold dinner to spend the night on the sofa, we reflect on the earlier events. We realize that in our hasty default to arrive at solution we had misunderstood the context of our spouse's agitation, completely misdiagnosed the problem, and failed to devise a conceptual framework to achieve a positive outcome. Keep in mind that we being the STEM, type A, "git'er done" people we are, it is in our DNA to default to solution. We could no more "not default" to solution than quit breathing. However, the strategist must never determine a solution before understanding context, defining the problem, and thinking through the desired parameters for solution development.[11]

Another way of examining the differences between strategist and planner comes in a second vignette, from the world of architecture.[12] In his book *How Designers Think,* Bryan Lawson describes an architectural firm in need of a new building (the problem). The firm is a medium-sized one that does both commercial and residential design and is looking to expand its market share in a community with over a million people and several other very competitive architectural businesses (the context). The company's leadership employs three teams to develop a design for a new facility for the architectural firm itself (framing design concepts).

The first team sets to work using a functional framework for analysis. Its members look at the design challenge as one of creating the most efficient workspace possible for the employees. Their rationale is, of course, one predicated on the idea that efficiency will provide the customer the best design at the best price—in other words, the classic efficiency/effectiveness idea. Their key assumption is that in the competitive world of architectural design, the cost of doing business will be the driving factor.

The second group, however, takes a different approach; its members focus on the customer. Their design seeks to make future customers' experience with their firm the best one possible. So, they consider every element, from the customer's initial entry into the lobby to finding exactly the right department within the company, and so build their design from the customer's perspective. They also think of common activity areas, like billing and drafting, placing them between the two major functional departments of the firm, commercial and residential design. They even consider how to lay out the parking lot to bring the customer to the front door efficiently. Their focus on the customer dictates the design logic for their approach, and their key assumption mimics the old adage, "The customer is always right."

The last team takes yet another approach to the building designs. This group thinks about the competitive context in which their firm does business. They decide on an aesthetic approach to the project. Their idea is to create a visually stunning statement that would indicate the creativeness of its architects and serve to bring customers to its door. As such, their design took advantage of the site location and its surroundings, as well as making a visual statement to the community. Their key assumption is one of "form over function."

As one considers the vignette above, there are at least three key points to take away. First, design is not about finding the "one right answer" to a problem in a given context. Wicked problems in social and societal contexts do not have single solutions. *The* right answers simply don't exist—only some answers that are better than others. Second, each approach above represents a framework in the context of the firm and the problem. The firm could use any one of these approaches (or "courses of action," in our parlance) for solution development. I highlight this point because the approach is not the solution. The solution translates, eventually, into the blueprints that a builder uses to construct the new building. What guides the development of those blueprints is the choice between functional, customer, and aesthetic perspectives. There are likely many courses of action for construction and a best one for any given building project. Finally, we can ask ourselves, "Which design framework did management choose?" One can speculate that management chose to optimize the final design, influenced by each of the others, to achieve a blended solution that the structural architects and engineers would turn into blueprints and building schedules.

This section has given us an idea of who we are and of some of the challenges we face as strategists, as well as ideas of how strategists and planners differ. In the next two sections we will examine what it is that strategists and planners do. This examination will help us to delineate the tasks between the two activities. However, one does not do strategy in some pure vacuum—the strategist does it with the purpose of achieving some larger purpose. For wicked problems, achieving something of significance requires careful planning and a well-designed course of action, with a detailed operational plan. So, as we transition to these next sections, keep in mind that the strategist and the planner are interlinked in an iterative process.

STRATEGISTS: DOING AND EDUCATING

Describing what strategists do reminds me of "job guidance" I received from a boss back in the day. I was new to my job, and he asked me if I had any questions about my duties. I told him I would simply work everything that came my way and figured he would let me know if I screwed something up. He pondered that point for a moment and then laid out his views on my duties: "Take care of everything, and do it perfectly." This story may not convey the duties of a strategist, but it captures the expectations placed on them. For the strategist, we could rephrase to say, "Think of everything, and do it perfectly."

The duties of the strategist are many; however, they collect around three broad activities in support of decision makers.[13] First, the strategist works to develop understanding of the context surrounding a given wicked problem (or set of them). Next, the strategist works to define the problem. Lastly, the strategist develops the guidance that provides the design concept for solving a specific problem in a given context. The architecture vignette provides an example of these three elements. It almost sounds easy, does it not?

However, making coherent strategy is a tough task, as evidenced by the overabundance of poor strategy.[14] An example of the kind of poor thinking that leads to poor strategy is the DoD effort directing the services to implement language programs by which all officers in the rank of O-1 and O-2 would achieve basic proficiency in a foreign language. The "office of primary responsibility" directed that implementation of this initiative occur within a seven-year time frame.[15] As in this case, sometimes someone issues you a solution and demands an implementation plan in return. Often when such an initiative arrives at the strategist's door, he has to work the issue backward to understand what strategy is in use, to understand what problem the higher headquarters is attempting to address, and in what environmental context.

Setting aside the challenges of implementation, and they were many, I offered the following assessment of this initiative to my counterparts on the Air Staff. In a general sense, I sought to understand what problem the lead office thought it was trying to solve. So, I started with a basic question: "For what problem in the USAF is this the solution?" I thought about officers in international air forces and realized that with very few exceptions these airmen, as they grew in experience and rank, increased their proficiency in English. I surmised that the same dynamic was at work with diplomats and politicians. Therefore, it seemed to me that the level of language proficiency could not be the central problem. For example, if one were to extrapolate such an issue into the future, one could ask, "Which language will be the language du jour of the next crisis?" Arabic? Pashtu? Chinese?

The second point I pondered was that of a requirement for USAF airmen to have foreign-language expertise. To highlight this issue, I posed this question to my Air Staff compatriots, "What is the international language of aviation?" The answer of course is English. The International Civil Aviation Organization within the United Nations has established that, among many other forms of guidance for aviation. So, I asked again, "For what Air Force problem is this DoD initiative the answer?" Continuing our reverse engineering of this strategy/planning guidance, let us look at the context of this initiative and its key underlying assumption.

The context primarily centered on the two wars the United States was fighting in the 2000s; DoD's language strategy and its key assumption built from this environment. By 2005 the United States was at war in Afghanistan and Iraq, and neither effort was going well for U.S. forces. Many problems were occurring that illustrated a lack of cultural understanding and highlighted shortfalls in U.S. doctrine and training.[16] As often happens, the "let's do something, anything," pressure was building, and one solution had led to the DoD initiative on language training. Continuing to work this problem in reverse, we ask ourselves, "What was the underlying assumption if the issue was culture and the solution was language?" The answer could only be that for the designers of this strategy, cultural expertise = language expertise. Poor, if not necessarily faulty, assumptions have led more than one strategist astray in the design of a strategy to solve a given problem in a given context. Here too, smart people used a flawed assumption as guidance and so developed a poor solution. I have often wondered if the "strategic corporal" needed much more language skill in Iraq or Afghanistan than "Thank you for the tea, your home is lovely," and "Stop, or I will shoot you."

Granted, we need language as well as culture experts (not always the same people), but no language-training course could produce either result in a few short weeks or even a few months. Years of education and training, as well as a similarly long incubation period living within the culture in question, are required to yield experts capable of shaping such environments at the individual level. In addition, in STEM disciplines we found it difficult if not impossible to "squeeze" language training into an already packed course of study.

Now, let's return to the three tasks of the strategist and think of "how" these jobs get done, keeping in mind that sometimes the strategist starts with little or no guidance and sometimes with a solution for which he must find context, problem, and design. In the first task, we should note that leadership seldom issues context to us. Often we get problems dumped on us and solutions (if not design) issued to us, but seldom will anyone provide context.

The first step in doing strategy is to develop the context—get to know the key actors, relationships, factors, and challenges. I start by grappling with those things that make for good versus bad strategy in general and transition to issues relating to context. Under "context," the strategist examines the strategic and operational environments and looks for the actors who foment or affect the challenges that bring about the problems of the day, as well as those who might resolve these issues. In addition, the strategist spends time looking at conflict termination, to ensure strategies focus as much on the future and the continuing advantage sought as on the initiation of the struggle.[17] Finally, as the strategist looks to put concepts into practice, she explores the making of strategy using a top-down methodology. She starts at the national policy level (drawing in international policy where and when required) and works down to the operational strategy level, most often the combatant and component commander levels.

The next task of the strategist is to understand the problem (or problems) he is facing. The strategist examines problems from the perspective of the *kinds* of problems the strategy group is likely to face and how to define problems so the design focuses on the main issue or challenge facing the nation and the joint team. He works to understand the "wicked" nature of the social and societal challenges and the difficulty of understanding each test in its unique context. One of the most important determinations one makes in problem definition is that of causal versus symptomatic elements of the problem. In some wicked problems, the military strategist finds that the military instrument of power addresses only symptoms, not causes. The counterinsurgency wars in Iraq and Afghanistan illustrate this point.

Tackling wicked problems leads one to concepts like chaos, complexity, and systems dynamics. For strategy students, it is always interesting to study predictability and unpredictability in a chaotic environment. Learning how complexity multiplies in the social and societal contexts of the wicked problems with which strategists deal helps them understand the Clausewitzian adage that in war, even the simplest thing is difficult.[18] Strategists typically find that using systemic approaches (operations design and others) help to refine one's thinking about wicked challenges yet do not prescribe rules or processes for designing the guidance that leads to solution development.

This last task requires the strategist to develop a design concept that ties national/international goals and objectives to the guidance that will drive the planning process and the development and subsequent selection of a course of action. As one might guess, this effort ties the problem and its context to the mission guidance required for operational planning, as found in the Joint Operation Planning Process. The development of an operational design serves to tie strategic goals, objectives, and direction to the kinds of operational missions one expects combatant commanders and their components to accomplish—that is, as the *M* in the DIME (diplomacy, information, military, and economic) instruments of national power. Using a strategy-task methodology, strategists and planners link the strategic level to goals and activities at the operational and even tactical levels of operation.

There is good news and bad, however, in the development of operational design. The good news for students of strategy is that operations design is finding its niche in service and joint doctrine. For example, Air Force Doctrine Document 3-0, *Operations and Planning,* discusses how the USAF uses the operational design concepts in designing air operations.[19] Joint Publication 5-0, *Joint Operations Planning,* has a chapter detailing the application of operational art and operational design in the JOPP.[20] The bad news is that once "we" place a conceptual approach into doctrine it tends to become a process, then a checklist; finally it loses its connection with the original intent, to be a way to think about wicked problems, and becomes just another "cake mix" of instructions to follow and steps to perform. In short, it gets EBO'd.[21]

As much as I would like to, I cannot tell the new strategist how to solve the wicked problems he will face in his career as a strategist. I can promise that every problem she faces will be unique to her in terms of the problem and its context, if for no other reason than that the human element will always be new. No matter how similar a problem looks to one that occurred in the past, the context will be different, and so one must develop unique operational designs tying together context, problem, and guidance for the development of solution(s). At SAASS, our motto "From the Past, the Future" is our way of saying that the past prepares the mind but never equates to the future. Accordingly, our focus is always on teaching the strategist how to think rather than what to think. As I transition to thinking about planning, I leave you with the following thoughts by Richard Rumelt on good strategy:

> The core of strategy work is always the same: discovering the critical factors in a situation and designing a way of coordinating and focusing actions to deal with those factors.[22]

> The key insight . . . is the hard-won lesson of a life-time of experience at strategy work . . . [that a] good strategy does more than urge us forward

toward a goal or vision. A good strategy honestly acknowledges the challenges being faced and provides an approach to overcoming them. And the greater the challenge, the more a good strategy focuses and coordinates efforts to achieve a powerful competitive punch or problem-solving effect. Unfortunately, good strategy is the exception, not the rule.[23]

PLANNERS: DOING AND EDUCATING (AND TRAINING)

As we begin to think about what planners do, I want to clarify our lexicon a bit. I have made a clear distinction between strategists and planners. In reality, the literature, doctrine, and common usage are not nearly so clear or distinct. Similarly, the use of the term "strategy" versus "planning" in common usage lacks the sharp definition offered here. For example, the joint community discusses operational design in a separate chapter of the JOPP; however, the Joint Staff title for the publication JP 5-0 is *Joint Operations Planning*. So, as strategists, one of the most important tasks is to serve as the "universal translator" in the discussions of strategists and planners, strategy and planning, and Planning, which, with the capital *P*, most likely includes both strategy and planning activities. (Keep in mind that the one thing sure to reign supreme in a crisis-action group is confusion. Moreover, much of the confusion will be over naming conventions.)[24] Now, let us turn to and examine the things that planners do.

A good planning team cuts to the heart of its efforts, asking, "What do we have to do and what do we have to do it with?" What planners imply in such a question is that someone has told them what to do and what will be available to do "it" with in response to the crisis du jour. This point illustrates a key difference between strategy and planning—strategists are not necessarily constrained in terms of ways and means; planners usually are. For example, when President Roosevelt declared "unconditional surrender" as the operational end state of military operations for World War II, the Allied powers still lacked the means with which to accomplish such a task.[25] The strategy included building such capabilities and capacities.

In the real world, of course, there are no absolutes. Many of the crises the United States has faced since the end of the Cold War have been come-as-you-are events; only in the long wars in Afghanistan and Iraq could we say ways, means, and ends had time to evolve significantly over time. In Bosnia, Kosovo, and Libya, for example, strategists had to provide their input to the planners with many of the same limitations as to ways and means that constrained the planners.[26] One twist in this discussion results from recent operations in Libya, Operations

Odyssey Dawn (OOD) and Unified Protector (OUP).[27] In these operations, the U.S. approach to strategy and planning of "just add more," operative and repeated in every conflict since World War II, ended. Despite repeated requests for additional forces, OOD leaders, strategists, and planners ended up "making do" for the most part with forces available within the European theater.[28] This "constraint" became more apparent during OUP, as the other NATO allies carried the bulk of operations while keeping significant forces engaged in operations in Afghanistan. For the first time since World War II, the United States, its allies, and coalition partners had to plan a sequential war in a way that at times, because of limited capacities and capabilities, could only respond to the crisis of the moment. There were no "overwhelming forces" to call upon. Future strategists and planners would do well to consider whether such a condition was a "one-off" or "one to remember."

Planners too must cover a lot of ground in the tasks they perform. In this regard, there are many "process guides." Each of the services has its variation. For example, the Army has MDMP—the Military Decision-Making Process; the Navy its Navy Planning Process; the Marines the Marine Corps Planning Process (MCPP); and the Air Force its operations planning and execution. Each of these is a variation on theme of the joint operational planning process of the joint community. Over the years, the service and joint processes have steadily converged, such that, ostensibly, the services can talk and work together as a planning team either in a joint setting or in service component commands. However, the reality still diverges from the preferred path.

The planning world still struggles to get everyone on the same page. The Army and the Marines are the best trained in planning processes. From the earliest stages of their careers, soldiers and marines use MDMP and MCPP, respectively, as their basic mission planning schemes. No "back of the envelope" planning here; they have these processes down and use them for nearly every activity—the Air Force and the Navy, not so much. I will leave our seafaring brethren on their own and focus on the Air Force.

The Air Force loves mission planning; however, it equally loves the "county option."[29] I suspect a survey of airmen when asked who/what JOPP-A is would produce responses falling in a range from believing it to be an emerging rap group to a few recognizing it as the air variation of the joint operational planning process. We love to be different. So most airmen, when thrown into a joint setting, are unfamiliar with the process and the lexicon of joint planning. Ah, I dream of the day when the Air Force creates a system for the development of tactical expertise and opts to have such a center, or centers, use a process not unlike the JOPP/JOPP-A to train its planners not only to do mission planning but to do so in a manner compatible with the rest of the joint team.[30]

Planners, like strategists, must endure demands to "solve world hunger" with every operational crisis or planning task. In the main, they actually accomplish two key tasks: one, they develop solutions and work toward solution selection; and two, they build the blueprints, the plans that put forces into motion. With the commander's design guidance (from the strategy group/cell), planners analyze the mission in light of the tasks and allocated resources and create the solution options—courses of action (COAs). Using criteria developed in the context of how the overall commander and subordinate levels of command defined success, planners evaluate the COAs using criteria developed with the commander and the strategy group.[31]

Once the commander selects a course of action, the hard toil of turning ideas into action begins, and planners work to produce the blueprint—the operations plan or concept plan that puts the detail into the process. This detail moves the force onto the field of battle and then sustains it through to mission completion. The various annexes in a plan provide the details, from operations to sustainment and the time-phased force deployment data to move forces, people, and equipment. A typical plan for a major operation can easily run to over a thousand pages of detail and represents a herculean effort by planners. In a twist on an old adage, "the job can't start until the paperwork is done."

A warning: the single most important "safety tip" I can offer you about the strategy-to-planning nexus is that the efforts of these two activities never stop, that the strategist and planner must function in an iterative way to ensure that ways and means achieve desired ends within the unique conflict context. Too often, strategists and planners fail to accomplish this iterative interaction or do it in a perfunctory manner. For example, common sense dictates keeping assumptions ever at the forefront of thought. However, in Operation Iraqi Freedom, who challenged the assumption that the Iraqis wanted "freedom," let alone freedom as leaders in the United States understood it? Recall that it took months of growing insurgency before this basic assumption fell before the reality of an insurgency and of an Iraq of various factions holding very different views of "freedom"—an Iraq that was more factional than inclusive. An honest and iterative review of such assumptions should prevent the "rose-colored glasses" syndrome from hiding the light of unwelcome truth. As strategists and planners, we must focus on reality and not wishful thinking.

So, how does one train and educate planners? In the Air Force, the education of planners typically begins with intermediate development education (IDE).[32] The Air Force begins training, however, early in a career. Aviators begin the process in pilot/navigator training, planning what events go into each flight or mission. So too for combat support officers—from technical training throughout their careers, support officers plan the efforts that support and sustain the mission. At schools like the USAF Weapons School and the Mobility Operations School, airmen receive advanced training and education in air planning and operations.

As mentioned in the previous paragraph, education in planning for most Air Force officers begins at IDE. For example, the Air Command and Staff College provides seminars in joint planning as part of the joint professional military education (JPME) requirements for joint education. The faculty also provides a planning elective that does a "deep dive" into operational planning, designed for planners at the component and combatant-commander staff levels.

There are other opportunities for planner training and education. For Air Force planners assigned to a component/combined/joint air and space operations center (C/JAOC), the 505th Command and Control Wing at Hurlburt Field, Florida, provides exceptional programs to prepare airmen for duties as air, space, and cyber planners from the tactical to the operational levels. In addition, the wing offers courses to prepare airmen for senior leadership positions in the C/JAOC.

In addition, the LeMay Center for Doctrine Development and Education provides a series of courses at the intermediate- and senior-officer levels. At the intermediate level, the center offers courses in joint air operations and contingency wartime planning, as well as information operations application. For senior leaders, it runs courses for the combined/joint air component commander, a warfighting course for joint flag officers, and executive courses in cyberspace operations and Air Force warfighter perspectives.

BRINGING TOGETHER STRATEGY AND PLANNING

The following depiction gives us "a way" to link a perspective on critical thinking to the preparation and activities of strategists and planners. I readily admit that the figure below is a composite of a lifetime of thinking about strategy and planning, as well as the influences of many others pondering these same issues. In short, the ideas here are not mine but an amalgamation of those of many other people to whom I am indebted for the education of a lifetime. The figure illustrates how one creates strategists (and planners) who can lead "big P" planning.

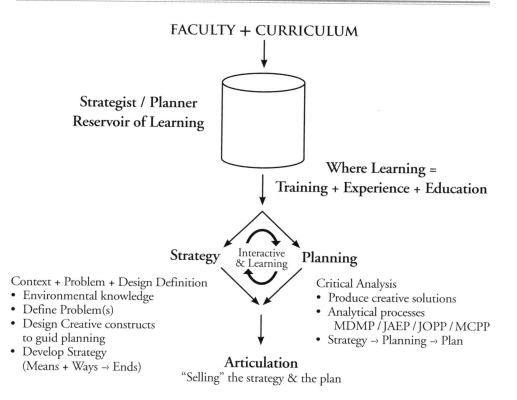

FACULTY + CURRICULUM

Strategist / Planner
Reservoir of Learning

Where Learning =
Training + Experience + Education

Strategy   Interactive & Learning   Planning

Context + Problem + Design Definition
• Environmental knowledge
• Define Problem(s)
• Design Creative constructs
  to guid planning
• Develop Strategy
  (Means + Ways → Ends)

Critical Analysis
• Produce creative solutions
• Analytical processes
  MDMP / JAEP / JOPP / MCPP
• Strategy → Planning → Plan

Articulation
"Selling" the strategy & the plan

The most critical elements of the figure are the faculty and the budding strategist and planner. A quality faculty can create the kind of curriculum that inspires students to learn and to master concepts, abstract and specific. Of course, the clay the faculty molds—the student—must be equal to the task. The Air Force has a great record of providing superb "clay" for this task. As we follow the depiction in the figure from top to bottom, the progression should by now be familiar. The depiction, of course, is one of a "perfect world"—a world where the creation of strategy and planning begin with the development of context for a problem situation/condition, leading to the development of a design that provides creative option paths that guide critical analysis in the planning section.

Another key element in the figure is the learning and iteration loop. It is there to remind one that strategy is always about getting something done and that to accomplish anything requires one to acknowledge the real world. While the strategist works continuously to refine the design with context and problem-definition updates, he must include the real-world limitations encountered by his planner counterpart. The planner, of course, works to merge concept with reality and to get from solution options to solution selection and "blueprint" development. Through the depicted iteration loop, the planner feeds her limitations or exploitation opportunities back to the strategist so that both can balance ways, means, and ends for decision makers. Indeed, the strategist and the planner are two sides of a single coin, as strategy simply has no purpose without a plan, and a plan without a strategy is a headless vector capable of achieving purpose only through blind serendipity.

It is important to keep in mind the key challenges that the strategist or planner faces. First and foremost are the critical three: context, context, context. Getting the context correct is the most critical element in strategy and planning. Keep in mind, the strategist and planner need the context of every participant—state and nonstate actors alike—in the crisis/contingency; one cannot be satisfied with knowing only one's own context.

The strategist must also be clear as to exactly what problem requires resolution. Recall the earlier DoD language-proficiency example and the issue it involved of identifying the real problem. As the strategist works to refine the problem statement, it is very important to determine if the problem entails issues of causation or symptoms or both. For example, one could say the United States sought to wipe out terrorism in Afghanistan by ending the al Qaeda presence there. If true, the best one could say is that the United States eliminated symptoms of terrorism—al Qaeda extremists—but not the causal factors that led to the terrorism problem that began the conflict. In addition, while it is important to distinguish causal factors from symptomatic ones, it is even more important to know the limits of the military instrument of national power in addressing either symptoms or their causal factors. The strategist works iteratively with the planner to ensure that national and military ways and means serve to meet the desired ends of national leaders.

For planners, the key challenge is to avoid "groundhog day." As George Santayana said, "Those who cannot remember the past are condemned to repeat it."[33] However, no matter how much a crisis today looks like one from yesteryear, each is unique to its context and the human element experiencing the current event. It is very easy to default to the past as a crutch for dealing with the complex problems of today. So, while at SAASS we say, "From the past, the future," that is very different from "the past = the future." The past informs us but does not dictate. In addition, knowledge of the past can let us know of pitfalls that we could avoid or anticipate better and more successful outcomes.

Another crutch is to satisfice with regard to a crisis—in other words, to build solutions based upon a set of criteria that may or not cover the entirety of the problem within its unique context. For example, I have seen many crisis simulations derail when a leader says solve for *A, B, C,* and *D.* Sure enough, all the leader gets back are answers to the four listed points. Interaction between strategists and planners helps to mitigate this tendency of human nature.

CONCLUSION

The basic premise of this chapter is that although strategy and planning are different, they are two sides of the same coin, that the former is not relevant without the latter and the latter is unguided without the former. Moreover, in addition to activity differences, the strategist and the planner are dissimilar. The former must be able to think in abstract terms that develop conceptual frameworks, the latter in more linear terms to produce solutions and the blueprints to implement them.

The development of a strategist requires the study of theory, concepts, and application in order to multiply, virtually, the experience base of each student of strategy. Strategists could never "experience" more than a handful of life-changing events in any one job, assignment, or even lifetime. However, through education one can experience hundreds, even thousands of other people's experiences in multiple contexts with the wicked problems of their eras as the grist for learning how to grind in the intellectual mill of the mind.

At the School of Advanced Air and Space Studies, our task is clear—to "educate strategists for the Air Force and the nation." This task from Gen. Larry Welch continues to serve as true north for the school and for the Air Force as it develops both strategists and planners. As I tell thesis students at SAASS, there are many "rabbit holes" one can follow—many "bright and shiny objects" to distract—yet we must focus on *the* problem, wicked and complex though it may be, in whatever context surrounds it in order to design the concepts that direct energy and effort toward a successful outcome. We educate strategists.

NOTES

1. Department of Defense, *Joint Operation Planning,* Joint Publication 5-0 (Washington, D.C., 11 August 2011) [hereafter JP 5-0], IV-2 to IV-3, http://www.dtic.mil/doctrine/new_pubs/jp5_0.pdf (accessed 11 January

2012). Chapter 4 provides the detailed explanation of the JOPP. In addition, the executive summary, xxv–xxviii, gives a brief introduction to the subject.

2. So named because the Iraqis always seemed to stir up trouble in the fall, ruining the Thanksgiving or Christmas holiday seasons.

3. Sun Tzu, *The Art of War,* trans. Samuel B. Griffith (London: Oxford University Press, 1963, 1971), 84.

4. Although the focus of recruiting is STEM, actual accessions include a variety of education backgrounds, owing in part to the demand in other endeavors for STEM graduates.

5. Saul McCloud, "Type A Personality," Simply Psychology, 2011, http://www.simplypsychology.org/personality-a.html#sthash.2krGukbQ.dpuf (accessed 1 February 2013). Of course, the downside to people with these personalities is that they can be overbearing, stubborn, and narrow-minded in thinking and action.

6. Theatrical acknowledgments to Austin Powers in *Austin Powers: International Man of Mystery.*

7. Horst W. J. Rittel and Melvin M. Webber, "Dilemmas in a General Theory of Planning," *Policy Sciences* 4 (1973): 160.

8. Chairman, Joint Chiefs of Staff, *Capstone Concept for Joint Operations: Joint Force 2020* (Washington, D.C., 10 September 2012), 3, http://www.jcs.mil//content/files/2012–09/092812122654_CCJO_JF2020_FINAL.pdf (accessed 28 September 2012).

9. School of Advanced Military Studies [hereafter SAMS], *Art of Design: Student Text,* version 2.0, 119, http://usacac.army.mil/cac2/CGSC/events/sams/ArtofDesign_v2.pdf (access confirmed 1 February 2013).

10. My apologies up front for the male orientation. Mea culpa.

11. I usually convey this vignette as a "survey" question to students. Very few admit to having found themselves in this circumstance, although nearly all sheepishly look down at their notes and quietly laugh.

12. Bryan Lawson, *How Designers Think: The Design Process Demystified,* 4th ed. (London: Routledge, Taylor & Francis, 2005), 181–99. Lawson discusses this vignette in a chapter (11) in his book; however, I paraphrase here and adapt the storyline (and improvise a bit) in the text to highlight the differences between the strategist as designer and the planner. Lawson's is the better prose, but I hope the reader here understands the point I am trying to convey.

13. The School of Advanced Air and Space Studies (SAASS) has taught the elements of context, problem definition, and problem framing (logic construction) since its inception. That said, our colleagues at the School of Advanced Military Studies did the work to codify these concepts with a supporting body of work. See SAMS, *Art of Design,* 120 (and chap. 3 for expanded concepts).

14. For a good discussion on good versus bad strategy, see Richard P. Rumelt, *Good Strategy, Bad Strategy: The Difference and Why It Matters* (New York: Crown Business, 2011).

15. The author served on the Air Force team that analyzed the implications for USAF implementation of this DoD directive.

16. One can find many sources to examine that range from screed (at both ends of the extreme spectrum) to "no problem here" relating to these points. The Army published a manuscript in 2006 that provides a reflective review of this issue. See William D. Wunderle, *Through the Lens of Cultural Awareness: A Primer for US Forces Deploying to Arab and Middle Eastern Countries* (Fort Leavenworth, Kans.: Combat Studies Institute Press, 2006), 2–4. These pages summarize selected common problems and doctrine and training shortfalls.

17. "Continuing advantage" is a concept put forth by my colleague Everett C. Dolman in his book *Pure Strategy: Power and Principle in the Space and Information Age* (New York: Frank Cass, 2005), 4, 18.

18. Carl von Clausewitz, *On War,* ed. and trans. Michael Howard and Peter Paret (Princeton, N.J.: Princeton University Press, 1976), 119.

19. U.S. Air Force, *Operations and Planning,* Air Force Doctrine Document 3-0 (9 November 2012), https://wwwmil.maxwell.af.mil/au/lemay/main .asp.

20. JP 5-0.

21. By "EBO'd" I am referring to the odyssey of effects-based operations from a concept in the 1990s to anathema for Gen. James Mattis at Joint Forces Command in the 2000s. Sadly, contractors at JFCOM took the original concepts and built an ossified edifice of process that completely compromised the original ideas. Similarly, "new" contractors at JFCOM attempted the same thing with operational design. Their first draft was a "how to" operations design procedures manual exceeding 250 pages in length.

22. Rumelt, *Good Strategy, Bad Strategy,* 2.

23. Ibid., 4.

24. At moments like these, I like to call things "bob." No matter which way you spell it, you get "bob." The circularity of naming arguments will make your head hurt, and so I offer, "bob" as a way forward. Again, please note that the sharp distinction between strategy and planning I draw here is not so clear in the real world.

25. Recall that Franklin D. Roosevelt and Winston Churchill announced this objective at the Casablanca Conference in January 1943, just over a year after the United States entered the war. It would be a year and some before the "arsenal of democracy" began to overwhelm Germany and Japan in terms of military production.

26. One could include the initial phases of Afghanistan and Iraq as come-as-you-are events too. As secretary of defense, Donald Rumsfeld stated at a

town hall in-theater, "As you know, you go to war with the Army you have. They're not the Army you might want or wish to have at a later time." See William Kristol, "The Defense Secretary We Have," *Washington Post,* 15 December 2004, A33, http://www.washingtonpost.com/wp-dyn/articles /A132–2004Dec14.html (accessed 28 February 2013).

27. OOD was the U.S.-led coalition that conducted the first days of the Libyan conflict, OUP being the NATO-led coalition that carried the conflict to termination some eight months later.

28. Maj. Gen. Margaret H. Woodward, "Defending America's Vital National Interests in Africa" (remarks at the Air Force Association's 2011 Air & Space Conference & Technology Exposition, National Harbor, Md., 21 September 2011).

29. "County option" is a colloquialism meaning "do it however you want." Often one finds different planning tools and methods in use by the various weapon-system planners, unguided by a standardized process. The results are often creative, if equally often hard to relate to the work of planners in the sister services.

30. One day, yes, one day, there will be a USAF Weapons School where instructors could teach these processes and students could learn, master, and propagate such teachings throughout the force. One day, one day—but I digress. In reality, Air Force planners could easily adjust mission planning to JOPP/JOPP-A and subsequently integrate it seamlessly with their joint compatriots.

31. The evaluation criteria for COA analysis are always unique to context, problem, and mission. Most criteria include strengths and weaknesses of the plan, opportunities and threats (which might drive branches or sequels in the plan), risk to the COA and probability for success, timing issues/ criteria, and the ability of the plan to meet or contribute to the accomplishment of mission objectives (the ends, to include those at the national/ international level), constraints and restraints, and the ways and means available to meet requirements. Keep in mind I mean this list only to be representative of criteria, not to be all-inclusive.

32. Note that in 1990, then–Chief of Staff Larry Welch chartered SAASS to develop strategists. As throughout this article, in our focus on strategy and strategists at SAASS, we try not to forget the interactive and iterative processes that must ensue between the two activities. I would be remiss if I did not note that our colleagues at Air Command and Staff College (ACSC) provide an exceptional course in operational planning, a course that we at SAASS encourage prospective applicants to our program to take advantage of while at ACSC.

33. George Santayana, *Life of Reason* (New York: Charles Scribner's Sons, 1955), 4.

CONCLUSION

Coming Full Circle

MARK O. YEISLEY

The need for strategy is constant in times of peace and war, yet the nature of strategy is protean and unclear. Volumes have been written about the subject as it relates to national security, nuclear surety, battlefield maneuver, and business, yet when asked its most basic meaning, many are unsure how to answer. This book has attempted to clarify the issue for those who study (or wish to impart) strategic wisdom; in doing so it has drawn from widely different disciplines that individually and collectively inform the study of strategy. While this work focuses on military strategy, it should be clear that numerous applications to other fields exist as well.

Lest the reader be unduly disappointed, this book does not clearly answer the question of what strategy *is*; instead, it focuses more on how strategy should be sought and outlines multiple approaches for doing so. As Dolman avers in chapter 1, it is not necessary for us to define strategy before we study it or discover its profound implications. Tacticians, he writes, seek to culminate their efforts on fields of battle, where all is known and victory and defeat are clearly defined and immutable. Strategists, while dependent on proper execution of the tactical, seek options that will expand available choice sets; thus continuation of planning, rather than culmination, is the goal of strategy. While strategy is about the plans and actions of political and military leaders, it is also intensely contextual; both the environment being studied and the perceptions and beliefs of the strategist studying it profoundly affect the strategy derived. What is important, Dolman

253

reminds us, is that strategy is dynamic, a deliberate search for continuing advantage. Strategists seek to understand all that *can* be known and to plan for and mitigate to the maximum degree possible what *cannot.* In this way the "fog of war," as Clausewitz famously described uncertainty, can be correspondingly minimized.

Moving away from the purely theoretical, Winton explores in chapter 2 the relationship between military theory and the military profession. Although it is clear that underlying truths make the relationship between theory and the military profession problematic, theory should educate the strategist's judgment and provide concrete guides for military action. When tested against the experiences of Generals George Patton and Ulysses S. Grant, however, surprising truths are discovered. Winton finds that Patton used theory as "Clausewitz intended it to be used"—as something to be absorbed by the military mind at the deepest levels. While Patton possessed a genius for war prepared by a deep understanding of military theory, Grant preferred novels to professional reading yet still became a commanding general who learned "on the job" through intense observation and reflection. Though military theory can be a valuable ingredient to the military mind, it more often serves a greater purpose in augmenting military genius.

International relations, as a field of study, seeks to understand the causes of war and the conditions necessary for peace; each of these is essential for the strategist to grasp. Of the many theories outlining how states compete for relative advantage, none is more enduring than realism. From Thucydides' account of the Peloponnesian Wars to the modern offerings of neorealism, no other single theory has demonstrated such predictive power concerning international interactions. Realists insist that survival is the most fundamental goal of states; with no one else looking out for them, states have no choice but to pursue their interests if they are not to risk destruction. Given that strategists must comprehend how states compete within a system having only limited power to restrain them, such theoretical mastery is mandatory. Yet Forsyth in chapter 3 reveals that realism remains an insufficient explanatory tool; the relentless pursuit of self-interest without regard for morality can often lead states to destruction. The strategist must therefore remember the moral component of strategy; failure to do so can result in tragically suboptimal outcomes.

No understanding of strategy can occur without an extensive foundation of history, as Tucci avers in chapter 4; the imbroglio he sets forth in his Socratic dialogue is a vivid summary of the importance of the study of classical history for the modern strategist. Important and enduring lessons can be learned from classical Greek and Roman writings; Clausewitz, Alfred von Schlieffen, and airpower theorist John Warden all relied heavily on classical history to inform their insights into the strategy process. Thucydides' writings on the Peloponnesian Wars provide an early account of great-power politics that informs international relations theory to this day. The Roman republic yields profound lessons for modern civil-military relations theory, and the effects of technological development on strategy and battle were no less remarkable in the classical era than they are on the modern battlefield. While the trireme, lance, and battle chariot may have faded away, the lessons of the ancient Greeks and Romans remain valuable to this day; the modern strategist who ignores them does so at his or her own peril.

The modern strategist must also be cognizant of the symbiotic relationship that exists between strategy and technology. While technology can transform the context of strategy, strategy can also, as Chiabotti adroitly observes in chapter 5, transform technologies. The evolution of the nuclear age provides proof of such a phenomenon: the discovery of nuclear fission, strategically implemented by the United States and others, led to the development of the nuclear weapon, which in turn transformed international security and military strategy for several decades (as of this writing). Considering the pace of technological change of the early twenty-first century, the modern strategist must in turn closely observe this evolutionary (or revolutionary) process to maximize predictive prowess and meet the challenge of concurrent strategic reassessment and change.

In its formative years the U.S. Air Force eschewed historical study almost entirely, focusing instead, until the end of the Cold War, on current affairs, staff and leadership skills, and technology. Indeed, Muller in chapter 6 suggests the Air Force believed there was little to gain from any examination of the past; the 1930s bombardment course as written had no historical content whatsoever. Air Command and Staff School, the Air Force midcareer officer education source, had no military or airpower history in its curriculum until the 1980s; no full-time civilian history professors were on its faculty until 1991. Congressional inquiry in the late 1980s and U.S. involvement in the first Gulf War provided the impetus for Air Force educational programs to embrace military and airpower history. According to Muller, history links airmen to a rich heritage, helps legitimize doctrine, provides lessons from past events, and helps the force consider the complex interactions of people and specific contextual factors that inform strategy development.

As a logical follow-on to Muller's comments, Jeffrey Smith argues in chapter 7 that before an effective airpower strategy could be developed, the U.S. Air Force had to develop and then institutionalize an underpinning airpower theory. Smith argues that prewar airpower thinkers failed to recognize two vital requirements for developing an effective airpower strategy: that contextual realities must be considered before translating such a theory into practice and that airpower strategy would have to be modified when these realities prevented that translation from occurring. This was the case during World War II, when the combined bomber offensive failed to achieve bombardment goals in the face of German resistance. The nuclear airpower strategy adopted by Strategic Air Command after World War II failed to translate airpower theory effectively within a politically constrained context. Similarly, he argues, the current fighter-centric airpower theory of gaining air superiority and precisely targeting enemy infrastructure and combatants has failed to challenge and defeat adversaries effectively in unconventional conflicts. To regain its effectiveness, U.S. airpower strategy must therefore consider all aspects of air, space, and cyber domains to meet the current and future contextual realities that will confront us.

Currently no greater or more rapid technological evolutions are occurring than in the realms of space and cyber; as of this writing the Mars Rover continues its exploration of the Martian surface, while NASA seeks to capture an asteroid with a robotic spaceship and place it in a stable orbit about the moon for future study. Space has become far more than just "the final frontier," as Gene Roddenberry once claimed; it now is, as M. V. Smith asserts in chapter 8, a strategic center of gravity (pardon the pun) and thus a crucial dimension of state power. Strategists must consider both the peacetime and wartime aspects of space protection, as space-based platforms perform a myriad of functions that support U.S. interests in war and peace simultaneously. These assets support diplomacy and military might through intelligence gathering and communications support while enhancing cultural and informational soft-power initiatives via data transmission that supports weather and climate information, as well as international trade. Maintaining and protecting these capabilities is vital to the modern strategist, for by doing so astutely he or she can accomplish the primary role of spacepower—that of preventing future war.

The evolution of global cyber capability is arguably progressing even faster and in a more revolutionary fashion than that of spacepower. Its rapidly changing nature has made it difficult to define cyberspace and respond to its nascent technologies; in addition, disagreement over its potential in war makes the development of proper strategy for its use and protection challenging indeed. Yet Bailey in chapter 9 shows how these formidable challenges pale in significance when compared to the social and political tensions that exist between quests for liberty versus order, notions of cooperative behavior as compared to isolationist tendencies, and the need for both transparency and privacy. The need for monitoring is vital, yet monitoring smacks of Big Brother; cooperation breeds stronger relationships but can also enhance vulnerabilities, and transparency also means the loss of privacy rights. Each of these conundrums makes a coherent future cyber strategy difficult indeed.

As a counter to the demands of future warfare, Yeisley in chapter 10 urges the modern strategist not to forget the lessons of conflicts past. While interstate warfare becomes increasingly uncommon as the pace of globalization quickens, the likelihood of irregular war between state and nonstate actors disaffected by globalization's residual effects remains significant. The problematic nature of irregular conflict (unpredictability of winners and losers, its lengthy and costly nature, and the destabilizing regional effects it can have) makes it essential that strategists have the necessary understanding to address it properly. They must understand the conditions that mobilize groups that foment irregular conflicts, identify the motivations that can drive individuals to leave hearth and home despite the sanctions they and their family are likely to face, and discern the political and social ends these challenger groups seek. Thus informed, the modern strategist will be better able to guide the strategic employment of U.S. assets to assess, plan for, and combat these difficult and costly conflicts in the future.

Still, the education of the strategist is incomplete until the skills of proper planning for the acquisition of desired political and military goals are learned and mastered. It is to this task that chapter 11 is devoted; Wright lays out a cognitive path for the strategist to follow that will obviate the need to explore many of the more common pitfalls that lie on the path from strategy to execution. The strategist cum planner must understand herself and her environment in order to develop a keen understanding of the context of the problem before her; this helps to define the problem itself and sets the stage for the development of an array of possible solutions. Probably the most difficult transition from strategist to planner is in the realm of possibility, as strategists are not necessarily constrained in ways and means, while planners always are. Nevertheless, the strategist as planner must ensure that ways and means achieve desired ends within the unique context of the conflict at hand. As Wright reminds us, strategy is never about wishful thinking.

So what can the student strategist take from all of this? One obvious conclusion that is often reached is that "strategy is hard"—any armchair historian can point to the results of the Vietnam War, Iraq, and Afghanistan and snidely remark that if the world's greatest military suffered three failures in a row, surely strategy is not easy. Yet in truth he would be right—making useful and relevant strategy in uniquely contextual situations with constrained resources is deucedly difficult. While this volume does not dispute that fact, it does attempt to mitigate the difficulty of strategic design by pointing out the diversity of subjects that inform the study of strategy. Clearly understanding the complexity inherent in strategic design and informed by the myriad of subjects that support a comprehensive grasp of the subject, novice strategists will be better prepared to meet the demands of the twenty-first-century strategic environment. It is our fervent hope that this book accomplishes just that.

SELECTED BIBLIOGRAPHY

Ackerman, Spencer. "Bradley Manning Takes 'Full Responsibility' for Giving WikiLeaks Huge Government Data Trove." *Wired.* 28 February 2013. http://www.wired.com/threatlevel/2013/02/bradley-manning/.

Adams, Henry. *The Education of Henry Adams.* Boston: Houghton Mifflin, 1918.

Air Corps Tactical School. *Attack Aviation Course 1937.* Maxwell Air Force Base, Ala.: USAF Historical Research Agency 168.7045–30, 6.

Atran, Scott. *Talking to the Enemy: Faith, Brotherhood and the (Un)Making of Terrorists.* New York: HarperCollins, 2010.

Axelrod, Robert. *The Evolution of Cooperation.* New York: Basic Books, 1984.

Bassford, Christopher. "John Keegan and the Grand Tradition of Trashing Clausewitz: A Polemic." *War in History* 1 (November 1994): 319–36.

Beaufre, Andre. *An Introduction to Strategy.* New York: Praeger, 1965.

Becker, Carl L. *Everyman His Own Historian: Essays on History and Politics.* New York: F. S. Crofts, 1935.

Betz, David J., and Tim Stevens. *Cyberspace and the State: Toward a Strategy for Cyber-Power.* London: International Institute for Strategic Studies, 2011.

Beyerchen, Alan. "Clausewitz, Nonlinearity, and the Unpredictability of War." *International Security* (Winter 1992/93): 59–90.

Biddle, Tami Davis. *Rhetoric and Reality in Air Warfare.* Princeton, N.J.: Princeton University Press, 2002.

Bijker, Wiebe E., Thomas P. Hughes, and Trevor Pinch, eds. *The Social Construction of Technological Systems: New Directions in the Sociology and History of Technology.* Cambridge, Mass.: MIT Press, 1987.

Blumenson, Martin, ed. *The Patton Papers 1940–1945.* Boston: Houghton Mifflin, 1974.

Bousquet, Antoine. *The Scientific Way of Warfare: Order and Chaos on the Battlefields of Modernity.* New York: Columbia University Press, 2009.

Boyle, Robert. *The Sceptical Chymist or Chymico-Physical Doubts and Paradoxes.* London: F. Caldwell, 1661.

Bradley, Mark, ed. *Classics and Imperialism in the British Empire.* New York: Oxford University Press, 2010.

Brate, Adam. *Technomanifestos: Visions from the Information Revolutionaries.* New York: Texere, 2002.

Brenner, Joel. *America the Vulnerable: Inside the New Threat Matrix of Digital Espionage, Crime, and Warfare.* New York: Penguin Books, 2011.

Brenner, Susan W. *Cyberthreats: The Emerging Fault Lines of the Nation State.* Oxford: Oxford University Press, 2009.

Brockman, John, ed. *This Explains Everything: Deep, Beautiful, and Elegant Theories of How the World Works.* New York: HarperCollins, 2013.

Brodie, Bernard. *Strategy in the Missile Age.* Princeton, N.J.: Princeton University Press, 1959.

Brodie, Bernard, and Fawn M. Brodie. *From Crossbow to H-Bomb: The Evolution of the Weapons and Tactics of Warfare.* Bloomington: Indiana University Press, 1973.

Brownlee, Romie L., and William J. Mullen III. *Changing an Army: An Oral History of General William E. DePuy, USA Retired.* Carlisle Barracks, Pa.: U.S. Military History Institute, n.d.

Builder, Carl H. *The Icarus Syndrome: The Role of Air Power Theory in the Evolution and Fate of the U.S. Air Force.* New Brunswick, N.J.: Transaction, 1994.

Bull, Hedley. *The Anarchical Society.* New York: Columbia University Press, 1977.

Burrows, William E. *This New Ocean.* New York: Modern Library, 1999.

Callwell, C. E. *Small Wars: Their Principles and Practice.* Lincoln: University of Nebraska Press, 1996.

Carse, James. *Finite and Infinite Games: A Vision of Life as Play and Possibility.* New York: Ballantine, 1986.

Catton, Bruce. *The Army of the Potomac: A Stillness at Appomattox.* Garden City, N.Y.: Doubleday, 1953.

———. *Grant Moves South.* Boston: Little, Brown, 1960.

———. *Grant Takes Command.* Boston: Little, Brown, 1968.

Chairman, Joint Chiefs of Staff. *Capstone Concept for Joint Operations: Joint Force 2020.* Washington, D.C., 10 September 2012. http://www.jcs.mil//content/files/2012–09/092812122654_CCJO_JF2020_FINAL.pdf.

Chung, Clayton S. *Defending Space: US Anti-Satellite Warfare and Space Weaponry.* New York: Osprey, 2006.

Clarke, Richard A., and Robert K. Knake. *Cyber War: The Next Threat to National Security and What to Do about It.* New York: HarperCollins, 2010.

Claude, Henry de. "Scientific Uncertainty and Fabricated Uncertainty." *The Stockholm Lectures.* Stockholm: Royal Swedish Academy of Sciences, 15 December 2011. http://sciences.blogs.liberation.fr/files/texte-de-claude-henry.pdf.

Clausewitz, Carl von. *On War.* Edited and translated by Michael Howard and Peter Paret. Princeton, N.J.: Princeton University Press, 1976.

———. *Vom Kriege.* Edited by Werner Hahlweg. 19th ed. Bonn: Ferd. Dümmlers Verlag, 1991.

Clodfelter, Mark. *The Limits of Air Power: The American Bombing of North Vietnam.* New York: Free Press, 1989.

Cohen, Eliot A. *Supreme Command: Soldiers, Statesmen, and Leadership in Wartime.* New York: Free Press, 2002.

Collier, Paul. "Rebellion as a Quasi-Criminal Activity." *Journal of Conflict Resolution* 44, no. 6 (2000).

Collier, Paul, and Nicholas Sambanis, eds. *Understanding Civil War: Evidence and Analysis.* Washington, D.C.: International Bank for Reconstruction and Development, World Bank, 2005.

Conger, Arthur L. *The Rise of U.S. Grant.* 1931. Reprint, New York: Da Capo, 1996.

Corrin, Amber. "Pentagon Staffing Up to Address Cyber Concerns." FCW: The Business of Federal Technology, 28 January 2013. http://fcw.com/articles/2013/01/28/cyber command-hiring.aspx.

Corum, James S., and Wray R. Johnson. *Airpower in Small Wars: Fighting Insurgents and Terrorists.* Lawrence: University Press of Kansas, 2003.

Corum, Robert. *Boyd: The Fighter Pilot Who Changed the Art of War.* New York: Back Bay Books, 2002.

Crane, Conrad C. *Bombs, Cities and Civilians.* Lawrence: University Press of Kansas, 1993.

D'Este, Carlo. *Patton: A Genius for War.* New York: HarperCollins, 1995.

Dale, Andrew. *Sources in the History of Mathematics and Physical Science.* Vol. 13. New York: Springer Verlag, 1994.

David, Fred R. *Strategic Management Concepts: A Competitive Advantage Approach.* Upper Saddle, N.J.: Prentice Hall, 2013.

David, Steven R. *Catastrophic Consequences: Civil Wars and American Interests.* Baltimore, Md.: Johns Hopkins Press, 2008.

Davis, Richard G. *On Target: Organizing and Executing the Strategic Air Campaign against Iraq.* Washington, D.C.: Air Force History and Museums Program, 2002.

Department of Defense, *Annual Report to Congress: Military Power of the People's Republic of China, 2006.* Washington, D.C., 2006.

————. *Joint Operation Planning*, Joint Publication 5-0. Washington, D.C., 11 August 2011. IV-2–IV-3. http://www.dtic.mil/doctrine/new_pubs/jp5_0.pdf.

Department of the Air Force. *Air Force Basic Doctrine,* Air Force Doctrine Document 1. Maxwell Air Force Base, Ala.: Headquarters, Air Force Doctrine Center, 1997.

————. *Basic Aerospace Doctrine of the United States Air Force,* Air Force Manual 1–1. 2 vols. Washington, D.C., 1992.

Department of the Army. *Operations*, Field Manual 100–5. Washington, D.C., 1982.

————. *Operations*, Field Manual 100–5. Washington, D.C., 1986.

Dolman, Everett C. *Astropolitik: Classical Geopolitics in the Space Age.* Portland, Ore.: Frank Cass, 2002.

————. *Pure Strategy: Power and Principle in the Space and Information Age.* New York: Frank Cass, 2005.

Donnelly, Jack. *Realism and International Relations.* London: Cambridge University Press, 2000.

Douhet, Giulio. *The Command of the Air.* Edited by Joseph Patrick Harahan and Richard H. Kohn. Tuscaloosa: University of Alabama Press, 2009.

————. *The Command of the Air.* New York: Coward-McCann, 1942.

du Picq, Ardant. "Battle Studies." *Roots of Strategy, Book 2.* Harrisburg, Pa.: Stackpole Books, 1987: 121–22.

Eccles, Henry E. *Logistics in the National Defense.* 1959. Reprint, Washington, D.C.: Headquarters United States Marine Corps, 1989.

Edgerton, David. *The Shock of the Old: Technology and Global History since 1900.* Oxford: Oxford University Press, 2007.

Ennels, Jerome, and Wesley P. Newton. *The Wisdom of Eagles: A History of Maxwell Air Force Base.* Montgomery, Ala.: Black Belt, 1997.

Esposito, Vincent J., ed. *The West Point Atlas of American Wars.* 2 vols. New York: Praeger, 1967.

Farnsworth, Timothy. "China and Russia Submit Cyber Proposal." *Arms Control Today (online),* November 2011. http://www.armscontrol.org/act/2011_11/China_and_Russia_Submit_Cyber_Proposal.

Fearon, James. "Ethnic Mobilization and Ethnic Violence." In *Oxford Handbook of Political Economy,* ed. Barry R. Weingast and Donald Wittman. Oxford: Oxford University Press, 2006.

————. "Rationalist Explanations for War." *International Organization* 49, no. 3 (Summer 1995).

Fearon, James D., and David Laitin. "Ethnicity, Insurgency and Civil War." *American Political Science Review* 97, no. 1 (February 2003).

Fetzer, Joel S., and J. Christopher Soper. *Muslims and the State in Britain, France, and Germany.* Boston: Cambridge University Press, 2004.

Finnemore, Martha. *The Purpose of Intervention: Changing Beliefs about the Use of Force.* Ithaca, N.Y.: Cornell University Press, 2003.

Finney, Robert T. *History of the Air Corps Tactical School, 1920–1940.* Washington, D.C.: Center for Air Force History, 1992.

Fitzpatrick, John C., ed. *The Writings of George Washington from the Original Manuscript Sources.* Washington, D.C.: U.S. Government Printing Office, 1940.

Foch, Ferdinand. *The Principles of War.* Translated by Hilaire Belloc. New York: Henry Holt, 1920.

Forsyth, James W., Jr., and Richard R Muller. "'We Were Deans Once, and Young': Veteran PME Educators Look Back." *Air & Space Power Journal* 25, no. 3 (Fall 2011): 91–99.

Fox, Jonathan. *Religion, Civilization and Civil War: 1945 through the Millennium.* Lanham, Md.: Lexington Books, 2004.

Freedman, Lawrence. *Strategy: A History.* New York: Oxford University Press, 2013.

Fuller, J. F. C. *The Generalship of Alexander the Great.* New Brunswick, N.J.: Rutgers University Press, 1960.

———. *The Generalship of Ulysses S. Grant.* 1929. Reprint, New York: Da Capo, n.d.

Futrell, Robert Frank. *Ideas, Concepts, Doctrine: Basic Thinking in the United States Air Force.* Vol. 2, *1961–1984.* Maxwell Air Force Base, Ala.: Air University Press, 1989.

———. *The United States Air Force in Korea.* Washington, D.C.: Air Force History and Museums Program, 2000.

Galula, David. *Counterinsurgency Warfare: Theory and Practice.* Westport, Conn.: Praeger Security International, 2006.

Gillespie, Paul G. *Weapons of Choice: The Development of Precision Guided Munitions.* Tuscaloosa: University of Alabama Press, 2006.

Gilpin, Robert. *War and Change in World Politics.* New York: Cambridge University Press, 1981.

Glantz, David M. *Soviet Military Operational Art: In Pursuit of Deep Battle.* London: Frank Cass, 1991.

Goldsworthy, Adrian. *The Punic Wars.* London: Cassell, 2000.

Grant, Ulysses S. *Personal Memoirs of U.S. Grant.* 2 vols. 1885. Reprint, New York: Bonanza Books, n.d.

Gray, Colin S. *Another Bloody Century: Future Warfare.* London: Phoenix, 2006.

———. "Irregular Warfare: One Nature, Many Characters." *Strategic Studies Quarterly* (Winter 2007).

———. *Modern Strategy.* Oxford: Oxford University Press, 1999.

Green, Brian. *Elegant Universe: Superstrings, Hidden Dimensions, and the Quest for the Ultimate Theory.* New York: Alfred A. Knopf, 2000.

————. *The Fabric of the Cosmos: Space, Time, and the Texture of Reality.* New York: Vintage, 2005.

Green, William. *Warplanes of the Third Reich.* New York: Galahad Books, 1986.

Greenblatt, Stephen. *The Swerve: How the World Became Modern.* New York: W. W. Norton, 2012.

Griffin, H. Dwight. *Air Corps Tactical School: The Untold Story.* Maxwell Air Force Base, Ala.: Air Command and Staff College, 1995.

Griffith, Samuel B. *The Illustrated Art of War.* Oxford: Oxford University Press, 2005.

Guevara, Ernesto "Che." *Guerrilla Warfare.* Lanham, Md.: Scholarly Resources, 1997.

Gurr, Ted Robert. *Why Men Rebel.* Princeton, N.J.: Princeton University Press, 1970.

Gurswamy, Krishnan. "India Tricks US Satellites." Associated Press, 19 May 1998, n.p. http://abcnews.go.com/sections/world/DailyNews/India980519_nukes.html.

Hagerman, Christopher. *Britain's Imperial Muse: The Classics, Imperialism, and the Indian Empire, 1784–1914.* New York: Palgrave Macmillan, 2013.

Hale, Henry. "Explaining Ethnicity." *Comparative Political Studies* 37, no. 4 (May 2004).

Hansell, Haywood S. *The Air Plan That Defeated Hitler.* Atlanta, Ga.: Higgins-MacArthur, 1972.

Hayward, Joel, and Tamir Libel. "Reflections on the Maxwell 'Revolution': John Warden and Reforms in Professional Military Education." *Royal Air Force Air Power Review* 14 (Spring 2011): 11–33.

Hechter, Michael. *Containing Nationalism.* Oxford: Oxford University Press, 2000.

Heuser, Beatrice. *The Evolution of Strategy: Thinking War from Antiquity to the Present.* New York: Cambridge University Press, 2010.

History of the Air Command and Staff College: Twentieth Anniversary Command Edition. Air University History, AUOI Series no. 18. Maxwell Air Force Base, Ala.: 15 February 1966.

Hofsteder, Douglas. *Gödel, Escher, Bach: An Eternal Golden Braid.* New York: Basic Books, 1979.

Holton, Gerald. *Thematic Origins of Scientific Thought: Kepler to Einstein.* Cambridge, Mass.: Harvard University Press, 1980.

Horowitz, Donald L. *Ethnic Groups in Conflict.* Los Angeles: University of California Press, 1985.

Howard, Michael. *The Franco-Prussian War: The German Invasion of France, 1870–1871.* London: Rupert Hart-Davis, 1961.

————. "Military Science in an Age of Peace." *Journal of the Royal United Services Institute for Defence Studies* 119 (March 1974): 7.

Huntington, Samuel P. *The Soldier and the State: The Theory and Politics of Civil-Military Relations.* Boston: Belknap, 1957.

Joint Chiefs of Staff. *Joint Operations Planning,* Joint Publication 5-0. Washington, D.C., 11 August 2011. http://www.dtic.mil/doctrine/.

Jomini, Baron de. *The Art of War.* Translated by G. H. Mendell and W. P. Craighill. 1862. Reprint, Westport, Conn.: Greenwood, 1971.

Jones, Seth G. *"The Future of Irregular Warfare" (CT-374, RAND Corporation), Testimony Presented before the House Committee on Armed Services, Subcommittee on Emerging Threats and Capabilities on March 27, 2012,* Washington, D.C.

Jullien, Francoise. *A Treatise on Efficacy: Between Western and Chinese Thinking.* Translated by Janice Lloyd. Honolulu: University of Hawaii Press, 1996.

Kalyvas, Stathis N. *The Logic of Violence in Civil War.* New York: Cambridge University Press, 2006.

Kalyvas, Stathis N., and Laia Balcells. "International System and Technologies of Rebellion: How the End of the Cold War Shaped Internal Conflict." *American Political Science Review* 104, no. 3 (August 2010).

Kaplan, Robert D. "The Coming Anarchy: How Scarcity, Crime, Overpopulation, Tribalism, and Disease Are Rapidly Destroying the Social Fabric of Our Planet." *Atlantic Monthly* 273, no. 2 (1994).

Keegan, John. *A History of Warfare.* New York: Alfred A. Knopf, 1993.

Kennan, George F. *Realities of American Foreign Policy.* Princeton, N.J.: Princeton University Press, 1954.

Kilcullen, David. *The Accidental Guerrilla: Fighting Small Wars in the Midst of a Big One.* Oxford: Oxford University Press, 2009.

Kiras, James D. *Special Operations and Strategy: From WWII to the War on Terrorism.* New York: Routledge, 2006.

Kissinger, Henry. *Diplomacy.* New York: Simon and Schuster, 1994.

Kramer, Franklin D., Stuart H. Starr, and Larry K. Wentz, eds. *Cyber Power and National Security.* Dulles, Va.: Potomac Books, 2009.

Krepon, Michael, and Samuel Black. *Space Security or Anti-Satellite Weapons?* Washington, D.C.: Stimson Center, 2010.

Kristol, William. "The Defense Secretary We Have." *Washington Post,* 15 December 2004. http://www.washingtonpost.com/wp-dyn/articles/A132–2004Dec14.html.

Kugelman, Michael, and Robert M. Hathaway, eds. *Running on Empty: Pakistan's Water Crisis.* Washington, D.C.: Woodrow Wilson International Center for Scholars, Asia Program, 2009.

Kuhn, Thomas S. *The Copernican Revolution: Planetary Astronomy in the Development of Western Thought.* Cambridge, Mass.: Harvard University Press, 1957. Reprint, Cambridge, Mass.: Harvard University Press, 1999.

———. *The Structure of Scientific Revolutions.* Chicago: University of Chicago Press, 1996.

Kurzweil, Ray. *The Age of Spiritual Machines: When Computers Exceed Human Intelligence.* New York: Penguin Books, 1999.

Lambeth, Benjamin S. *Air Power against Terror: America's Conduct of Operation Enduring Freedom.* Santa Monica, Calif.: RAND, 2005.

Lanning, Michael Lee. *The Military 100: A Ranking of the Most Influential Military Leaders of All Time.* New York: Barnes and Noble, 1996.

Lawson, Bryan. *How Designers Think: The Design Process Demystified.* 4th ed. London: Routledge, Taylor & Francis, 2005.

Lazenby, J. F. *The First Punic War.* Stanford, Calif.: Stanford University Press, 1996.

———. *Hannibal's War.* Norman: Oklahoma University Press, 1978.

Libicki, Martin C. *Conquest in Cyberspace: National Security and Information Warfare.* New York: Cambridge University Press.

———. *The Mesh and the Net: Speculations on Armed Conflict in a Time of Free Silicon.* Washington, D.C.: National Defense University, 1995.

Liddell Hart, B. H. *Scipio Africanus: Greater than Napoleon.* New York: Da Capo, 1994.

———. *Strategy.* 2nd edition. New York: Penguin Books, 1991.

Lonsdale, David J. *The Nature of War in the Information Age: Clausewitzian Future.* London: Frank Cass, 2004.

Luttwak, Edward N. *The Grand Strategy of the Byzantine Empire.* Cambridge, Mass.: Harvard University Press, 2009.

———. *The Grand Strategy of the Roman Empire.* Baltimore, Md.: Johns Hopkins University Press, 1976.

———. *Strategy: The Logic of War and Peace.* Cambridge, Mass.: Belknap Press, 2003.

———. *Strategy: The Logic of War and Peace.* Cambridge, Mass.: Belknap, 1987.

Luvaas, Jay. *The Military Legacy of the Civil War: The European Inheritance.* 1959. Reprint, Lawrence: University Press of Kansas, 1988.

Machiavelli, Niccoló. *The Art of War.* Translated by Ellis Farneworth, with an introduction by Neal Wood. New York: Da Capo, 1965.

MacKenzie, Donald. *Inventing Accuracy: A Historical Sociology of Nuclear Missile Guidance.* Cambridge, Mass.: MIT Press, 1990.

Mackinder, Halford. "The Geographical Pivot of History." Reprint of 1904 article. *Geographical Journal* 170, no. 4 (2004): 298–321.

Mackinlay, John. *The Insurgent Archipelago.* New York: Columbia University Press, 2009.

Mahan, Alfred T. *The Influence of Sea Power upon History: 1660–1873.* Mineola, N.Y.: Dover, 1890.

———. *Mahan on Naval Strategy: Selections from the Writings of Rear Admiral Alfred Thayer Mahan.* Edited by John B. Hattendorf. Annapolis, Md.: Naval Institute Press, 1991.

McCloud, Saul. "Type A Personality." Simply Psychology, 2011. http://www.simplypsy chology.org/personality-a.html#sthash.2krGukbQ.dpuf.

McFeely, William S. *Grant: A Biography.* New York: W. W. Norton, 1981.

McNeill, William H. *Technology, Armed Force, and Society since A.D. 1000.* Chicago: University of Chicago Press, 1982.

McPhee, John. *The Curve of Binding Energy: A Journey into the Awesome and Alarming World of Theodore B. Taylor.* New York: Farrar, Straus, and Giroux, 1974.

Meacham, Jon. *American Lion: Andrew Jackson in the White House.* New York: Random House, 2009.

Mearsheimer, John. *The Tragedy of Great Power Politics.* New York: W. W. Norton, 2001.

Meilinger, Philip, ed. *The Paths of Heaven.* Maxwell Air Force Base, Ala.: Air University Press, 1996.

The Military Maxims of Napoleon. Translated by George C. D'Aguilar. Introduction and commentary by David Chandler. New York: Macmillan, 1988.

Millis, Walter. *Arms and Men: A Study in American Military History.* New Brunswick, N.J.: Rutgers University Press, 1956.

Mitchell, William. *Winged Defense: The Development and Possibilities of Modern Air Power, Economic and Military.* New York: Dover, 1988.

Morgan, Forrest. *Crisis Stability and Long-Range Strike: A Comparative Analysis of Fighters, Bombers, and Missiles.* Santa Monica, Calif.: RAND, 2013.

Morgenthau, Hans. *Human Rights and Foreign Policy.* New York: Council on Religion and International Affairs, 1979.

———. *Truth and Power: Essays of a Decade, 1960–1970.* New York: Praeger, 1970.

Morozov, Evgeny. *The Net Delusion: The Dark Side of Internet Freedom.* New York: Public-Affairs, 2011.

Morrison, James L., Jr. *"The Best School in the World": West Point in the Pre–Civil War Years, 1833–1866.* Kent, Ohio: Kent State University Press, 1986.

Morrow, John H., Jr. *The Great War in the Air: Military Aviation from 1909 to 1921.* Washington, D.C.: Smithsonian Institution Press, 1993.

Mrozek, Donald J. *Air Power and the Ground War in Vietnam.* Maxwell Air Force Base, Ala.: Air University Press, 1988.

Nalty, B. C., ed. *Winged Shield, Winged Sword: A History of the United States Air Force.* Washington, D.C.: Air Force History and Museums Program, 1997.

Nardin, Terry, and David Mapel, eds. *Traditions of International Ethics.* London: Cambridge University Press, 1992.

Niebuhr, Reinhold. *Moral Man and Immoral Society: A Study in Ethics and Politics.* New York: Charles Scribner's Sons, 1932.

Niederman, Derrick. *The Puzzler's Dilemma: From the Lighthouse of Alexandria to Monty Hall, a Fresh Look at Classic Conundrums of Logic, Mathematics, and Life.* New York: Penguin Books, 2012.

North, Douglass. *Structure and Change in Economic History.* New York: W. W. Norton, 1981.

Nossiter, Adam. "Cholera Epidemic Envelops Coastal Slums in West Africa." *New York Times,* 22 August 2012.

Nussbaum, Emily. "Kids, the Internet, and the End of Privacy: The Greatest Generation Gap since Rock and Roll." *New York Magazine,* 12 February 2007. http://nymag .com/news/features/27341/.

Nye, Joseph S., Jr. *The Future of Power.* New York: PublicAffairs, 2011.

―――. *Soft Power: The Means to Success in World Politics.* New York: PublicAffairs, 2004.

Nye, Roger H. *The Patton Mind: The Professional Development of an Extraordinary Leader.* Garden City, N.Y.: Avery, 1993.

O'Connor, J. J., and E. F. Robertson. "Mathematical Discovery of Planets." MacTutor History of Mathematics Archive, n.d. http://www-history.mcs.st-and.ac.uk/Hist Topics/Neptune_and_Pluto.html.

O'Neill, Bard. *Insurgency and Terrorism: From Revolution to Apocalypse.* Washington, D.C.: Potomac Books, 2005.

Obama, Barack H. *International Strategy for Cyberspace: Prosperity, Security, and Openness in a Networked World.* Washington, D.C.: Office of the President of the United States, May 2011.

Olsen, John Andreas. *John Warden and the Renaissance of American Air Power.* Washington, D.C.: Potomac Books, 2007.

Osgood, Robert, and Robert Tucker. *Force, Order, and Justice.* Baltimore, Md.: Johns Hopkins University Press, 1967.

Pape, Robert A. *Bombing to Win: Air Power and Coercion in War.* Ithaca, N.Y.: Cornell University Press, 1996.

Pflanze, Otto. *Bismarck and the Development of Germany: The Period of Unification, 1815–1871.* Princeton, N.J.: Princeton University Press, 1971.

Pockock, John. *The Machiavellian Moment: Florentine Political Thought and the Atlantic Republican Tradition.* Princeton, N.J.: Princeton University Press, 1967.

Polyani, Michael, and Harry Prosch. *Meaning.* Chicago: University of Chicago Press, 1975.

Posen, Barry. "Crisis Stability and Conventional Arms Control." *Daedalus* 120, no. 1 (Winter 1991): 217–32.

―――. *The Sources of Military Doctrine: France, Britain, and Germany between the Wars.* Ithaca, N.Y.: Cornell University Press, 1984.

Powell, Robert. "Crisis Stability in the Nuclear Age." *American Political Science Review* 83, no. 1 (March 1989): 61–76.

Randolph, Stephen. *Powerful and Brutal Weapons: Nixon, Kissinger, and the Easter Offensive.* Cambridge, Mass.: Harvard, 2007.

Ratley, Lonnie O., III. "Air Power at Kursk: A Lesson for Today?" *Military Review* 62 (April 1978): 54–62.

Reardon, Carol. *Soldiers and Scholars: The U.S. Army and the Uses of Military History, 1865–1920.* Lawrence: University Press of Kansas, 1990.

———. *With a Sword in One Hand & Jomini in the Other: The Problem of Military Thought in the Civil War North.* Chapel Hill: University of North Carolina Press, 2012.

"Record Number of African Refugees and Migrants Cross the Gulf of Aden in 2012." *UN High Council on Refugees Briefing Notes.* Geneva, 15 January 2013.

Register of Graduates and Former Cadets. West Point: U.S. Military Academy, 2000.

Report of the Commission to Assess United States National Security Space Management and Organization. Washington, D.C., 11 January 2001.

Reveron, Derek S., ed. *Cyberspace and National Security: Threats, Opportunities, and Power in a Virtual World.* Washington, D.C.: Georgetown University Press, 2012.

Reynolds, Craig. "Flocks, Herds, and Schools: A Distributional Behavioral Model." *Computer Graphics* 21, no. 4 (1987): 25–34.

Rhodes, Richard. *The Making of the Atomic Bomb.* New York: Simon and Schuster, 1986.

Rid, Thomas. "Cyber Fail: The Obama Administration's Lousy Record on Cyber Security." *New Republic,* 4 February 2013. http://www.newrepublic.com/article/112314 /obama-administrations-lousy-record-cyber-security.

Rip, Michael Russell, and James M. Hasik. *The Precision Revolution: GPS and the Future of Aerial Warfare.* Annapolis, Md.: Naval Institute Press, 2002.

Rittel, Horst W. J., and Melvin M. Webber. "Dilemmas in a General Theory of Planning." *Policy Sciences* 4 (1973).

Romjue, John L. *From Active Defense to AirLand Battle: The Development of Army Doctrine 1973–1982.* Fort Monroe, Va.: U.S. Army Training and Doctrine Command, 1984.

Rosen, Stephen P. *Winning the Next War: Innovation and the Modern Military.* Ithaca, N.Y.: Cornell University Press, 1991.

Rumelt, Richard P. *Good Strategy, Bad Strategy: The Difference and Why It Matters.* New York: Crown Business, 2011.

Sabbagh, Dan. "Hillary Clinton's Speech: Shades of Hypocrisy on Internet Freedom." *Guardian,* 15 February 2011. http://www.guardian.co.uk/world/2011/feb/15/hillary -clinton-internet-freedom.

Sahay, Tara Shankar. "Pakistan Feels Let Down by US Spy Satellites." Rediff on the Net, 13 May 1998. http://www.rediff.com/news/1998/may/13spy.htm.

Schaffer, Ronald. *Small Wars Manual: United States Marine Corps 1940.* Manhattan, Kans.: Sunflower University Press, 2004.

Schelling, Thomas C. *Arms and Influence.* New Haven, Conn.: Yale University Press, 1966.

School of Advanced Military Studies. *Art of Design: Student Text.* Version 2.0. http://usacac.army.mil/cac2/CGSC/events/sams/ArtofDesign_v2.pdf.

Schweller, Randall. "Neorealism's Status-quo Bias: What Security Dilemma." *Security Studies* 5 (Spring 1996): 90–121.

Segall, Glen M. "Thoughts on Dissuasion." *Journal of Military and Strategic Studies* 10, no. 4 (Summer 2008). http://www.jmss.org/jmss/index.php/jmss/article/viewFile /73/83.

Seidler, Christoph. "How Iran Silences Unwanted News." ABC News/International, 1 April 2010. http://abcnews.go.com/International/iran-jamming-satellite-signals -carrying-foreign-media/story?id=10258000.

Sheehan, Neil. *A Fiery Peace in a Cold War: Bernard Schriever and the Ultimate Weapon.* New York: Random House, 2009.

Showalter, Dennis. *Railroads and Rifles: Soldiers, Technology, and the Unification of Germany.* Hamden, Conn.: Archon Books, 1975.

Shwedo, Bradford J. "BJ." *XIX Tactical Air Command and ULTRA: Patton's Force Enhancers in the 1944 Campaign in France.* Maxwell Air Force Base, Ala.: Air University Press, 2001.

Simpkin, Richard. *Deep Battle: The Brainchild of Marshal Tukhachevskii.* London: Brassey's Defence, 1987.

Smith, Jeffrey J. *Tomorrow's Air Force: Tracing the Past, Shaping the Future.* Bloomington: Indiana University Press, 2014.

Smith, M. V. *Ten Propositions Regarding Spacepower.* Maxwell Air Force Base, Ala.: Air University Press, 2002.

Smith, Rupert. *The Utility of Force: The Art of War in the Modern World.* New York: Vintage Books, 2008.

Snow, C. P. *The Two Cultures and a Second Look.* London: Cambridge University Press, 1964.

Stepanova, Ekaterina. *The Role of Information Communication Technologies in the "Arab Spring": Implications beyond the Region.* PONARS Eurasia Policy Memo 159. Washington, D.C., May 2011.

Stephens, A., ed. *The War in the Air.* Fairbairn, Australia: Air Power Studies Center, 1994.

Strassler, Robert B. *The Landmark Thucydides: A Comprehensive Guide to the Peloponnesian War.* New York: Free Press, 1996.

Sun Tzu. *The Art of War.* Translated by Ralph D. Sawyer. Boulder, Colo.: Westview, 1994.

———. *The Art of War.* Translated by Samuel B. Griffith. London: Oxford University Press, 1963.

Taber, Robert. *War of the Flea: The Classic Study of Guerrilla Warfare.* Washington, D.C.: Brassey's, 2002.

Thompson, Kenneth W. *Moralism and Morality in Politics and Diplomacy.* Lanham, Md.: University Press of America, 1985.

Thucydides. *History of the Peloponnesian War.* Translated by Rex Warner. London: Penguin Books, 1972.

Tilford, Earl H. *Setup: What the Air Force Did in Vietnam and Why.* Maxwell Air Force Base, Ala.: Air University Press, 1991.

Tooze, Adam. *The Wages of Destruction: The Making and Breaking of the Nazi Economy.* New York: Penguin Books, 2008.

Trinquier, Roger. *Modern Warfare: A French View of Counterinsurgency.* Westport, Conn.: Praeger Security International, 2006.

U.S. Army/Marine Corps Counterinsurgency Field Manual 3-24. Chicago: University of Chicago Press, 2007.

Waltz, Kenneth N. *Man, the State, and War.* New York: Columbia University Press, 1959.

———. "Structural Realism after the Cold War," *International Security* 25, no. 1 (Summer 2000): 13.

———. *Theory of International Politics.* Boston, Mass.: McGraw-Hill, 1979.

Walzer, Michael. *Just and Unjust Wars.* New York: Basic Books, 1977.

Warfighting: The Marine Corps Book of Strategy. New York: Currency-Doubleday, 1994.

Watts, Barry. *Clausewitzian Friction and Future War.* McNair Paper 52. Washington, D.C.: Institute for National Strategic Studies, 1996.

Webster's Encyclopedic Unabridged Dictionary of the English Language. New York: Gramercy Books, 1996.

Weingast, Barry R., and Donald Wittman, eds. *Oxford Handbook of Political Economy.* Oxford: Oxford University Press, 2006.

Weinstein, Jeremy. *Inside Rebellion: The Politics of Insurgent Violence.* New York: Cambridge University Press, 2007.

Wendt, Alexander. *Social Theory of International Politics.* New York: Cambridge University Press, 1999.

White, Lynn, Jr. *Medieval Technology and Social Change.* Oxford: Oxford University Press, 1962.

Wilkening, Dean, Ken Watman, Michael Kennedy, and Richard Darilek. *Strategic Defenses and Crisis Stability.* Santa Monica, Calif.: RAND, 1989.

Williams, T. Harry. *McClellan, Sherman, and Grant.* 1962. Reprint, Westport, Conn.: Greenwood, 1976.

Winton, George Peterson, Jr. "Ante-Bellum Military Instruction of West Point Officers and Its Influence upon Confederate Military Organization and Operations." Ph.D. dissertation, University of South Carolina, May 1972.

Winton, Harold R. *Corps Commanders of the Bulge: Six American Generals and Victory in the Ardennes.* Lawrence: University Press of Kansas, 2007.

———. "Reflections on the Air Force's New Manual." *Military Review* 72 (November 1992): 20–31.

Wolfram, Stephen. *A New Kind of Science*. Champaign, Ill.: Wolfram, 2002.

Woodward, Margaret H. "Defending America's Vital National Interests in Africa." Remarks at the Air Force Association's 2011 Air & Space Conference & Technology Exposition, National Harbor, Md., 21 September 2011.

Worden, Mike. *Rise of the Fighter Generals: The Problem of Air Force Leadership 1945– 1982*. Maxwell Air Force Base, Ala.: Air University Press, 1998.

Worden, S. Pete. "Future Strategy and Professional Development: A Roadmap." Paper submitted to the National Defense University Space Power Theory Team, 2006.

Wunderle, William D. *Through the Lens of Cultural Awareness: A Primer for US Forces Deploying to Arab and Middle Eastern Countries*. Fort Leavenworth, Kans.: Combat Studies Institute Press, 2006.

Wylie, J. C. *Military Strategy: A General Theory of Power Control*. 1967. Reprint, Annapolis, Md.: Naval Institute Press, n.d.

Yeisley, Mark O. "Bipolarity, Proxy Wars and the Rise of China." *Strategic Studies Quarterly* 5, no. 4 (Winter 2011).

Young, James Russell. *Around the World with General Grant*. 2 vols. New York: n.p., 1879.

Zukav, Gary. *The Dancing Wu Li Masters: An Overview of the New Physics*. New York: Morrow, 1979.

INDEX

ABOUT THE EDITORS

RICHARD J. BAILEY JR. is an associate professor of strategy and security studies, USAF School of Advanced Air and Space Studies, Maxwell Air Force Base, Alabama. He earned his PhD in the Department of Government at Georgetown University. Rick is an active-duty U.S. Air Force colonel, with over 3,500 flight hours in various Air Force aircraft. His research interests include military strategy, cyberpower, and civil-military relations.

JAMES W. FORSYTH JR. is the dean of the Air Command and Staff College at Maxwell Air Force Base, Alabama. He received his PhD in international studies from the Joseph Korbel School of International Studies, University of Denver. While there he studied international and comparative politics, as well as security studies. His research interests are wide ranging, and he has written on great power conflict and war.

MARK O. YEISLEY is a former colonel and associate professor at the School of Advanced Air and Space Studies and holds a PhD in international relations from Duke University. While on active duty he served in various operational and staff assignments, and he currently teaches for the Air Command and Staff College. His research interests include contemporary irregular war, ethnic and religious violence, and political geography.

The Naval Institute Press is the book-publishing arm of the U.S. Naval Institute, a private, nonprofit, membership society for sea service professionals and others who share an interest in naval and maritime affairs. Established in 1873 at the U.S. Naval Academy in Annapolis, Maryland, where its offices remain today, the Naval Institute has members worldwide.

Members of the Naval Institute support the education programs of the society and receive the influential monthly magazine *Proceedings* or the colorful bimonthly magazine *Naval History* and discounts on fine nautical prints and on ship and aircraft photos. They also have access to the transcripts of the Institute's Oral History Program and get discounted admission to any of the Institute-sponsored seminars offered around the country.

The Naval Institute's book-publishing program, begun in 1898 with basic guides to naval practices, has broadened its scope to include books of more general interest. Now the Naval Institute Press publishes about seventy titles each year, ranging from how-to books on boating and navigation to battle histories, biographies, ship and aircraft guides, and novels. Institute members receive significant discounts on the Press' more than eight hundred books in print.

Full-time students are eligible for special half-price membership rates. Life memberships are also available.

For a free catalog describing Naval Institute Press books currently available, and for further information about joining the U.S. Naval Institute, please write to:

Member Services
U.S. NAVAL INSTITUTE
291 Wood Road
Annapolis, MD 21402-5034
Telephone: (800) 233-8764
Fax: (410) 571-1703
Web address: www.usni.org